UNNATURAL DEATH

Jean Orloff was found alone in her apartment, nude and facedown on her bed. Part of the bed was burned and the phone was off the hook, but she was pronounced dead from natural causes—probably a heart attack. Her family and friends made plans for a cremation and memorial service.

They weren't prepared for the phone call. The coroner's office investigator had taken one look at Orloff's body and exclaimed, "This woman was murdered!"

There were abrasions on Orloff's face and deep furrows in her neck where she had been strangled. The muscles of her voice box were cracked and there were indentations on her tongue where she had bitten down while being strangled. The sixty-year-old woman had been sexually assaulted, and bruises discolored her left collarbone, left upper arm, left forearm, right thigh, both lower legs, and both hands.

This was no natural death. Jean Orloff had fought desperately for her life . . . and lost.

<u>BOOK YOUR PLACE ON OUR WEBSITE</u> <u>AND MAKE THE</u> <u>READING CONNECTION!</u>

We've created a customized website just for our very special readers, where you can get the inside scoop on everything that's going on with Zebra, Pinnacle and Kensington books.

When you come online, you'll have the exciting opportunity to:

- View covers of upcoming books
- Read sample chapters
- Learn about our future publishing schedule (listed by publication month *and author*)
- Find out when your favorite authors will be visiting a city near you
- Search for and order backlist books from our online catalog
- Check out author bios and background information
- Send e-mail to your favorite authors
- Meet the Kensington staff online
- Join us in weekly chats with authors, readers and other guests
- Get writing guidelines
- AND MUCH MORE!

Visit our website at
http://www.kensingtonbooks.com

BODY DOUBLE

Don Lasseter

PINNACLE BOOKS
Kensington Publishing Corp.
http://www.kensingtonbooks.com

Some names have been changed to protect the privacy of individuals connected to this story.

PINNACLE BOOKS are published by

Kensington Publishing Corp.
850 Third Avenue
New York, NY 10022

All Kensington Titles, Imprints, and Distributed Lines are available at special quantity discounts for bulk purchases for sales promotions, premiums, fund-raising, and educational or institutional use. Special book excerpts or customized printings can also be created to fit specific needs. For details, write or phone the office of the Kensington special sales manager: Kensington Publishing Corp., 850 Third Avenue, New York, NY 10022, attn: Special Sales Department. Phone: 1-800-221-2647.

Pinnacle and the P logo Reg. U.S. Pat. & TM Off.

First Printing: June 2002
10 9 8 7 6 5 4 3 2 1

Printed in the United States of America

One

"Whenever I was at my grandmother's house," said Sherry Davis, "I always knew someone was spying on me from next door. I would see a pair of eyes, peeking from a window, peering from the interior darkness. It gave me chills."

Still, Davis visited her grandmother as often as possible, seldom letting more than a week elapse without seeing her. The older woman functioned as a role model in many ways for Sherry, nourishing a bond between them that extended well beyond blood ties. Myra Davis's successful career in motion pictures and television had inspired Sherry's own achievements in show business. Delighting in her granddaughter's accomplishments as a model and actress, Myra took special pride in Sherry's choice to use the Davis surname even after she married John Flock, a man with a bright future of his own in film and television.

One special phase of Myra Davis's work in movies, Sherry recalled, was her participation in making Alfred Hitchcock's 1960 horror classic, *Psycho*.

The movie drew huge audiences worldwide. Viewers recoiled in horror watching the notorious, intense shower scene in which Janet Leigh, in the role of

Marion Crane, is murdered in a shower. A hand repeatedly plunges a butcher knife into the naked body of Crane, and blood swirls down the drain. Shrill, bloodcurdling music screeches in the background creating the impression of a woman's terrified screams. When movie buffs think of *Psycho,* the first image that comes to mind is the shower scene. Fans knew the stars, of course, but few people realized they saw snippets of a performance by Myra Davis.

Sherry Davis recalled the scenes. "My grandmother loved her association with Janet Leigh in that film and several others. She was Janet's stand-in, but she was also the woman in the rocking chair, Anthony Perkins's mother. And you know that shot of the hand holding a knife, plunging it at Janet Leigh in the shower? That was my grandmother's hand."

The contrast between the knife-wielding psycho in the movie, and the real-life Myra Davis, could not have been more divergent. Sherry described her grandmother as extremely moral, gentle, and always willing to help anyone in need. A deep love existed between the two women, and Sherry couldn't wait to finally tell Myra some exciting news she'd been holding back: she was in her fourth month of pregnancy. She prayed, though, that she hadn't waited too long.

Rushing to Myra's Cheviot Hills home, on a warm Sunday morning, July 3, 1988, Davis fretted about a telephone call she had received that same morning. Ordinarily, the commute from her house in Playa Del Rey, near the beach and not far from Los Angles International Airport, would take no more than fifteen minutes in light weekend traffic. This morning, though, she had to fight an urge to drive a little faster than usual.

"I hadn't spoken to my grandmother for about a week," Davis later recalled. "She knew that I'd been involved in preparations for my best friend's wedding, which was held about thirty miles down the coast in Newport Beach, so she understood why I hadn't contacted her. That Sunday morning, my uncle called from Idaho. He said, 'I've been trying to get hold of Mom for a couple of days, but she's not answering the telephone. The line just keeps ringing and ringing. I called the operator and her line seems to be fine.'

"He had tried several times on Saturday, and again Sunday morning," Sherry recalled. "He wondered if I had heard from her and I told him I hadn't. 'Could you go over,' he asked, 'and see if she's OK?' "

Davis instantly agreed, hung up, and dialed the familiar number, only to hear the intermittent sounds of ringing. "We knew it wasn't like my grandmother to leave the house early unless she had a movie or TV job. She'd usually hang around at least until noon before going shopping or to the food market." Sherry's husband, John, expressed concern and asked her if she wanted him to go. "No," she replied. "I'll just run over there. You stay with the baby." If something was wrong, it wouldn't be a good idea to take their two-year-old son along.

Peeling off the Santa Monica Freeway, Davis sped north on Beverly Drive. Slowing in front of Myra's home, she pulled over to the curb in front of a cozy white one-story structure built in the late 1940s, shortly after World War II. She could see the drapes were closed behind the big sixteen-pane front window. A bird-of-paradise plant and the leaves of a birch tree obscured her view of the front-porch entry.

Leaving her car, Davis trod nervously up the driveway and felt a sudden rush of blood to her face and a tightening in her stomach. A pile of undisturbed newspapers sat fading in the July heat near the front entry, under a roof that extended over the driveway to make a portico. "I knew something was terribly wrong. That was not like her. She always did the crossword puzzles and she would never let the papers lay there. I just knew." It also disturbed Davis that Myra's dust-covered brown-and-tan Chevrolet Malibu sat parked deep in the driveway instead of being garaged at the rear of the house. "That alone wouldn't have freaked me out, but combined with the newspapers, I knew it was bad."

A thousand thoughts flooded her mind with indistinct, dark images, but she couldn't allow any of the frightening scenarios to snap into focus. Searching for soothing explanations, she wanted to rationalize the alarming clues.

"I had a key to her house, but I just didn't want to go in. I was scared." Somewhere in the back recesses of her consciousness, the notion came to Davis that if something terrible had happened, she didn't want to disturb the interior of the home. "I really wasn't thinking about a crime, but the thought of her being dead from some other causes did occur to me. It didn't make much sense, though. At age seventy-one, she was really healthy. Oh, she complained about a little arthritis now and then, but nothing else. She'd always eaten well, never drank, never smoked. I just wasn't sure what to think."

Still hoping for the best, Davis tried the front door and found it locked. She could see no damage indicating a possible break-in. "So I started wondering if maybe she'd had a heart attack or something."

Edging around to the side, Davis cupped her hands to the sides of her face and looked through a window. No evidence of ransacking. "But the light was still on at ten-thirty in the morning. That didn't seem right. Being very frugal, my grandmother never kept the lights on in daylight hours."

Her nerves on edge, Davis moved to another window at the exterior of Myra's bedroom. The drapes were tightly drawn. "That was normal. She always kept them closed." Entering a screened-in patio at the back of the house, Davis passed a third widow also blanked by drapes. She knew, though, that nothing obscured the view through a small, open pane of glass higher on the wall. Myra's beloved pair of cats had learned to climb a trellis and use the opening for access in and out of the house. Pulling a table to a spot below the high window, Davis climbed up, took a deep breath, and looked inside. Streaks of light beamed through the small pane directly toward the bed as if orchestrated by a lighting specialist on a movie set.

"I saw her on the bed lying on her back. I immediately knew she was dead!"

Fighting her emotions, Davis could see that Myra's body had started to decompose. "You could tell. She was mostly nude and her stomach was distended. I couldn't see any blood. I took one look and it freaked me out. When it sunk in, I left. I couldn't remember any of the details."

Time and space spun in crazy circles for Sherry Davis, and an overwhelming sadness darkened the bright day. Now her beloved grandmother would never know of the new baby coming. There would be no more laughing together, no sharing show business experiences, no holidays together. Nothing would be the same.

Trying to make some sense of it, Davis told herself that Myra had died of natural causes. "I knew that she was half naked, but I thought maybe she was getting ready for bed and had a heart attack. So I left to get some help."

Davis's first thought was to ask a neighbor for assistance, but she deliberately avoided going next door. Those leering eyes from a dark window had frightened and angered Davis too many times. "I knew that family," she later growled in a disgusted voice.

A quick mental inventory of other local residents didn't help. "I had known another lady across the street for a long time, but she was losing her mind, so I couldn't disturb her." It flashed back to Davis that a woman down the street had been raped several years earlier. "Some guy came through her window. She lived alone with her two dozen cats and people called her the cat woman. My grandmother was so distressed." As a little girl, "I'd spent a lot of time in that neighborhood, but everyone I knew had either died or moved away," Davis recalled.

Dropping the idea of appealing to neighbors, Davis drove to a nearby gas station. "I knew there was a pay phone there, but I drove round and round and couldn't find it." Under stress, everything familiar seems to vanish or change. Finally, she could think of nothing else but to return home into the comfortable arms of her husband. She drove there in a daze.

In a rush of words, she explained to John what she had seen and asked him to call 911. Accepting his offer to go to Myra's home himself to see what he could do, Sherry gave him her grandmother's house keys. She gently asked, "When the paramedics arrive, please don't go in with them." She didn't want him to see her poor grandmother lying there nude.

John Flock respected his wife's wishes. He arrived at Myra Davis's home simultaneously with the emergency medical technicians and waited outside while they examined her. The subsequent events turned out to be far different from what he'd expected. Not long after the fire department emergency team arrived, police vehicles screamed to a halt at the curb.

After waiting interminably, Flock reeled in astonishment when a detective informed him that Myra Davis had not died of natural causes.

Someone had raped her and strangled her to death.

Two

Over the years, Myra Davis had opened her home to several of her relatives, allowing them to temporarily live with her. When investigators discovered this, one of the boarders soon became a prime suspect in the search for her killer.

Three people had stayed with the gentle woman over varying periods of time. Her own mother, Grace Jones, occupied a bedroom in the home for years until her death in 1985. Earl Porterfield, Grace's brother-in-law, stayed there until he passed away in 1986.

Sherry Davis's own brother Corey was the most recent resident in Myra's home. In addition, a male friend of his had also spent about three weeks doing handiwork for Myra in return for a bed and bath.

Among Davis's five younger siblings, four brothers and one sister, Corey was the eldest brother according to Sherry Davis. "He had some problems over the years. If he wasn't drunk, he was high on drugs. I think he got high with a couple of the people who lived next door, including the guy who peeped at me when I visited my grandmother. She was the only one who would give Corey money and a place to sleep.

My husband and I often helped his kids, but we wouldn't contribute to his irresponsibility."

Los Angeles Police Department homicide detective Gary Fullerton arrived at the Beverly Drive home early Sunday afternoon. The July sun increased a natural redness in his full face, partially covered by a bristling goatee. A burly, muscular man, Fullerton had removed his sport coat before entering the stifling interior, revealing a damp shirt threatening to burst at the seams. He checked the condition of the front entry and noted no evidence of a forced entry.

In the master bedroom, Fullerton observed the body of an "elderly" white female lying faceup across the bed, near the pillows. It was still neatly made up, covered by a brown quilted bedspread. Her legs were bent at the knees, with feet on the floor. She wore nothing but a disarranged rose-colored blouse and a white bra pulled up to expose her chest.

Taking notes as he inspected the crime scene, Fullerton later used them to report: "She was nude from the waist down. Her blouse had been pulled up and her bra opened." Rigor mortis had been present and blood had settled into her back and the lower parts of her body, a condition called lividity. "Her stomach was distended and maggots were present in the nose and mouth." She had probably been dead for "days."

A mostly empty purse lay next to the corpse. The contents, along with an assortment of papers, lay scattered on one corner of the bedspread and on the floor. All five drawers in a chest had been pulled open. A nightstand had been rifled.

Due to the victim's position, her open blouse, bra out of place, and other indications, it appeared that a possible sexual assault had occurred. Fullerton called for the Los Angeles Coroner's Office to send someone out with a rape kit.

Senior Criminalist Lloyd Mahamay was dispatched to answer Fullerton's request. He'd been visiting crime scenes for ten years, and his arched eyebrows under a thatch of unruly graying hair gave him a surprised expression at each one. His duty involved examining all of the victim's body cavities and taking fluid samples. The sex kit is a sealed box, ten by two by eight inches, containing the necessary materials. Breaking the seal, Mahamay withdrew several swabs, something like oversize Q-Tips, and probed the victim's mouth, vagina, and anus. In addition, he touched the cotton tip to the breasts and other epidermal areas to collect fluids left anywhere on the external body surfaces. Afterward he carefully sealed the swabs, marked the containers for identification, and carried them to the coroner's laboratory for analysis.

A search of the house turned up no money.

Both Fullerton and Mahamay could see the probable cause of death. A ligature had been used around the victim's neck. A pair of nylon panties had been wrapped around her throat, and the plastic handle of a pot scrubber, probably taken from the kitchen, had been used like a tourniquet to twist and tighten the ligature "extremely hard." Her glasses and a delicate chain attached to the frames had been caught up in the twisted garment.

From the evidence, it seemed reasonable to conclude that a burglary had taken place in the course of rape and homicide.

Coroner's technicians removed the body of Myra Davis and transported it to a laboratory for autopsy. Dr. William Swalwell, a veteran of the department, performed the procedure, which revealed that Davis had died in agony. Placement of the ligature led him to conclude that the perpetrator had faced the victim while twisting and tightening the death weapon, gradually cutting off her air supply. Petechial hemorrhaging, rupture of tiny blood vessels in the eyes and gums, helped confirm a finding of death by strangulation. It is caused, said the coroner, by the blood supply being cut off and "trying to return to the heart." He also found the left hyoid bone below the jaw, inside the neck, was fractured. "The tongue bled from compression of the voice box." Violent application of a ligature causes it to "protrude and the victim bites down on it. Then a lack of oxygen to the brain causes seizure. The carotid arteries on both sides of the neck are occluded. With no blood going to the brain, the heart slows down; then death occurs."

The victim couldn't scream due to firm pressure on the voice box and because of hyoid bone damage. When compression of the carotid arteries takes place, the victim will remain conscious for ten to fifteen seconds; then the arms go limp and the body relaxes. Within four to six minutes, there is irreversible brain damage. But it no longer matters because the victim dies within 1 to 1 1/2 minutes of maximum pressure being applied.

Dr. Swalwell examined the victim's genitalia and concluded that she had been raped. "There was no vaginal trauma. This is not unusual. When a perpetrator makes penile penetration, he sometimes enters only the outer labia, then ejaculates."

In another part of the coroner's facilities, the serology unit, a criminalist used the swabs collected by
Mahamay to make smears on glass slides. Examination
under a microscope revealed semen and sperm cells,
confirming that Myra Davis had been raped.

The swabs and slides were stored under refrigeration, then frozen. They would be kept for a future
possibility of comparing the evidence to blood samples taken from a suspect. If one could ever be found.

After hearing that Myra Davis had been murdered,
John Flock returned home and tenderly broke the
news to his wife, Sherry Davis. Wishing to spare her
any additional pain, he didn't mention that the
woman had also been raped. It would be a long time
before Sherry learned of the brutal violation her
grandmother had endured.

That evening, she telephoned her father in San Diego and her uncle in Idaho. Both men drove to Los
Angeles to help make arrangements for cremation
and a funeral service.

The family gathered at Myra's home three days after the body was found. "There was black fingerprint
dust everywhere, on the door frames and on her
dresser drawers, which had been ransacked. The police had removed all the bedding," Davis said.

Detective Fullerton escorted Sherry outside. Standing between Myra's home and the house next door,
he asked if she had any idea who might have any
reason to harm her grandmother. "The only person
I can think of," she answered while gesturing toward
the adjacent house, "is the guy next door." She meant
George Green, the man she thought spied on her

when she visited Myra. Fullerton nodded, made some notes, and said he would look into it.

In his investigation of the family next door, Detective Fullerton encountered more residents than he'd expected. From time to time, at least nine people and a dog occupied the three-bedroom house, similar in size, architecture, and color to the adjacent Davis home except for a white brick fireplace. Dora Green, the matriarchal owner, seemed to be in charge. Fullerton learned that she operated a manicure business in a beauty salon on Pico Avenue, a few miles away. He met the other occupants, including both of Dora's adult daughters, Betty and Glenda; Glenda's husband, Tom Vale; their three offspring; Betty's boyfriend, "Sonny"; and George Green. A blond cocker spaniel named Ginger rounded out the family.

Detective John Rockwood, Fullerton's partner, questioned Sonny, asking if he knew Myra Davis. The solidly built young man acknowledged an acquaintance with her, but said he hadn't seen her for at least a week. Neither had George Green.

Green, according to Sherry Davis, was probably the one who kept her under surreptitious scrutiny when she did yard work for her grandmother. "It was eerie," Davis recalled. "It wasn't like I wore a bikini or anything. I was fully dressed, but he would stare at me. And quite often, whenever he would see me, he'd come over and follow me around. Just talk, talk, talk. When he'd see my car in the driveway, he'd come over and knock on the door and want to come in the house. He made my grandmother nervous. She told me once that she had seen someone peeking in her window." Davis had advised Myra to install an alarm system, or at least subscribe to a service providing a panic button worn at the neck. Even without the danger of an intruder, such a device might help in the case of a health emergency. But Myra said she'd lived there forty years and had survived without such a contraption. "I even tried to get her to sell the house and move to a smaller condominium. She wouldn't hear of it."

If George Green, in his attention to Sherry Davis, hoped she would be attracted physically to him, he suffered a serious misunderstanding of her opinion. "He was overweight and sloppy. Not very tall. Always dressed in jeans and T-shirts. Definitely not a fashion plate. And he was a chronic liar, telling stories about everything. He lived over there in that house where there was always screaming and yelling, doors slamming, and sounds of fighting. My grandmother was really scared of him, and worried that he would hurt me."

Neither Sherry nor Myra knew that Green had been in trouble with the law.

While frightened by George Green, Myra seemed to like Dora and Sonny. She thought he seemed nice enough, volunteering to help her with repair jobs around the house and yard for minimal pay. His quiet, courteous behavior, which seemed to border on shyness, impressed Myra. Sherry popped in unannounced one day while Sonny labored with a plumbing problem under the sink. He seemed embarrassed in Sherry's presence and prepared to leave. Mumbling an apology as he departed, he said, "I don't have the right parts, so I'll have to come back tomorrow." His behavior contrasted sharply with George Green's fawning attempts to draw Sherry into conversation.

"Even though Sonny seemed nice enough, I still didn't feel comfortable with my grandmother hiring someone she knew nothing about," Davis said. "She told me that Dora asked her if she could use Sonny to do repairs because he was out of work and needed the money, and that he was really a good handyman."

Shaking her head in thoughtful retrospect, Davis described Myra as a good-hearted soul who always tried to help anyone in the neighborhood. "She was the first one to bake a cake or rush to the aid of people in distress." Concerned about the risk, Davis had offered to pay for professional plumbers or other service people, but Myra waved off the idea. "She felt sorry for Dora, that she had to live with that bunch of lunatics. And she wanted to help them if she could."

Sherry Davis felt certain that either George Green or Sonny told Detective Fullerton that her brother Corey had been in Myra's house at the time of the murder. "They both knew that Corey had stayed there not long before and that his friend lived in the house for about three weeks doing chores for her.

"Fullerton kept calling me. It soon became apparent that he thought my oldest brother had killed my grandmother, and maybe his pal had been an accomplice. I protested. He said, 'You don't understand. You live in a glass house. You don't know my job.' " The "glass house" reference seemed odd to Davis, but she began to wonder if Fullerton might be correct. When she learned that Corey apparently failed to provide a satisfactory alibi, doubts assailed her about his innocence. "The detective quoted me statistics about how many people kill members of their own families."

Confused and distressed, Davis asked Fullerton if he had interviewed the people next door. "He told me," she later recalled, "that he had spoken to them, and that 'everything had panned out.' None of them, he said, had seen my grandmother for a while."

Asking herself if her brother really could have killed their grandmother, Sherry Davis wrestled with serious doubts, but tried to keep an open mind. Later speaking of the dilemma, she said Corey had been troubled with substance abuse and had difficulty with accepting responsibilities. Davis tried to remember if her brother had ever been jailed, but could recall only a few incidents related to parking tickets. Two of his cars had been impounded over financial problems, and Corey hadn't even bothered to reclaim them. But to her knowledge, he'd never been involved in any felonies. His main problems centered on alcohol, drugs, and money. He seemed to be always short of funds, always in debt. Could he have attacked Myra in a stupor and accidentally killed her? Davis still didn't know that Myra had been sexually assaulted. If Corey had been desperate for money and asked Myra to give him more, the frugal woman might have rejected him. She willingly provided Corey with food, a place to sleep, and subsistence money, but she might have balked at handing over additional cash. Could he have exploded into a deadly rage and strangled her?

Or could the neighbor have been the killer? Could George Green have talked his way into the house, tried to steal valuable items, been caught, and strangled Myra to prevent being arrested? It didn't make sense considering that Myra had been found on her bed, partially nude. Nothing seemed to fit. More likely, Davis thought, the murder was committed by an intruder completely unknown to her or her grandmother. She could only hope the police would soon find the answers. For now, she planned to concentrate on taking care of Myra's home and possessions, in which she would find so many reminders of happier days.

The Davis family agreed to cremate the body of Myra. Sherry recalled, "There were no funerals on that side of the family. They were all cremated."

In recalling her grandmother's life, Davis remembered that Myra had always wanted to be a dancer, worked hard in the motion picture business, and later extended her career with success in television.

Born in Albuquerque, New Mexico, in 1917, Myra Davis focused all her energy on the study of dance. At fourteen, she migrated to California and soon found bit work at various movie studios around Hollywood and often at the sprawling complex called MGM in Culver City. In 1935, she appeared as one of the dancers in a musical hit titled *Folies Bergère*, starring Maurice Chevalier and Ann Sothern. Myra couldn't conceal her pride when the movie won an Oscar for dance direction.

Over the years, she found small roles, often as a stand-in or body double, in a number of movies. Her parts were never big enough to warrant screen credit. Sometimes, in auditioning for work, she used her maiden name, Myra Jones. While working at MGM, she met an aspiring cowboy actor named Robert Davis. Davis, nearly always dressed in western clothing, with a cowboy hat and boots, impressed Myra with his wit, charm, and humor, even if he did drink a bit too much. She married him and had two sons.

Robert, known among his friends and associates as

"Alabam," socialized frequently with two other actors who became well-known stars. One of them, Franchot Tone, performed in more than seventy movies, including *Mutiny on the Bounty,* with Clark Gable, and *The Lives of a Bengal Lancer,* with Gary Cooper. Between 1933 and 1937, Tone shared billing with Joan Crawford in eight films and made her his first of four wives in 1935.

To honor his close friendship with Tone, Robert Davis convinced Myra to name their first son after him. The boy, Franchot Davis, would later become the father of Sherry.

The third actor in the trio of close pals was Jacob Julius Garfinkle, a scrappy young man who'd survived a rough-and-tumble childhood on the Lower East Side of New York City. Barely escaping a life on the wrong side of the law, Garfinkle found salvation in the beckoning of theater. Acting lessons led to Broadway roles and eventual success in forty movies, where he achieved stardom using the name John Garfield. He played tough guys in most roles, such as *The Postman Always Rings Twice,* with Lana Turner, in 1946, but won acclaim as a blinded WWII marine in a post-war film titled *Pride of the Marines.*

Sherry Davis, speaking of her father, Franchot, said that he hated show business. "He didn't like it because his dad, Robert Davis, was a raging alcoholic. My grandfather ran with Franchot Tone and John Garfield. They were all drunks, and my father, as a teenager, used to have to go and find them in bars and bring them home. I've heard so many stories about him going from bar to bar looking for his dad."

Coping with a carousing husband and two sons, Myra continued to work, finding spots in various movies. She appeared in the 1956 epic *Around the World in 80 Days*, with David Niven and a host of stars doing cameos. That year, her life brightened considerably with the arrival of a tiny granddaughter named Sherry.

"I was born when my parents were only seventeen," said Davis. "They were divorced by the time I was three. My father joined the navy and remarried. My mother found another husband two years later. I spent a lot of time at my grandmother's house on Beverly Drive."

Fondly looking back, Davis revealed that Myra always wanted her to be in show business. "She had two sons and I was the only girl in her life. She put me in competition for a baby-food ad, to be the Gerber Baby. I was picked for it, but my father hated show business so much, he wouldn't sign the release forms." The setback, though, did not discourage Myra's ambitions for her granddaughter. "She tried to make connections for me to be a child actress. She loved the business. As soon as I turned eighteen and didn't need parental release, she signed me up at Central Casting. She called them and said she was sending over her beautiful granddaughter."

Sherry, though, wasn't too enthusiastic at first about movie aspirations. Perfectly satisfied as a part-time fashion runway model, she didn't particularly want to become separated from her social life and friends in Newport Beach, forty miles from Hollywood. "I was attending college in Newport and wasn't all that interested in working. I was in Orange County, and Hollywood was part of Los Angeles. That was the other side of the world. But, to satisfy my grandmother, I took my portfolio to Central Casting and they signed me up. I was in show business by the time I was nineteen."

Among Davis's earliest memories of her grand-mother, she recalled an incident while Myra worked as Janet Leigh's double. "When I was a baby, she took me to a movie set and into Janet Leigh's trailer dress-ing room. Janet held me. I've always wanted to ask her if she remembers that, and tell her I am Myra's granddaughter."

As Davis remembered, Myra wore her hair in the same style and color worn by Janet Leigh, always pre-pared to double for the star in various long-distance or hazardous shots. "If Janet wore a wig, Myra would wear a duplicate wig. My grandmother worked with Janet for years, not only in *Psycho,* but in *Bye Bye Birdie* and several other films. She also found employment in several Dean Martin and Jerry Lewis movies." Davis always looked forward, as a child, to seeing the para-phernalia Myra would bring home from movie sets: coffee mugs, T-shirts, photos of the stars and techni-cians, and endless other souvenirs.

Asked if Myra had functioned as a body double in the famous shower scene of *Psycho,* in which Janet Leigh's character is stabbed to death, Davis said, "No, she was not the one in the shower." She added, "My grandmother would never do any nude work. She was so modest. She would never have appeared naked. No, no, no, that was not my grandmother." In that classic film, Janet Leigh actually did the great majority of the shower-scene work herself. Specially made moleskin pieces, glued over vital parts to create an appearance of complete nudity, allowed the star to maintain a certain amount of modesty while spending an uncomfortable week filming the famous scene.

Leigh reported in her book about the film that the warm water sometimes caused the moleskin to peel off, and she had never before noticed so many male technicians perched in the catwalks above the set. Whenever it became necessary to shoot with a nude body double, a model name Marli Renfro was used. According to Leigh, she "was accustomed to being nude, it being all in a day's work." But Renfro "was not on camera during the shower scene." Leigh also revealed that the effect of dark blood swirling down the drain, filmed in black and white, was created by using diluted chocolate syrup. The traumatic effect of making the movie, Leigh later stated, prevented her from ever entering a shower again.

So while Myra was present and available during filming of the shower sequence, and wielded the murder weapon, she wasn't involved in any work requiring nudity.

Myra never tired of performing in movies, said Davis. She continued doing bits, doubles, and stand-ins for years, and especially liked the camaraderie stemming from working on film sets. "When you are on a project, from beginning to end, you become like a family. There's a continuity to it, and you work such long hours. You get to know everyone, about their children, who is having a baby, who is getting married, what their trips were like. You really learn the ins and outs of people you work with because you spend so much time together and there is a lot of dead time to stand around and talk. And Myra really enjoyed the community feeling on a set. Especially the long assignments, which were much better than working a day here and a day there."

A stand-in, explained Davis, is a person who replaces

the star during long, tedious setups in which lighting,
camera, and sound technicians prepare for the actual
shooting or at the time of rehearsals. A body double
actually replaces the star during filming, sometimes doing nude work or dangerous scenes that might jeop-
ardize the star's safety. Myra performed both as a body
double and as a stand-in, but loved being employed in
the latter category. "She always said she was one of the
fortunate ones because stand-ins got to work every
day."

Davis admired the way her grandmother maintained an upbeat attitude, always seeming happy, despite tragic events. Myra's husband, Robert Davis,
wrecked his own health with alcohol. His buddies
John Garfield and Franchot Tone were both dead before 1969. Garfield reportedly succumbed to a heart
attack in 1952, after being blacklisted during the infamous Communist witch-hunt conducted by HUAC,
the U.S. House of Representatives Un-American Activities Committee. Rampant rumors that he had committed suicide filled scandal sheets. Franchot Tone's
reputation was damaged at about the same time when
he and actor Tom Neal slugged it out in a bar over
B-movie sex goddess Barbara Payton. Tone eventually
married her, but she soon left him and returned to
Neal. Neal scorned her to marry Gail Evatt, whom he
wound up killing. Released from a six-year manslaughter term in 1972, he lasted only eight more months
before dying of heart failure. Tone enjoyed a revival
of his career by taking roles in television, and died in
1968.

Perhaps the barrage of turmoil and death led
Robert "Alabam" Davis to drown his sorrows in li-
quor. When surgeons removed part of his stomach

and warned him to stop drinking, he turned to amphetamines. "He could no longer drink, so he started taking pills," said Davis. "He took too many one night, when I was a teenager in 1971, and died of an overdose. We never knew if it was an accident or if he did it deliberately. He and my grandmother didn't share the same bedroom. She went in to wake him up and found him dead."

Myra's motion picture jobs tapered off in the late seventies. One of the last films she worked in was *Looking for Mr. Goodbar,* with Diane Keaton, in 1977. Sherry recalled, "She opened up the movie. It's her you hear screaming at the beginning."

It warmed Sherry Davis's heart, after she became a regular in the business, to hear the experienced personnel speak of her grandmother. "The casting people always said such wonderful things about her. And when I'd go to a set, as a stand-in or double for an actress, people who knew Myra would always come to me and compliment her."

Eventually, Sherry Davis would equal and surpass her grandmother, doing not only stand-in and body-double work, but would act in both movies and television. In 1991, she doubled for Demi Moore in *The Butcher's Wife.* Said Davis, "I got the job, even though I don't look anything like her. But in this movie, she had long blond hair, and at that time, my own hair was quite long. I went to the interview as one who fit her height and body structure. My hair perfectly matched the character she was playing. So they added a few more blond streaks, making it impossible to tell from the side or back that it wasn't really Demi Moore. They had to do retakes on two or three particular scenes, but she was already seven months pregnant, so they needed a double. Actually, Demi came back and filmed many of the shots herself, with the camera carefully avoiding her abdomen."

Activities in more than twenty-five movies, including bit parts and doubling, led Sherry into television roles. On the popular *Happy Days* series, she displayed her dancing skills, much as Myra had done fifty years earlier. A sitcom filmed by Paramount, called *Brothers and Sisters*, gave her a part as a "sorority prude." More recently, she performed in dramatic television series, including *The Practice* and *CSI*, or *Crime Scene Investigation*. In an episode of the latter show, she played a mother who was murdered by having her throat slit. The death of her own grandmother haunted her during the acting stint.

Another lucrative phase of television work for Sherry Davis soon developed: doing television commercials. "I did ads for hair products and fast food. And I did a commercial for Pepsi-Cola. There are so many things you can do in this business." Her new reputation in television jobs allowed her to return a favor.

"I'm the one who got my grandmother into commercials, just as she had arranged for me to join Central Casting. I said, 'You know what, Grandma, this is perfect for you. You are healthy, a good script reader, and talented. Jobs for your age group are so limited, but not in doing ads. Instead of having two hundred women interviewing for a part, there would be more like thirty people.' So I took her to my agent. They loved her." Thrilled, Myra Davis scored well in the new phase of her career. She worked in commercials for Hertz car rentals, International House of Pancakes, or IHOP, Country Time Lemonade, Grandma's

Cookies, and many more. "It tickled her to be recognized, and her friends would come up and say, 'Oh, I saw you on television.' But she was even more happy to be working in the industry she loved."

The happiness ended on a hot July day in 1988.

When Sherry Davis's family learned that investigators regarded Corey as a prime suspect in the murder, the news destroyed family relationships. Davis described it. "Myra's other son, my uncle, was furious with my father. He blamed him for Corey's very existence and for his substance abuse. Then they had a big fight over the sale of my grandmother's home, even though neither of them had ever contributed to its upkeep or furnishing. I was the only one who helped her take care of it. I bought furniture for her, carpeted the house, and took care of her. My father and my grandmother didn't really get along. He probably hadn't seen her in four years or more before she died. It was a mess. I hired painters and got the house sold. I've not spoken to my uncle since. And he doesn't speak to my father."

The troubles for Sherry Davis had just started. Tragedy struck twice more within eighteen days of her grandmother's murder. The four-month pregnancy ended in a miscarriage. She said, "My baby died. And a few days later, my stepfather, my mother's second husband, was hit by a car on his bicycle and killed. He'd been my stepfather since I was five. Both sides of my family were emotional wrecks."

Hope for early arrest and conviction of Myra Davis's killer gradually faded. Sherry Davis kept in contact with Detective Fullerton, hoping to hear that he'd found more evidence and could announce a pending arrest, but each telephone call ended in frustration. Doubts about her own brother's possible involvement troubled her. She later said, "I think Fullerton created this whole scenario about my brother. He even hinted that Corey's buddy, the one who had lived with my grandmother about three weeks, might have been there with him, and they were the ones who did it."

Still unaware that her grandmother had been sexually assaulted, Davis wondered about that possibility. She asked the detective, "What if there was a rape involved?" His answer, that they were still "checking it out," didn't satisfy her. "I pushed it," she recalled, "and he hinted that if a rape had happened, Corey's friend might have done it. I couldn't believe that. I asked, 'You mean he could have raped my grand-mother while my brother watched?' " As Davis remembered it, the detective suggested that Corey might have "passed out" at that point.

Three

When Dora Green later heard sharp criticisms of her family, her objections were nothing less than vitriolic. "I wish everyone would stop telling so many lies about us," she protested. In sharp contrast to accounts of dissension, she spoke of harmony and kindness.

She had known Myra Davis, who was a good neighbor. Before one of the babies was born to Green's daughter, Myra had gone to the trouble of knitting booties for the child. And when Myra had mentioned the need for some repairs to be done in her home, Green had volunteered her other daughter's boyfriend, Sonny, to help out.

Sonny, said Green, was like her own son. He even called her "Ma." She'd once laughingly said, "I'm not your mother." Sonny had replied, "Yes, you are." He married Betty on November 20, 1988, a few months after Myra Davis died. Before the marriage, Green explained, Sonny had been living in her home. She hastened to point out that he'd slept on a "hide-a-bed" couch. "I'm not naive about premarital sex," said Green, "but didn't want it going on in my house. He respected me enough not to do it."

Dora Green felt that Sonny had been treated unfairly in life. He'd joined the army in 1987, but after successfully completing basic training in Fort Jackson, South Carolina, and serving several months, he'd been discharged due to some "prior arrest." Upon returning to civilian life, he met Betty and started dating her. Looking for work, he was hired by an ambulance service, but fired when they discovered an arrest record. He took other jobs, Green said, as a limousine driver and then as a construction worker helping to build the Los Angeles subway known as the Red Line. These gigs didn't last long.

His willingness to work, according to Green, extended to the home. "While he lived with me, he did all kinds of handiwork, including cooking, cleaning, gardening, and making repairs."

It pleased Green that Sonny converted to the Jewish faith to marry Betty. "In Jewish culture," she said, "it's important to marry within the faith. My son didn't and neither did my other daughter. But Sonny went to classes and adopted the faith a few months before the wedding, just to make me happy. It meant a great deal to me. I tried to raise my kids in our religion."

The wedding, said Green, was more important to her than her own. "They were two very special, beautiful young people." She thought it especially touching that her aging uncle and his wife, who "treated Sonny as if they had adopted him," walked him down the aisle at the wedding. Not one person from his own family bothered to attend.

The uncle's wife, Green recalled, was a brilliant woman and a school principal. Then in her eighties, she was lost with anything electronic. "She would call frequently, like once or twice a week, and ask for help with electrical appliances, and Sonny would drop everything to show her how to use them or make repairs."

In another gesture toward Judaism, Sonny made it a point to learn about the appropriate food. Smiling, Green said, "My uncle loved horseradish. Sonny tried to copy him." He slathered a generous amount on a serving of gefilte fish. "When it hit him, he didn't know what to do. He never tried that again."

Blessed with an artistic flair, Sonny used spare time to make pencil drawings. Green beamed when she displayed his portraits of family members and even Ginger, the dog. Looking at photographs of his wedding to Betty, Sonny drew portraits of himself and his new wife. He also sketched excellent likenesses of young girls as winged angels.

Stricken by carpal tunnel syndrome, Dora Green worried that she would never be able to work again. "I'm a manicurist. I was really scared. It looked like I would never be able to use my hands again." Sonny, she said, was like a savior to her. He helped in every way he could, cutting her food for her, trying to make her laugh when depression struck. "One time, in a restaurant, he was cutting my meat, and I teased him by telling him not to throw it at me. So he did. And we had a big food fight right there in the restaurant."

As therapy to help her recover from the ailment, Sonny suggested finger exercises to Green and taught her to play an electronic Nintendo game. "I became addicted to it," she said, giggling.

He helped her through another affliction, too. Her vision was blurred by cataracts in both eyes. "I thought I was going to be blind in my early fifties. It was like looking through a sheet of wax." She underwent surgery in 1991, and needed applications of eyedrops afterward, two or three times daily. "I couldn't do it, and my daughter was too squeamish to help. But Sonny made a big joke of it and put the eyedrops in. He was really loving and caring."

Once again, Dora Green's health failed when breast cancer struck in 1994. She underwent long, uncomfortable radiation and chemotherapy treatments. The side effects—hair loss, radiation burns, nausea, and constant medication—were almost as bad as the disease. Sonny was elsewhere, but when he returned on July 12, 1997, he resumed his role as caretaker, trying constantly to cheer her up.

Sonny's empathy extended not only to her, but to her sick German shepherd, Ursus, as well, said Green. "Ursus was my deceased husband's dog. He was an eighty-pound German shepherd, and he got very sick. He got jaundice and his liver shut down." When the dog fell ill and couldn't drink, Green's son-in-law carefully lifted the animal's head and gave it water. When the dog threw up, so did Sonny. "He couldn't handle the sight of vomit and would usually walk away." But his compassion was big enough to assist the dog. "We called the veterinarian, and he said to bring Ursus over, so Sonny picked him up and carried him like a baby to the car, held him in his lap while I drove over to the veterinarian." With pride, Green said that after Ursus had to be euthanatized, Sonny gave the same kind of attention to Ginger, the blond cocker spaniel. "He had a doggy toothbrush. Ginger had bad teeth, had lost most of them, but Sonny even brushed her [remaining] teeth. He bathed her, groomed her, and walked her.

"Ginger always had behavior problems," recalled Green. She had a stroke and always yelped. "You'd think she was being beaten. And when she took a walk, she always had to be in front. Sonny loved her."

One of Green's most prized possessions was assembled by Sonny. She told of family movies, on sixteen-millimeter film, beginning to deteriorate. Sonny rented a projector and worked for weeks transferring them to videotape. In her honor, she said, he even dubbed in music, using her beloved Frank Sinatra tunes, although he hated them.

To Dora Green, her family joy seemed to center on her beloved Sonny. In her reminiscences, she never once mentioned her own son, George Green.

Four

Beverly Drive slices in reckless curves downhill through a canyon flanked on both sides by lavish, expansive hillside homes of Hollywood luminaries. Leveling out, it cuts south into the shopping pinnacle of the rich and famous, Beverly Hills. Between Sunset Boulevard and Wilshire, its four lanes are jammed with Rolls-Royces, Mercedes-Benzes, and Jaguars. Continuing south, the street loses a bit of its glamour. By the time it crosses Olympic and reaches the Santa Monica Freeway, it has once again narrowed into a residential street of smaller homes in a respectable zip code location called Cheviot Hills. The neighborhood in which Myra Davis lived was regarded as a safe community. But a series of bizarre attacks on six women, over a period of two years, gripped the area.

Tina Joye felt no fear as she strolled the peaceful sidewalk along Castle Heights Avenue, shepherding two children entrusted to her by their parents. The little ones, ages three and four, toddled along with her, only a few blocks from their home. In her duties as nanny, or au pair, Joye felt certain of their safety. Her own vulnerability didn't even occur to her.

She paid little attention to a sandy-haired young

man keeping pace with her, a few yards behind. By the time she realized that he'd increased his speed and closed the distance between them, it was too late to react.

Without warning, she felt a pair of hands groping her buttocks over the skirt she wore. Later speaking of the encounter, she said, "I felt a hand slide between my legs." As the stranger probed and squeezed, intimately grabbing and fondling, shock paralyzed her. "I was very scared."

Within a few seconds, an indignant fury replaced her fright, and she yelled the first insult that came into her mind. "Stupid!"

The assailant returned her shout with a string of loud, vulgar obscenities, making reference to her body. "He was very angry." He raised a clenched fist in what she perceived as a threat to punch her in the face. "I thought he was going to hit me."

Perhaps his reluctance to be arrested, or her feisty reaction to his bizarre attack, discouraged the mugger. Continuing his barrage of invectives, he suddenly turned, and walked away, in no special hurry.

Trembling in a rush of anger, embarrassment, and fright, Joye grabbed the hands of both children and hurried back to their home. She called the police to report a strange case of sexual battery. Only later did it occur to her that she might have narrowly escaped a far more serious fate.

As the months slid by, Detective Gary Fullerton uncovered no additional leads in the murder of Myra Davis. Two men remained under suspicion, but noth-

ing turned up that would solidly link them to the
crime.

Early traffic buzzed past Roxbury Park in the south-
west corner of Beverly Hills on May 15, 1989, nearly
ten months after Myra Davis was raped and strangled
in her home, about two miles away.

Planning to board a city bus, Mary Lotolo, twenty-
five, strode briskly along the Roxbury Drive sidewalk
toward Olympic Boulevard. Vivacious and lively, just
slightly over five feet tall, Lotolo had short red hair,
olive skin, and dark eyes that gave her an exotic look.
She had allowed herself enough time to enjoy the
daily walk past lawn and trees en route to her job.

In Lotolo's peripheral vision, she caught a glimpse
of a young man sitting in the driver's seat of a parked
tow truck, obviously staring at her. Being ogled by
men was nothing new to her, so she shrugged it off
and continued on her way. As she started to cross the
street, she heard the sound of heavy footsteps behind
her, seemingly in a hurry. As a simple matter of courtesy, she moved aside to let the impatient pedestrian
pass.

A hand touched her back. Before she could react,
another hand reached between her legs and roughly
gripped her pubic area through her clothing.

Shocked beyond belief, Mary Lotolo screamed as
loud as she could. The assailant released her and ran,
but not before she got a good look at him. She
guessed him to be about six feet tall, muscular, dark
sandy hair, with a heavy brow and a brushy blond mustache.

Angry and distressed, Lotolo couldn't even think

about going to work. She rushed home and called the police.

The rape and murder case of Myra Davis gathered dust in the LAPD files, becoming a lingering bad memory on the first anniversary of her death. Sherry Davis and her family still maintained a faint hope that it would one day be solved. No arrests had been made. No additional evidence turned up. Whoever killed her was still free.

On Exposition Boulevard, just three-quarters of a mile from the home where Myra Davis had lived and died, Susan Deane, thirty-six, meditated and chanted her prayers as she walked toward a temple along the residential street. She thought it seemed deserted in the early morning in October 1990, and didn't notice a shadowy figure emerge. Her heart leaped when a hand touched her buttocks. Shocked, Deane spun around to face a young man. She felt her face flush and tears form when she saw that he gripped a knife in his right hand, which he waved threateningly at hip level. Unshaven, with tousled sandy hair and rumpled clothing, he appeared to have just climbed out of bed. Even more frightening to Deane, she later said, was the "wild look" in his eyes. It didn't help when she saw that his "zipper was open and his penis was exposed."

Feeling as if she had entered a horrible nightmare, Susan Deane stood still as the muscular man ranted at her in vulgar, obscene, insulting language, his blond mustache bristling. She nearly collapsed with relief when he inexplicably retreated and vanished.

Thankful that she hadn't been injured or killed, she rushed home to telephone the police.

Still trying to recover on the following day, Deane couldn't believe it when she caught sight of the assailant driving by near the same spot. He sat behind the wheel of a blue 1970s pickup truck. It terrified her when their eyes met, and he began screaming "horrible things" at her. Fortunately, he was traveling in the opposite direction, so she darted out of sight, ran home, and called the police again.

Yet a third time, a few days later, she spotted him driving on nearby Robertson Boulevard. Again he shouted demeaning insults and obscenities. Growing angrier, she rushed to a pay phone and dialed the police department.

No more than three weeks had passed before the sex groper made another appearance, this one even more violent. On the first day of November, Elsa Beebe, returning from Santa Monica City College shortly after noon, walked along Castle Heights Drive, paralleling Beverly Drive, one block east. Carefree after classes, the tall, striking eighteen-year-old chewed on an apple and thought about her future. Answering an inner call to help unfortunate people, she planned to become a missionary. She had seen more than her share of poverty during her childhood in a war-torn Central American country and wanted to work toward erasing such misery. With that goal, she worked part-time as a nanny to pay her way through school.

Speaking later of the incident that changed her life, Beebe said, "I was attacked. Someone grabbed me from behind and forced me to the ground on my knees. I fought hard to get up. But he grabbed me around the neck."

While holding her down with an arm around her throat, the muscular, sandy-haired assailant rubbed Beebe's body and buttocks. "He was horribly lewd, telling me he wanted to have sex with me. I was screaming and fighting and finally broke loose from his grip. I ran away."

Beebe could hear the man yelling behind her. "Hey, if you don't want to give it up, let me pay for it." She accelerated her flight. "Don't bother running," he shouted. "I know where you live."

What she didn't mention in her recollection was the horror she'd experienced as a four-year-old child when she was raped, and the longstanding effects of posttraumatic stress disorder resulting from the brutal violation of her young body.

Despite her report to the police, the thug persisted in giving her trouble. "Afterward, I was getting lewd calls from a man who sounded like him. He was breathing heavily and said he was masturbating. When I stopped answering my phone, he left messages on my answering machine, saying he was going to kill my cat. I don't know how he knew I owned a cat."

A few days later, she returned home. It was evident that someone had been in her apartment, and her cat was locked in a closet.

Terrified, Elsa Beebe installed extra locks on her door and began sleeping in the dead-bolted bathroom. Unable to sleep or study, she eventually moved to San Francisco, where she underwent long months of therapy. She gave up on her plans to become a missionary.

* * *

In early February 1991, another woman fell victim
to the bizarre sexual attacks. Bonnie Rosen, thirty-
four, attractive, petite, with long black hair, while walking home from work, heading south on Beverly Drive,
saw a young muscular man approach head-on. The
stocky six-footer, with a light-colored mustache,
blocked her path, reached toward her, grabbed her
left breast through her clothing, and smirked. "Nice
tit!" he told her. She jerked away, ran, and later called
the police.

Five

Bernard Davis and his wife, Shirley—no relation to Myra or Sherry Davis—followed their customary habit, on the beautiful sunny morning of Friday, March 6, 1992, of walking the few blocks to Von's grocery market. A soft breeze had nudged the coastal overcast back toward the sea, leaving blue sky and a clear view of the mountains north of their home in the Palms section of West Los Angeles, near Cheviot Hills.

At age sixty-seven, Bernard enjoyed reasonably good health, as did Shirley who was a couple of years younger. Standing no more than five-seven and five-five, neither of them would tip scales much more than 110 pounds. Bernard might even be considered frail by larger men.

With Shirley pushing their wheeled shopping cart along Palms Boulevard, the couple stopped short of their destination, aghast at the scene they witnessed. It was the second time in two days they'd endured watching the same man apparently abusing his dog.

About five or six yards in front of the couple, the muscular fellow, about six feet tall, mid-twenties, pulled a leash against which a blond cocker spaniel barked and seemed to be resisting. Appearing angry, the man began kicking at the little dog.

Appalled, Shirley Davis called out, "Don't do that. You shouldn't kick your dog."

Turning toward them, the man's face darkened in fury. He shouted, "Mind your own fucking business. It's my fucking dog. I'll do what I damn well please with it."

Bernard Davis, from a generation that didn't use such words in the company of ladies, recoiled and spoke up. "Be quiet! I don't like anyone to use that kind of language in front of my wife."

Shirley later spoke of the incident: "I whispered to my husband, let's just walk away, that the guy was a very angry person. Then the man came toward us. He kicked my cart and put a dent in it. He put his hands on it and pushed it at me. I was grateful the cart was between him and me, for fear that he might have hit me."

The dog owner, letting go of the cart, clenched a fist, lunged toward Bernard Davis, and threw a punch into the smaller man's face. The blow fractured his cheekbone and opened a cut. Davis fell backward, landed on the pavement, and struck his head against the cement.

According to Shirley, the assailant saw her husband lying still on the ground, spun around, and ran away, taking the dog with him.

A passing motorist saw the stricken couple and called the police. Paramedics arrived a few minutes later. As they attended to him, Davis opened his eyes. Groggy, he groaned and tried to rise. "Let me up," he demanded, "I want to go to the market." Within a few minutes, he passed out again. The EMTs loaded him into an ambulance for transportation to a nearby hospital. Shirley rode with him, observing that his right eye was closed and blood flowed from his cheekbone.

He remained under care until the next day, when he was released for transfer to a Bay Vista convalescent hospital for observation and treatment by his own physician. Davis was able to stand and walk to a police officer's car for a ride to the second hospital.

That night, he lapsed into a coma. Ten days later, seemingly on the verge of regaining consciousness, Davis tried to move and found he was paralyzed. Shirley's hopes for his recovery dimmed as his condition deteriorated. Bernard Davis died on the last day of March, a little more than three weeks after being struck.

In the interim, on March 16, Lana Martin, thirty-one, walking home from a bus stop in Cheviot Hills, at about seven-thirty in the evening, nearly collided with a dark-haired young man as he came around a corner. Starting to excuse herself, Martin was interrupted by his vulgar comments about the size and appearance of her breasts. Horrified, she stood staring at him in shock. "Then he reached out and touched my vagina through my clothing."

Martin recoiled, screaming. The assailant jumped into a car parked adjacent to them. She ran. He started the car, lurched it up onto the sidewalk, and accelerated toward her. Trying to scramble away, she twisted her ankle and fell. At the last second, he twisted the wheel, rolled back onto the pavement with tires squealing, and roared away. A woman witnessed the whole sequence from her apartment window and rushed out to help Martin. She drove the crying victim home and helped her call the police.

Detectives investigating the assault of Bernard Davis interviewed his wife, Shirley, on March 25. After noting the facts, he showed her a "six-pack" of photos depicting different men with similar characteristics. Without hesitation, she identified photo number three as the assailant.

His name was Kenneth Dean Hunt. Some people called him "Sonny."

A check into Hunt's background revealed that he'd been involved in a series of strange attacks on women. During the past two years, six female victims had picked him from photo lineups as the man who had sexually attacked them on public sidewalks in the Cheviot Hills area and had sexually groped them. Two of the cases had occurred only two blocks from the spot where Bernard Davis had been struck. Hunt had been arrested and charged with sexual battery against Mary Lotolo and Bonnie Rosen, but imposition of sentences was suspended in both cases. Instead, he was put on probation and given a list of specific orders by the court. "Obey all laws, stay away from the women who had identified him, do not commit a similar offense, and submit to one year of sexual abuse counseling."

A Los Angeles County deputy medical examiner conducted an autopsy of Bernard Davis and certified that Davis had died as a direct result of blunt-force trauma to the head.

Four months later, Hunt entered a negotiated plea of guilty to voluntary manslaughter. Charges of felony cruelty to animals, for allegedly kicking his dog, were dropped.

Ordered to serve six years, he went to state prison. His wife, Betty, and his mother-in-law, Dora Green, visited him as often as possible. When Dora underwent treatment for cancer, Hunt was still behind bars, so he couldn't give her the loving care she later described. He benefited, however, from a generous policy in force at that time that allowed felons to be paroled after serving about half of their sentences. He was released, on parole, November 22, 1995. John Widener, an energetic, stout, goateed agent of the California Department of Corrections (CDC), would be in charge of helping Hunt adjust to life in the community and avoid pitfalls that might lead to future criminal acts.

Conditions imposed on Hunt were typical for most parolees. He couldn't engage in any criminal conduct; he must not own, possess, or have access to any weapon; he must comply with instructions from his parole agent, John Widener.

The job of supervising Kenneth Hunt hadn't been made easy by CDC officials. In 1998, nearly 125,000 inmates were released from state correctional facilities, all of them on parole. But the budget had been sharply cut for parole services, nearly doubling the caseloads for each of the 1,800 parole agents. Every one of them, including Widener, would be responsible for eighty to one hundred parolees. That meant regularly visiting each person, attempting to oversee their routines, their housing, medical care, education, and social activities, and to provide counseling.

For some, the job seemed overwhelming, but not for Widener. Respected among his peers and col-

leagues, he had a reputation for hard work, thorough-
ness, and fair treatment of his "clients." He let none
of them slip through the cracks. He also supervised
Hunt's brother-in-law, George Green, who had crossed
paths with the law through forgery.

Kenneth "Sonny" Hunt moved back into the house
on Beverly Drive with his wife, mother-in-law, and several others. He worked at odd jobs, unable to keep
any regular employment. His treatment of both
women convinced them that he was a wonderful, loving person.

On a rainy night in January, while driving home,
Hunt spotted an attractive woman trying to keep dry.
He pulled over and scanned her well-packed 105
pounds on a five-four frame, her tousled brown hair
streaked with blond, her seductive brown eyes and full
lips. He offered her a ride. Tina Moore smiled and
accepted. It wasn't the first time she'd entered an
automobile of a man she didn't know. Her behavior
would later come under scrutiny with a revelation that
she had been convicted of a misdemeanor called
"moral turpitude," more commonly known as prostitution.

Moore's background meant nothing to Hunt. Finding her likable and sexy, he gallantly provided transportation to her home. The warmth and feelings that
began on a cold, rainy January night developed into
a relationship that lasted into the warm breezes of
mid-June. It ended when she found out he hadn't
been entirely honest with her. "We had an argument," she later said, "because I found out he was
married."

According to Moore, she and Hunt met for a few
drinks. "I knew he was living with a lady, like a lady

friend in the same home. And I don't remember how I found out he was married. I was ranting and raving. And that is when he backhanded me across the bridge of my nose." She added that Hunt was a big, strong guy, and the blow left black-and-blue bruises. She described herself as having "raccoon eyes."

The attack startled her. "Everything happened so fast." Moore couldn't recall many details about the confrontation. "I do remember the backhand," she groaned. Given reminders, she didn't deny that Hunt had grown tired of her. "I was drinking," she said, "and he told me he wanted to cut off our relationship and that he was going back to his wife." She said she couldn't remember whether she had slapped him or not. After another gentle reminder, Moore said it was possible that she had kicked him in the groin before he hit her.

If Tina Moore's memory failed months later, the incident was quite clear in her mind on June 17, 1996, when she informed parole agent John Widener of the incident. Kenneth Hunt was charged with assault and battery.

The CDC rules are quite clear. A parolee is supervised by a CDC agent and must follow certain conditions. If a violation is committed, the Board of Prison Terms can revoke parole and order the offender to serve a parole revocation term.

Kenneth Dean Hunt returned to the lockup to serve another year, from July 24, 1996, until July 12, 1997.

Once again, his wife, Betty, and his mother-in-law showed their faith in him through visits and letters. When he returned home again, Hunt sported tattoos over several parts of his body. His wife's name deco-

rated his chest; his own nickname, "Sonny," was inked
onto his left forearm, flanked by a pair of skulls.

During the entire period of incarceration, no blood
relative ever came to see him.

Six

The onslaught of problems for Dora Green's son-in-law troubled her. She just couldn't believe Hunt had been involved in any criminal behavior, and welcomed him home in the summer of 1997 after he'd served additional time for violating parole. Resuming the relationship, she accepted his solicitous treatment and love he proffered as if she'd given birth to him. He voluntarily helped around the house and nursed her through various ailments. Green hoped the bad times were over.

Hunt faced difficulty finding regular employment again, so Green watched for any opportunity to help. She sometimes found it among her customers at the manicure business she ran on Pico Boulevard, a short distance from her home on Beverly Drive.

Among Green's most faithful clients was an attractive fifty-nine-year-old divorcée who looked no more than forty. Jean Orloff had patronized the manicurist for several years. She drove semiweekly from her apartment in a modern three-story building on South Bentley Avenue in West Los Angeles, not far from Cheviot Hills. Vibrant and beautiful, Orloff kept herself in perfect shape, used makeup sparingly, and insisted on keeping her nails properly manicured. She liked Dora Green's service so well, she recommended it to her own mother, Elizabeth Davis (no relation to either Myra Davis or Bernard Davis), who also became a regular customer of the little salon on Pico.

During one of Orloff's manicure sessions, Kenneth and Betty Hunt dropped in for a quick visit. Dora introduced Jean to them. A few weeks later, Orloff mentioned a problem she had been enduring a long time in her apartment. A large mirror, she said, had been twisted from its wall mounting by an earthquake in 1995, and she'd had no luck in getting it fixed. Green immediately offered help. She said, "You met my son-in-law. He does this kind of work."

Not only could Sonny be useful, said Dora, but his wife could also provide a service. She sold Avon products. So Orloff became a part-time employer of Hunt and a regular client of his wife, Betty.

Near the end of October, 1997, while showing Orloff her wares, Betty mentioned the annual Halloween party to be held at her home on Beverly Drive. Orloff had previously heard both Hunt and Green describing in glowing detail the lavish decorations for Halloween they'd prepared in other years. It sounded like an exciting event, so Orloff said she would love to attend and would bring her neighbor, Barbara Kappedal.

Kappedal, close to Orloff's age, also lived alone in the same apartment building, on the second floor, one flight down from Jean. The two women had been close friends for years. They contrasted noticeably in appearance. Orloff was a sun worshiper and kept her skin well tanned, complementing her long dark hair and accenting her blue-green eyes. Kappedal bore classic Nordic characteristics: lean, high cheekbones, light complexion, and bobbed blond hair cut short, parted, and combed back.

They shared interests in movies, the Los Angeles Kings hockey team, dinners together, and even rock concerts. The Rolling Stones with Mick Jagger weren't exactly Kappedal's favorite musicians, but Orloff loved them and talked her into going to two of their concerts, one at Dodger Stadium, on a hill north of downtown Los Angeles. For that one, a friend had provided her with "pit passes," enabling them to sit up close. Acquaintances teased them about it, but, Kappedal said, "Jeannie just laughed it off. Young at heart is definitely the best way to describe her."

Another characteristic both women shared was love for their cats. When Barbara adopted a pair of kittens, Jean made it a point to visit every night to play with the frisky balls of fur, much to the disgruntlement of her own purebred chocolate-point Balinese cat, Frankie. Frankie, friends said, had replaced her elderly Siamese, Tiffany, after the latter's death at age seventeen, and was like Jean's child. Sometimes, sunbathing on her apartment balcony, Orloff would hold conversations with Kappedal, who relaxed on her own balcony below, while Frankie sat on the ledge, staring down on Barbara, then back to Jean as they spoke. With an imperious expression, he seemed to understand everything they said. As a dedicated animal lover, Orloff collected photographs of friends' pets and kept them in an album. She also worked as a volunteer at the Humane Society when she had time off from her professional duties as a dental surgical assistant.

Kappedal accepted Orloff's invitation to join her at Dora Green's Halloween party. They marveled at the

elaborate and creepy decorations, the carved pump-
kins, and the food.

A big part of Orloff's social life involved food. She
liked to experiment with cooking techniques and new
recipes. During dinner preparations, she would frequently telephone Kappedal and say, "I just made
something, do you want to come up and have a bite
to eat?" Barbara seldom refused.

Another regular food event regularly brought Orloff together with her family. Monthly, without fail,
she met her mother, Elizabeth Davis, and her sister,
Lois Bachrach, at various restaurants for lunch.

Bachrach, attractive, stylish, and sophisticated, married to an advertising executive, later reminisced about
those events. She said, "Jeannie had Wednesday afternoons off. At least once a month, the three of us would
take advantage of that to have lunch together. We ate
at a number of places, but at least twice a year we would
meet at this one little place. When we were growing up
in Chicago, we had a maid, Bunny Armstrong, who
made the best fried chicken. We found this great fam-
ily-owned restaurant on Pico and they made fried
chicken just like Bunny's. In the spring and fall, we
would go there and have our 'Bunny' lunch, fried
chicken and yams."

It amused Lois to see the interplay between Jean and
their mother. "Mom and Jeannie fought like cats and
dogs. They loved each other to pieces, but they always
argued about silly, trivial things. It was funny. Both of
them were very scrappy. I was always the low-key one,
not an arguer."

About Dora Green's 1997 Halloween party, Bachrach said, "For years her manicurist had talked to my
sister about how they really do up their house for the

occasion. I suppose because Sonny Hunt had started doing handyman work at Jeannie's, and Betty was her Avon lady, that Jeannie and Barbara decided to attend." It took place just six days after Jean's sixtieth birthday.

On Wednesday, March 18, 1998, Lois, Jean, and their mother, Elizabeth, had their "Bunny" lunch at the little restaurant on Pico. Jean and Elizabeth had their usual good-natured argument, while Lois laughed. She informed Jean and her mom about an upcoming trip to Kansas City with her husband. They chatted, ate, giggled, then went their separate ways.

It was the last time Lois or Elizabeth ever saw Jean Orloff.

"My earliest memories of my sister," recalled Lois Bachrach, "were when I was two or three years old. Jeannie was born on October 25, 1937, when we lived on Drexel Boulevard in Chicago, so she was about eight years older than I." Orloff's parents, Robert and Elizabeth Weiss, had divorced, and Elizabeth had subsequently married Myron Davis, a prominent attorney with *Esquire* magazine. Mr. Davis legally adopted baby Jean, but did not change her name. Lois came along in 1945, into an affluent, comfortable lifestyle.

"I think I was like a little doll to Jeannie," said Bachrach. "She was probably the best older sister anyone could have. She played games with me; she included me with all her friends, took me roller-skating, to the park, and to movies. I can even recall the first movie I ever saw. It was with Jeannie and her boyfriend." The teenagers took Lois to see *There's No Business Like Show Business,* starring Ethel Merman and

Dan Dailey, a brassy musical featuring a young beauty named Marilyn Monroe, who performed a torrid dance while singing "We're Having a Heat Wave." The youngster also tagged along to a showing of "the scariest movie I've ever seen." It was *The House of Wax*, with Vincent Price. A few years later, Bachrach watched another scary thriller. She would never forget Anthony Perkins and Janet Leigh in a black-and-white movie called *Psycho*.

Movies reminded Bachrach of her sister, but piano music would always bring more tender memories. "I remember the day the piano came. By then, we had moved to Cornell Avenue and lived on the twenty-first floor of a big apartment building. I was five and Jeannie was thirteen. I was not allowed to touch the piano. So when our parents would go out and my sister would baby-sit me, she would let me sit with her and put my hands on the forbidden keys. She taught me how to play a few silly little tunes, like 'Chopsticks.' She was very talented with her hands and could play quite well. I remember my parents discussing Jeannie's piano teacher, who said she was an incredibly gifted child at thirteen.

"Not only did Jeannie have gifted hands," Bachrach said with a nostalgic laugh, "but she had prehensile toes! My sister could pick up things with her feet! And I don't know why she didn't pursue the piano as a career. I think maybe she was simply a teenager who really didn't love it. But she would play for our pleasure."

Jean's first romance, Bachrach recalled, was with a boy named Kenny. "My sister was extremely beautiful and bore some resemblances to a popular actress at that time named Pier Angeli." Bachrach referred to a gorgeous, diminutive Italian actress who moved to Hollywood in the early 1950s appeared with stars such as Kirk Douglas and Paul Newman, and died at age thirty-nine from a drug overdose. "There was another guy in our building, Eddie, who had a crush on Jeannie. I remember Kenny and Eddie literally fighting over her, a fistfight out in the park. My father had to go and break them up."

"I wouldn't say Jeannie was defiant, but she pressed the envelope. She was somewhat of a rebel and not a very good student. My parents imposed a curfew, but she seldom met it. She was a handful. I was little and remember her coming in late. My parents had these discussions with her that I could overhear from my bed. Jeannie was very popular, and a social butterfly."

In the mid-1950s, recalled Bachrach, *Esquire* magazine moved its headquarters from Chicago to New York, necessitating a move for the Davis family. "I was about ten, and it was the summer before Jeannie's senior year in high school. We moved to White Plains, and Jeannie hated it." Forced to leave her friends and familiar environment, the teenager's reaction could certainly be expected. She made it clear she wanted to return to Chicago as soon as possible. But, gradually, she made adjustments, met new friends, and graduated from White Plains High School. Instead of rushing immediately back to Illinois, Jean enrolled at Westchester Community College to become a medical technician. Shortly after completing the curriculum, she finally made the move, returning to Chicago.

In the Windy City, Jean found employment as a medical technician, began dating, and met the man she thought was "mister right." She married him in

1959. Their only child, Debby, came along the next year. For Jeannie, though, things didn't work out as well as she had expected in Chicago or in her marriage. Mild irritations between the couple grew to unrest, then discord, and finally unbearable friction. Realization settled in for both Jeannie and her husband that it wasn't going to work. They divorced after two years. Jean needed the comfort of her family, so she and her little daughter returned to White Plains into the same apartment building where her parents and sister lived.

"It was tough for her," said Bachrach. "Her ex-husband didn't provide for her or for little Debby. We were still very close, but I soon completed high school and went off to Ithaca College." Bachrach earned a bachelor of science degree in physical therapy and accepted a position with the Westchester County Department of Health. She married Charles Bachrach in 1968, but continued working. "I would go into low-income projects and provide physical-therapy home care for disabled people, such as stroke victims." She recognized her vulnerability to attack, but thought little of it until she was mugged in one of the neighborhoods. "I wasn't seriously injured, but it scared me. My husband insisted I change jobs, so I went to work for a general hospital in Porchester, New York." It didn't take the intelligent and hardworking young woman long to become a department head at the hospital. "Then I got pregnant." Her own daughter, Jennifer, made her world debut on March 27, 1972. "After that, I worked only part-time for thirteen years."

At about the same time of Jennifer's birth, Jean Orloff needed a big change in her life. She stunned everyone by announcing she wanted to relocate to the West Coast. A short time later, she packed up and moved, with her little daughter, to California, where she stayed temporarily with a relative in the San Fernando Valley.

After a few months, Orloff found a charming one-bedroom apartment on Bentley Avenue in West Los Angeles. Two blocks of the street, lined with deciduous trees and towering Mexican fan palms, was filled with upscale apartment buildings within walking distance of shopping on busy Santa Monica Boulevard. Orloff's residence, on the top floor of a three-story white building, seemed secure enough. Visitors were required to use an intercom at the front entry and could gain access only through a door electronically controlled by the residents.

At night school, Orloff took courses to qualify her as a surgical dental assistant and found regular employment in that profession.

Southern Californians are perhaps the most automobile-dependent society in the country. Freeways crisscrossing the big basin flow with rivers of rubber and steel, spewing pollutants, roaring, jamming, fraying nerves, but ultimately delivering drivers to their destinations. Jean Orloff soon discovered it was necessary, when in the City of Angels, to do as the Angelenos do. She bought a new Chevrolet Malibu, red with a white top, black interior, and whitewall tires. "She was so meticulous with that car," said her sister, "and took unbelievable care of it." She would have preferred to park it in a closed garage, but the apartment offered spaces under the building.

Lois and Jean missed each other sorely, so made it a point to travel cross-country as often as possible for reunions, with Lois doing most of the commuting. In Los Angeles, she observed that Jean "was a wonderful mom, but like many single parents, felt it necessary to work long hours, which left Debby as a latchkey kid. Like all kids with too much freedom, she got into a little trouble here and there. Nothing serious. And there were financial problems. Basically, I was always there to bail her out because Jeannie couldn't afford to. So I'd get a call saying, 'I need some help.' "

Being the daughter of a single parent had no serious detrimental effects on Debby McAllister. Years later, as the mother of her own teenage son, she reflected on the relationship with her mom. Speaking in a melodious, upbeat voice full of charm and humor, she said, "I guess I was a pretty good kid. I was fine until I reached fifteen or sixteen." With a quick smile, she added, "Maybe I wasn't so fine. I don't know. I've had a great life. I mean, I'm an only child and I was totally spoiled. We used to go places and do things together. She took wonderful care of me. There's really nothing bad to say. She always worked hard and gave me the best of everything."

Most of McAllister's comments about Jean Orloff resonated with compliments and love. But there is always something critical a daughter can say about her mother. McAllister was no exception. "Even though she was terrific in so many ways, Mom was a complex person. She had her agenda and I had mine, like most kids that age. I think we probably had the typical mother-daughter clash. As teenagers, we know everything and parents know nothing. And we're always right, and they are just old, dusty, and archaic, and don't know anything. I know now I was wrong." Another smile darted across her lips. "And if I knew then what I know now, I'd probably do the same things."

One thing that bothered her was her mother's chain-smoking. "I have this sensitive nose, like a hound dog's, and I couldn't stand the constant smell of her Kool cigarettes. The apartment and her car reeked of them. I am, by choice, a nonsmoker and a nondrinker." The cigarettes made her hate smoking.

Other than the stench of cigarette smoke in the one-bedroom apartment, Debby liked the place. "It was nice and light in there with all the big windows. Mom's theme was mostly whitewashed oak and mauve. She had a king-size bed. We shared it for a while, until she didn't believe me when I told her that she snored. I put it on tape and she moved into the living room."

McAllister had inherited enviable genes that were bestowed upon her grandmother, her Aunt Lois, and her mom, Jean. They all looked much younger than their true ages. Slightly over forty, McAllister retained a youthful freshness that would allow her to easily pass for twenty-five. Bright and free-spirited, she spoke in rapid-fire sentences loaded with intelligence and wit. And she tried to tread softly when dealing with one particular issue about her mom she had found even more troublesome than the cigarettes.

Asked if Jean had been an overly strict or too permissive mother, McAllister said, "No, neither one. But I thought at the time that she didn't understand me. She probably did understand. I think sometimes she was so— so—vain. There's no other way to put it. She was very into her youngness, clinging tenaciously to youth. Which is all fine and dandy. She was beautiful and she was attractive. The women in our family are very lucky because we don't look our age. I appreciate that. But I think it's hard when you are struggling with the aging process to have a kid who is growing up, and you have to see yourself as an older person. I think that created a lot of conflict. So things got much better when I didn't live with her anymore. She never asked me to leave, but I left because it was time to. I was seventeen and I had finished high school. Then, of course knowing everything, I moved in with my girlfriend. Rent was cheap and work was easy. If I had done everything I should have done, I would have been a veterinarian. That was my goal." She spoke from behind her desk as a regional administrator for General Electric Medical Systems, Clinical Services.

A new anxiety began troubling Lois Bachrach and Jean Orloff in 1981. Myron Davis had fallen ill. He suffered for two years, but appeared to be recovering. Bachrach recalled, "We thought he was going to be OK, so Chuck and I relocated to California in June 1984. But he suffered a relapse, so we arranged to move both my mother and father out here. He passed away the following October."

Orloff, raising her teenage daughter, remained single, dating a few men. Not long before Debby left the apartment, a striking young man caught Orloff's eye in a supermarket. He worked there bagging groceries while attending the University of California, Los Angeles (UCLA), in Westwood, only two miles north of Orloff's apartment. They began dating despite a marked age difference. Said Lois Bachrach, "She had a long relationship with Vittorio Amati that lasted about twenty years. She was about forty, and he was in his early twenties. She did like younger men. He was very big and tall, with dark curly hair. Jeannie was only about five-four, and she looked so much younger than she was. They both played the piano, and they hit if off really well. They were a good-looking couple."

Debby McAllister also recalled Amati. "He wasn't much older than I was, and from a very wealthy family. I thought he was kinda like a con man to her. This is my interpretation, that he promised her everything and gave her nothing. Well, he did and he didn't. He gave her a cat and some nice jewelry. But he promised her things. I'm not certain, but I think he had another woman in his life. It was like he led a double life, basically. I don't think many people knew about his relationship with my mom."

According to McAllister, Amati rented an apartment on the second floor of the building where she and her mother lived. "I would see him from time to time, but, to me, he was just the guy in the apartment building. I eventually knew there was something going on between them. He moved out about the same time I did. He found a house a few miles away, and I talked to him about renting a room from him, but decided that wouldn't be a good idea. After that, he was what I call 'the man of darkness.' That means he only came around at night, like a vampire. But after I left, I wasn't sure who Mom saw or what she did."

In the first part of 1998, tension flared between Vittorio and Jean. By then, as Lois Bachrach recalled, he had worked his way up the ladder of a large professional organization. His employer suggested that his corporate and social status would be enhanced if had a wife. Amati reluctantly agreed, and told Orloff. Only she wasn't his choice for marriage! His proposal was a little different than what she might have expected. He wanted to marry someone else, but keep on seeing Jean. She let him know, in unequivocal terms, that his suggestion was unsatisfactory. The parting left strained feelings in both of them.

If Orloff suffered a broken heart, it didn't stop her from going out. One evening in 1998, she drove the short distance to Westwood, a popular movie-going destination for nearby UCLA students, to see a new film. It was a remake of *Psycho*. The new version followed the original Hitchcock script.

Orloff's daughter, Debby, went through her own tribulations with men. While still living with her mom, she began dating a youth named John Serpico. "He was my boyfriend from the time I was fifteen until I was seventeen, and was also from a very wealthy Italian family. They had an Italian restaurant and knew a lot of movie stars. His aunt was married to that entertainer who used to make such weird music, Spike Jones. John used to play backgammon with Lucille Ball. I met all those people through John. It was a lot of fun."

When the romance cooled with Serpico, they still remained on good terms. "Mom loved him and kept in contact with him for years. When John got married, Mom and his wife became close pals."

A new love soon entered Debby's life, an enchantment that led to marriage. She became Debby McAllister in 1981. Following her mother's pattern, the union produced a child, then later disintegrated. The baby, Andy, entered the world at Cedars-Sinai Hospital on September 17, 1983. His mother chose to raise him in a beautiful coastal town, San Clemente, ninety miles south of Jean Orloff's apartment. Despite the distance, Andy's presence in Orloff's life made a remarkable change in her.

Debby remembered it. "She had been so involved with being young; then she became this wonderful grandmother when I had Andy. Maybe she was ready to express all those maternal urges. Maybe there had been a time in her life when things were so complicated for her because she didn't know who she was. To be so young and pretty, then to have a daughter who became a teenager, and to suddenly be forty. She was complex in many ways. But her and Andy, that was a whole different story. They did everything together. They traveled at least once a year. Went to San Francisco. I've never even been there. It was just so wonderful to see that." Orloff made it clear that when Andy reached the age of sixteen, she was going to give him her car, the beautiful red-and-white Malibu.

Andy McAllister would one day characterize the bond with his grandmother by saying, "We were, like, best friends." She took him to hockey games, movies, picnics, and to San Diego's SeaWorld. On reciprocal visits, said Andy, "she did a lot of special things with me, just me and her. My dad usually dropped me off at her house, sometimes for the day and sometimes to stay overnight." With her high energy level, Orloff had no trouble keeping up with young Andy. He recalled, "She started taking me to concerts when I was eight or nine. And at games, she yelled louder than everyone else. She was never sickly and acted like she was about twenty." Her fondness for animals impressed Andy, and they reveled together in a visit to the San Diego Zoo. For years, they talked about going to Florida together to visit Disney World. In February 1998, Orloff made the reservations, several weeks in advance, and bought the plane tickets. Andy couldn't wait. He and his mom both agreed that Jean Orloff was the best, and prettiest, grandmother in the world.

Just as Orloff found fulfillment in her grandson, the widowed mother of Jean and Lois Bachrach, Elizabeth Davis, found solace in her daughters. Said Bachrach, "She was a very young and vigorous seventy-three. She and Jeannie spent a lot of time together, because my sister lived alone by then."

In San Clemente, Debby McAllister and her son, Andy, spent much of their time with Troy Posner, who had been a big part of their lives for several years. He and Debby had talked about marriage, but reluctance to tie the knot again kept her from such a commitment. "We are better off not married," she said. One of the better aspects of their relationship stemmed from Posner's deep affection for Jean Orloff. He couldn't do enough for her, and thought she would be a terrific mother-in-law.

Doris Boesky, Jean Orloff's good friend and neighbor, grabbed up an important addressed envelope that needed to be mailed, on Saturday, March 28, 1998. It was already 3:45 in the afternoon, and the final postal pickup from the drop boxes outside the post office on Veteran Avenue would be at 4:00 P.M.. Fishing in her purse for her car keys, she rushed out of her residence, next door to Orloff's apartment building, planning to drive to the post office. It would take only about five minutes. Her heart sank when she reached the car. One of the tires had gone flat.

There just wasn't enough time to wait for the Auto Club to dispatch someone. Boesky knew precisely who would readily agree to help, her pal Jean Orloff. She telephoned. "Jeannie," she wailed, "I have car trouble and I need a ride to the post office. Can you help me out?"

"Sure," came the instant response. Within a few minutes, Orloff picked Boesky up in the red-and-white Chevy Malibu. Dressed casually in sweats and wearing no makeup, Jean joked about hoping no one would see her. They chattered amiably on the way, and Boesky mailed her letter.

Back in front of the apartment, the two women conversed for several minutes until about 4:30 P.M. Boesky would later say it was clear to her, from the way Orloff was dressed and from her comments, that she had no plans to go anywhere that evening. Boesky thanked her for the lift and waved good-bye.

Seven

The lives of Jean Orloff's family were devastated during the last weekend of March 1998. It all started with a series of telephone calls.

On Saturday morning, March 28, Jean Orloff called her daughter Debby in San Clemente. Debby's former boyfriend John Serpico and his wife had dropped by that morning to spend some time with Jean. She held a deep fondness for the couple and had frequently joined them on social occasions, and even sad ones. Orloff had recently attended the funeral of Serpico's mother. She wanted to tell Debby about the visit.

McAllister, busy with a pressing list of chores, listened as Jean shared the news. Wishing to hear all the details, but preferring to wait until she had a little more time to spare, she said, "Mom, I really want to hear what's going on with them, so can I call you a little later today?" Orloff said that would be fine.

That afternoon, needing a break, McAllister made her first attempt to keep her promise. She got a busy signal. Several more tries drew the same result.

Speaking of it in retrospect, she said, "Even though Mom had a busy life, she always seemed to be there when I called her. I don't know how that worked so well, but she always seemed to be available when I needed her. And I knew that the only time her phone was busy very long was when she took it off the hook to go to the laundry room. So I didn't think much of it. 'Oh, she's just doing laundry,' I told myself.''

On Sunday afternoon, when McAllister's phone rang, Troy Posner answered for her. He listened for a moment and gripped the handset until his knuckles turned white. Tears formed in his eyes. After he'd hung up, he took Debby's hand, hugged her, and spoke. "That was Barbara Kappedal. Your mom has died!"

Remembering the moment, McAllister said, "When he answered the phone and started crying, I thought maybe something was wrong with my grandmother or maybe she had passed away. But he told me about Mom. I couldn't believe it at first."

Lois Bachrach and her husband, Chuck, both weary after a long flight from Kansas City, had just walked into their Studio City hillside home. She had spoken with her sister three days earlier by telephone, and later recalled it with a smile. "Jeannie always, always remembered birthdays, and she called me at our hotel on March twenty-sixth because it was my daughter's birthday. She always did that to congratulate me for having had Jennifer."

Within moments after entering the house, they received a far different call. Lois answered the phone and heard the breaking, strained voice of Debby McAllister. "This is really weird. I just got a call from Barbara Kappedal telling me that Mom is dead! That Mom had died. I'm coming up. Will you go over there?"

Feeling herself start to tremble, Bachrach struggled

to control her own emotions. "Of course. I'll leave right away."

Fifteen minutes later, she and Chuck arrived at Orloff's West Los Angeles apartment on Bentley Avenue. "The first thing we did is go up to Jeannie's apartment. I knocked, and two young uniformed police officers came to the door. A man and a woman. I told them who I was, and one of them said, 'We suggest that you don't come in. You can if you want, but we strongly suggest that you don't. It's not a pretty sight. We are waiting for the coroner.' "

Not quite certain what to do, the couple said they would wait in Barbara Kappedal's apartment on the next floor below. The police thought that would be a good idea, and said they would come down and notify them when the coroner had finished his examination. Nodding, one officer commented that the paramedics had already left, then said to Lois, "Your sister died of natural causes. It was very quick and she didn't suffer."

In Kappedal's apartment, the minutes dragged by like hours. No one knew what to say, other than short, whispered attempts to comfort one another. It took maximum effort to hold back tears when Bachrach's mother, Elizabeth Davis, arrived, accompanied by her own sister. Within a little more than an hour, Debby McAllister showed up with her son, Andy, and Troy Posner.

After another interminable wait, the police officers made their appearance as promised and said, "OK, the coroner was here. He came; he saw; he left. He agreed it was natural causes. You can call the mortuary now, if you wish, and have her body transported to a funeral home."

Against her better judgment, Lois Bachrach decided she wanted to have a final look at her sister. She asked Posner to go upstairs with her. Trembling again, she edged gently through the familiar entry, stepped to the bedroom doorway, and forced her gaze toward the bed. "Jeannie's body was covered with an afghan blanket," Bachrach recalled. "All I saw was a hand."

When the mortuary attendants arrived, they first removed a few items of jewelry from Orloff's body, gave them to Bachrach, then placed the corpse on a gurney for transportation to a funeral home. Bachrach took another brief look around her sister's apartment. An odd odor of stale smoke lingered in the air. And it wasn't the usual cigarette smoke. Then they spotted something that jolted them. On one side of the king-size bed, the ruffled bed skirt had been damaged by a recent fire, accounting for the peculiar odor. A quick check of the smoke alarm, installed only six months earlier, revealed that it had been dismantled, with the wires hanging loose and the cover missing. An unsettled feeling swept over Bachrach. She knew there had been a fire in her sister's kitchen months earlier, and when Jean had the damage repaired, she also put in the new smoke detectors.

A look at the bed made Bachrach feel even worse. "There were bloodstains on the bedcovers, so Troy and I removed all the bedding, took it out back, and threw it in a Dumpster. This was on Sunday night, and they collect the trash there on Monday morning." A few spots could still be seen on the mattress, so they turned it over. In the kitchen, they disposed of raw chicken pieces lying in the sink. The meat had apparently been thawing, or was there to be washed before cooking.

When the coroner's investigator arrived, Kappedal asked why there was blood around Orloff's head. He replied, "Sometimes blood vessels break when a heart attack takes place." The answer didn't satisfy her.

Returning to Kappedal's apartment, Lois hugged Debby, who asked, "What does it look like up there? I can't go up." Bachrach assured her that the place looked as it always did.

McAllister later said, "I wanted to remember her and the place as I had always known it. I was afraid. And if there were horrible, gross smells, like blood or something, I couldn't have stood it. I felt so sorry, too, for Barbara. She saw my mother lying there. What a horrible vision to stay with you your whole life. So Troy went up there for me. He loved her dearly and it was not an easy thing for him to do."

At Bachrach's comforting assurance that everything seemed normal in the apartment, McAllister at last changed her mind. Moving through the apartment in a daze, she examined a few of her mother's personal possessions, including a jewelry box she decided to take with her, along with her mom's purse. She looked fondly at the amazing array of bottles on the dresser. Lotions, colognes, perfumes—a staggering assortment of cosmetics. All neatly lined up, waiting for Orloff to sit before the mirror and use them. Everything in its order. The image imprinted itself on her mind.

After selecting a few other items to carry out, Bachrach and her husband prepared to leave. McAllister took a last look around and picked up Frankie, the cat. Leaning against Posner, she walked out.

"We all agreed," said Bachrach, "that on Monday

morning, we would make funeral arrangements. We would come back and start cleaning the apartment on Thursday."

Nothing would turn out the way they planned.

Orloff's close friend Barbara Kappedal later described what led to her discovering the body and the strange sequence of events that followed. "I received a call from Jeannie's mother, Elizabeth, a little after five o'clock Sunday afternoon. I knew her voice because we'd previously had dinner together with Jeannie." Elizabeth Davis told Kappedal that she'd been trying to reach her daughter by telephone since two-thirty, but got only busy signals. She asked, "Would you mind going upstairs and tell her to call her mother?"

"I walked up," said Kappedal. "When I reached Jeannie's apartment door, I saw the Sunday paper still lying on the hallway floor. That was really unusual, because she read it early, did the crossword puzzle, and clipped coupons from it. If she was going to be away, she would have asked me to pick it up and also to feed Frankie, her cat."

Kappedal rang the doorbell. No answer. She knocked. Still no response. "I went back to my apartment and got the door key she had given me." When Kappedal inserted the key into the dead bolt, it surprised her to see that it had not been locked. "Jeannie always kept her door locked, even though the security apartment had an intercom to the front entry, and visitors had to be allowed in by a remote control that buzzed them in. She was kind of nervous about that."

It startled Kappedal even more when she found the

second bolt also unlocked. Cautiously pushing the door open, she peered into the entry and took a few tentative steps into the silent room. The odor of smoke irritated her nostrils. "I knew Jeannie smoked cigarettes, but this was a different smell, like cloth burning."

Edging forward, Kappedal came to a sudden stop. "I could see into her bedroom, through the open door. She was lying facedown on the bed with her feet over the end of it. There was some blood around her head."

Even though Kappedal realized her friend was apparently dead, she called out her name. "She was so still and her feet were blue. She was naked on top of the covers." The phone, she noticed, was not in its usual place on a nightstand, but rather on the floor with the handset out of the cradle. She also observed where the smoky odor originated. The dust ruffle, or bed skirt below the mattress, had been partially burned, not very long ago. "It looked like it had been on fire, but had gone out."

Another peculiar thing caught her eye. Orloff always kept towels neatly folded and stored, or placed carefully on towel racks. "There were towels in a pile on the bathroom floor." Passing through the kitchen, Kappedal noticed raw chicken pieces in the sink as if they were being drained in preparation for cooking. "But Jeannie normally cooked dinner at about five-thirty P.M. to eat at seven."

The whole scenario seemed strange to Kappedal. "As soon as I saw her, I thought she had been murdered. It was just the whole feeling in the apartment. Her body looked like it had been flung on the bed."

Sick at heart, Kappedal rushed back downstairs to

telephone 911. Paramedics and investigators arrived shortly.

Tall, lean, dark-haired, and with the sculptured face of a movie star, Captain Chadwick Spargo, of the Los Angeles Fire Department, supervised the engine company at fire station 59 in West L.A. He and his three-person paramedic assessment unit answered the call to an apartment on Bentley Avenue. "We were met outside by the woman who called 911," Spargo later said. "She directed us to her female acquaintance in a unit on the third floor. Inside the apartment, we observed the body of a nude female facedown on a bed, her arms splayed out with palms up. This was unusual. People who die naturally are very seldom found facedown with palms up." Spargo noted that he had seen hundreds of heart attack victims and they are nearly always supine, faceup. The telephone, which appeared to Spargo as if it had been knocked from the nightstand to the floor, also made him suspicious.

Even if those oddities hadn't caught his attention, Spargo was especially bothered by his observation that part of the dust ruffle had recently been burned. He had often seen arson attempts that looked quite similar.

Overseeing examination by the paramedics, Spargo noticed a slightly red crease on the dead woman's neck. "It didn't look like normal lividity to me."

Sergeant Christopher M. Giles, of the Los Angeles Police Department, West L.A. Patrol, later spoke of his visit to Jean Orloff's apartment. Called to the scene, he met a pair of his uniformed subordinates, who showed him into Orloff's bedroom. In his report, the stout, beefy cop said, "I saw a naked female facedown on the bed. Part of the bed was burned. I no-

ticed cigarettes in the room and heart medicine in
her cabinet. I saw the phone was disconnected." He
later changed "disconnected" to "off the hook."

Captain Spargo spoke with Giles and expressed his
concerns about the peculiar circumstances. Giles
seemed unimpressed. Spargo later said, "He didn't
agree with our assessment that it seemed unusual."
Giles concluded that "there appeared to be no evidence of anything other than death by natural causes.
My officers had called a doctor, who would sign off
that it was a natural death."

To both Spargo and Kappedal, Giles said, "I've
been to hundreds of homicides and this isn't one of
them. But we'll let the coroner decide."

Barbara Kappedal wondered if Sergeant Giles had
arrived at incorrect conclusions. "I tried to point out
to him my suspicions." One of the officers asked her
if the deceased woman took any medication. Kappedal
said that Orloff did, indeed, use medicine for a common heart condition. The investigators seemed to believe that Orloff may not have taken her pills, or hadn't
used the proper dosage. One said, "Well, she's an elderly lady, and she didn't take her medicine and died."
Kappedal's protests made little impact. She directed
Giles to the kitchen. Someone who feels sick doesn't
put chicken in the sink to thaw, then strip naked and
die on the bed. But the officers felt that nothing else
was out of place. The burned dust ruffles could have
been caused by a mislaid cigarette, discarded match,
or careless use of a lighter. He made no comment about
the disconnected smoke alarm.

The coroner turned Orloff's body faceup and covered her with an afghan robe taken from a chair. He

announced that it appeared she had died of natural causes, probably a heart attack.

Dreading the task of informing the family, Kappedal steeled herself. She knew Lois Bachrach and her husband had traveled to Kansas City, so she called Orloff's daughter, Debby, to break the tragic news.

Still trying to recover from the shock of her sister's sudden death, Lois Bachrach and her husband visited the mortuary on Monday morning to make final arrangements for cremation of Orloff's body. A consoling manager said to her, "We're going to send the death certificate off to her doctor. As soon as we get it back, it will go to the health department. When they sign off on it, we will be able to make final disposition of the body. We should have the signed authorization by tomorrow; then we can perform the cremation soon afterward."

Bachrach wiped away tears and nodded. The timing would allow them to follow through with plans for a memorial service on Wednesday. Later discussing it, she said, "We're Jewish. In our religion, you do it as quickly as possible. There are no wakes, nothing before final disposition. Any ceremony takes place afterward. Thinking that everything would be completed by Wednesday morning, we wrote the obituaries to appear in New York and Chicago newspapers, and of course in Los Angeles."

The smooth process fell to pieces on Tuesday with a telephone call to Bachrach from the mortuary. The manager said, "We have a little problem here. The health department said they could not accept the doctor's signature on the death certificate, even if he was willing to sign." In California, he explained, in order to certify a death certificate the physician must have seen the patient within a month. But Orloff hadn't seen her doctor for at least six months. When he was contacted, he pointed that out. He also didn't believe that her heart condition was serious enough to kill her. Without more information, the physician refused to sign the death certificate. "Just to let you know," the caller added, "I'm going to contact the coroner's office. They will send a qualified person out to get this thing completed."

Later the same day, the perplexed mortuary manager tried to call Bachrach, couldn't reach her, so telephoned Debby McAllister. "Now we have another problem," he said. His contact with the Los Angeles Coroner's Office had resolved nothing because they had been unable to find any record of Orloff's death. Apparently, the department's investigator who had examined the body at the apartment had not filed a report, nor had he taken photographs, or even registered a case number. "This is going to delay things a bit. We are not going to be able to cremate the body before the memorial service," said the manager. "Is this a major problem for the family?"

Not wishing to complicate matters any worse, McAllister said they didn't seem to have any choice. They had scheduled the memorial service for Wednesday, so they would go ahead with it. The manager assured her that a coroner's investigator would make a special visit to the mortuary, examine the body, and get the matter settled.

The service was held as planned, but with an empty casket instead of an urn containing Orloff's ashes. The grieving family was joined by Jean Orloff's friends and neighbors paying their last respects to the woman who had brightened their lives. Dora Green and her daughter Betty Hunt were among them.

Bachrach recalled, "Afterward, we invited everyone in the family to stay that night in our home. Then on Thursday morning, Debby and Troy went to Jeannie's apartment to start sorting her things. I wanted to go, too, but had an important dental appointment that morning. As I was sitting in the dentist's chair, my cell phone went off. It was Debby, freaking out! She said Jeannie had been murdered!"

The mortuary manager had called McAllister to report what took place when Sherwood Dixon, the coroner investigator, arrived. He had taken one look at the body and proclaimed, "No way is this a death by natural causes. This woman was murdered! She was strangled." Dixon drew his conclusion after observing a dark purple furrow around Orloff's neck, which hadn't been obvious during earlier examinations. Subsequent explanations for the oversight noted that bruising in human tissue often does not clearly show until a day or two after the impact that caused it. What had earlier appeared to be nothing more than a slightly red crease or fold had darkened into a distinct manifestation of traumatic injury. Dixon stated he would remove the body for a complete autopsy. In addition, he would notify the LAPD homicide unit.

Before ending his conversation with McAllister, the manager added, "If there's anything you want to take from your mother's apartment, you'd better hurry up because homicide is on their way. It will be a crime scene. You won't be able to touch anything."

Bachrach, sitting in the dentist's chair, stunned again by the incredible twists, shouted, "Stop. I'm

leaving!" She raced to her sister's apartment. "I arrived at the same time as the police, with their black-
and-whites everywhere. They were putting crime-scene
tape all over the place. Five days had passed since
Jean Orloff's death, and there they were, telling me
not to touch anything." Bachrach couldn't believe it.
She and her family had been in the apartment, had
removed several personal items, had thrown away bedding, turned the mattress, disposed of the thawed
chicken, and started the cleaning. It worried her that
they had possibly destroyed valuable evidence.

When McAllister and Posner arrived, the police confronted them, along with Bachrach, and told them the
autopsy would be performed on Friday. "We will let
you know what they find. Meanwhile, you will not be
allowed inside the apartment." They made us all leave,
said Bachrach.

A perplexing mental image kept running through
McAllister's mind; all those perfume and cosmetic bottles lined up neatly on top of the dresser. "I know my
mom, and I know she had every *tchotchke* in America.
And if you were to slightly bump into that dresser, something would fall down, but there was *nothing* displaced.
The passage between her bed and the dresser was quite
narrow. If there had been any kind of a struggle at all,
especially if the killer had thrown her around, there
would have been a lot of bottles tipped over. And I
can't see any rapist or killer in a bedroom taking the
time to put everything back in order." Especially if that
charred bed ruffle was indicative that he had planned
to burn the place down. It didn't make sense to her.
Maybe the orderly placement of *"tchotchke"* suggested
there was no struggle because the guy knew her. Like,
perhaps, a former lover.

The family met again at Kappedal's residence on Friday, where detectives fingerprinted each of them and asked a series of questions. The investigators wanted to know the names of Jean Orloff's friends, enemies, and associates. They made a list of her doctors, her physical therapist, her manicurist, and anyone she had hired to do handyman work. Inevitably, the name of her longtime boyfriend, Vittorio Amati, came up. The parting had not been amicable. Bachrach later said, "We all thought Vittorio might be involved in her death. And we told the police that."

The bizarre sequence of events resembled a mystery movie full of twists and turns. By a hairbreadth, the cremation of Jean Orloff's body had barely been avoided. Had it not, all remaining evidence of murder, not already lost due to the speedy police and coroner's work, would have vanished forever, along with any chance of catching her killer. Fate had dramatically intervened. No motive was clear and no suspects identified, only a myriad of questions. Who would have wanted to kill the beautiful, fun-loving woman?

Eight

In the presence of two LAPD detectives, Dr. Louis Pena, a forensic pathologist and deputy medical examiner for the L.A. County Coroner's Office, performed the autopsy of Jean Orloff's body. Over a long, distinguished career, he had completed more than 1,600 examinations of deceased human beings. He was well acquainted with another pathologist in the organization, Dr. William Swalwell, who had carried out the autopsy on Myra Davis ten years earlier.

Just as had been discovered on the body of Davis, Dr. Pena found extensive petechial hemorrhaging in the eyes of Orloff, indicating death by strangulation. Dark, ragged furrows in her neck, abrasions to her chin, to the right side of her mouth, and to the tip of her nose, along with bruising of her inner gums all suggested she had been brutalized and strangled with a ligature. "The multiple injuries," he said, "would be consistent with her being hit in the face, or her face being pushed violently against a hard surface." It also appeared that she had probably fought desperately, trying to grasp the ligature as it choked the life out of her.

Internal injuries to the victim included extensive

neck hemorrhaging. The muscles over her voice-box bones had been cracked, and the tongue bore indentations caused by her biting down as she was being strangled. The perpetrator had also inflicted blunt-force trauma to the back of her rib cage before death, perhaps by pushing a knee into it while subduing her. Bruises discolored her left collarbone, left upper arm, left forearm, right thigh, both lower legs, and her hands, all of which suggested a violent struggle.

In direct contrast to earlier assumptions that she had possibly died of a heart attack, conclusions made at the crime scene by the police and a coroner's investigator, Dr. Pena found that despite mild hardening of the arteries, Orloff had been in generally "good health." The heart medicine she took was for a common arrhythmia, or rapid beat, which is seldom life threatening.

One more similarity to the examination of Myra Davis turned up. Jean Orloff had been sexually assaulted, and the responsible man left traces of semen in her body.

Clearly, Jean Orloff had struggled and fought for her life. In all probability, the physical conflict could help investigators. If a suspect could be identified and questioned, he probably would be covered with scratches.

One of the investigating officers who had met Orloff's family at her Bentley Street apartment on Friday, April 3, after the stunning discovery that a murder had been committed, was Detective Francene Mounger. Standing no more than five feet two inches, she might not look imposing to bad guys, but neither does a vial of nitroglycerin. Mounger had graduated from the Los Angeles Police Academy in

1982. Despite being a mother of three daughters and one son, she kept pace with "a lot of young, rugged males fresh out of college." On one hand, she could be as firm as any street cop, but on the other she could use her radiant smile and soft hazel-brown eyes to reveal the bright, cordial, good-natured inner woman.

Three years after her birth in Durant, Oklahoma, Mounger's family had moved to Lubbock, Texas, the home of rock-and-roll icon Buddy Holly. Speaking of her life in the panhandle, Mounger said, "Waylon Jennings was a disc jockey on radio there when I was growing up. But I was never a country-western fan. My two older brothers were into Elvis Presley, so I liked rock and roll better." That preference helped when the family relocated again, this time to Los Angeles, where "hillbilly" music was not in vogue. "I'm a Hollywood High School graduate," she said, her eyes glittering with pride.

After high school, she met a handsome LAPD cop, married him, had four children, and worked in an assortment of jobs. "By 1982," she said, "I decided to try something different. I wasn't sure just what I wanted to do, but I knew what I *didn't* want to do. I didn't want to be confined in an office building or work any kind of sales. I like the outdoors. At that time, the LAPD went on a campaign of recruiting women. So my husband suggested I give it a try. There were far fewer women on the force then, and most of them didn't work patrol duty. At the academy, the physical part was tough, but I got through OK."

She worked patrol for several years out of the Hollenbeck Division, which contains a large Hispanic community. "There are a lot of street gangs there, but what impressed me was that most of the residents were really nice law-abiding people who were supportive of the police. On my first few patrol adventures, I recognized there could be danger, but, you know, I really wasn't nervous. That usually comes after a difficult situation is all over, and you begin to think about what might have happened."

Mounger's husband, Darryl, had moved from the adventures of the mean streets to the intrigue of courtrooms. After earning a law degree, he became a defense attorney specializing in representing police officers. Among his clients were cops in several controversial, high-profile cases. They included Stacey Koon, one of a group of officers who repeatedly struck an African-American man, Rodney King, after a high-speed chase. The incident, videotaped by a bystander, received national attention on television news. Another client, Mark Fuhrman, became well known as the investigator who found the infamous glove tried on by O. J. Simpson during his notorious murder trial.

Francene Mounger, after working robbery detail for several years, and interacting with homicide teams, joined the unit as a detective in 1998.

On the day a coroner's investigator decided Jean Orloff had been murdered, Mounger was off duty. "Sergeant Ron Phillips, my supervisor, called me at home. We are always on call. He said Lieutenant McWillies, from the coroner's office, had contacted him with information about an apparent homicide. A deputy coroner had gone to a funeral home to look at a deceased woman and discovered that she had obviously been strangled. The ligature marks were clearly evident, quite pronounced."

Mounger rushed to the station on Butler Avenue in West Los Angeles, where she met Ron Phillips for a drive to the coroner's office. "Doctor Pena looked at the victim's body. She had died from strangulation by ligature. He also directed that a rape kit be employed." The analysis proved that victim Jean Orloff had not only been murdered, but had also been sexually assaulted.

Observing the entire autopsy procedure, Mounger made notes of observations and potential leads. It is not an easy job to watch the dissection of a human being. Mounger, like all homicide investigators, couldn't allow thoughts of the victim's prematurely ended life to cloud her thoughts. Concentration must be objective, looking for any slight clue that might help answer questions about those horrible moments when that life was savagely snuffed out by a brutal killer.

Wearing a blue paper shirt and apron over her regular clothing, a surgical mask and goggles, along with plastic bootees, all the garb designed for protection from biohazards, Mounger listened and took notes. She heard Dr. Pena describe broken ribs in the victim's back, leading to a possible scenario of a perpetrator forcibly pushing his knee into Orloff's back while subduing her with one arm and using the other hand to twist a ligature that choked the life from her. Whether Pena said the killer might have been left-handed, or Mounger's mental image of the struggle created a picture of a left-handed man inflicting the injuries, she could not be certain. She noted "killer is possibly left-handed."

With the grisly autopsy duty behind them, Mounger and Phillips left the coroner's lab and drove to Orloff's residence on Bentley Avenue, where they joined Detective Bradford Roberts and Detective Bruce Oakley. The victim's family, distressed and confused, had also arrived. They wanted to cooperate, and were worried that they might have disturbed possible evidence several days earlier when officials concluded that Orloff had died of natural causes.

Gathering family members together, Detective Mounger assured them that everything possible would be done to solve the case. Taking them aside, one by one, she asked questions about Orloff's associates and activities. When the Scientific Investigation Division (SID) arrived, she helped coordinate the process of fingerprinting and taking of photographs. "There was no real crime scene," she would later observe. "So much of the furnishing in the apartment, and the victim's possessions, had been moved, packed up, or even disposed of."

Even though little chance of finding any usable evidence remained, Mounger and Phillips examined the interior of Orloff's apartment. "We saw burns on the dust ruffle on the bottom right side of the bed. The carpet and mattress were also scorched. Diagonally across the bed, we could see more evidence of burning." The earlier conclusion that Orloff might have caused the damage with careless smoking seemed remote. Mounger thought it appeared more like an effort to torch the place.

One other item caught Mounger's eye. "Near the bed, I found an electric massager with a twisted cord. I later took it to the coroner for analysis, and he confirmed that it 'could have been' the murder weapon, the ligature that made those marks on her neck.

"We began the long process of interviewing every-

one connected to the victim. We talked to family
members that day, well into the evening, along with
Barbara Kappedal and other friends and neighbors of
Orloff." No eyewitnesses to the actual crime could be
found.

Speaking later of the original decision by an LAPD
investigator who concluded that Orloff had died of
natural causes, Mounger expressed regrets, but recognized the human factor. "The sergeant who made the
decision was relatively new in the assignment. We are
not infallible, as much as we want to be. As with any
human being, we can make errors. It was certainly
difficult at that time to see the injuries to the victim's
neck and other parts of her body. Bruises generally
don't show up in those dark colors for a day or two.
It was evident that she was a smoker and there was
heart medicine in her cabinet. Who knows? People
making decisions can be distracted, exhausted at the
end of a shift, or simply make errors in judgment. We
would like to be perfect, but that doesn't always happen." It was fortunate that other circumstances occurred to prevent the body of Jean Orloff from being
cremated before it could be discovered that she had
been murdered.

Detective Ron Phillips, supervisor of the homicide
team in the West L.A. station, expressed pride about
his decision to assign the Orloff case to Francene
Mounger. She related well to the victim's family and
possessed the right instincts for the job. With more
than thirty years of experience on the force, Phillips
was a sound judge of skills needed to investigate murders.

Born in Arkansas, Phillips was ten days old when
his parents moved to southern California in 1945. His

father, like thousands of other young men, had just returned home from service with the U.S. Army in WWII, anxious to settle with his new family and start a career. He spent forty-seven years with the U.S. Postal Service. Ron chose a different path. From the age of ten, he wanted to do more than play cops and robbers. He realized that early in life he wanted to be a cop. "When I was just a kid, I knew a policeman and liked him. My best friend's uncle was with the Alhambra Police Department, and another buddy's dad was with the Los Angeles Sheriff's Office. I guess that had a lot to do with my choice." He achieved his goal in 1966.

"I worked my first homicide case in 1972, and was in and out of homicide units for years." By the time the Orloff case broke, he had been promoted several times, finally to Detective III (senior detective). He supervised not only the four investigators of murder in West L.A., but also the gang unit of two detectives and seven patrol officers. To anyone visiting his office, it's clear that he has not only the respect of his colleagues, but their deep friendship as well. A husky man, Phillips's deep-set brown eyes under a high forehead reflect a capability of penetrating through any facade a bad guy might assume. Somehow, despite years of cornering killers and con men, he has retained a sharp sense of humor and a ready laugh.

When the notification came that Jean Orloff had not died a natural death, but had been murdered, Phillips called Francene Mounger at home. "She didn't have a partner then, so I went with her on the interviews."

After the autopsy, Phillips huddled with Mounger and Roberts to brainstorm the facts and plan the next moves. With the murder of a single woman, it often turns out that ex-husbands, boyfriends, or casual lovers are linked to the crime or know something about it. "We knew that Jean Orloff was single, and wondered if she had any boyfriends or other men in her life that perhaps her family didn't know about. Francene came up with a great idea."

"Being female," said Mounger, "I know we talk about our lives to our hairdressers and our manicurists. We use them as sounding boards. I had talked with Jean Orloff's mother, Elizabeth, and learned that a manicurist named Dora Green had been doing the nails of both Elizabeth and Jean for several years." Tracing the name and her place of business, they learned that Green lived on Beverly Drive in Cheviot Hills, only a few miles from the police station.

"So Ron Phillips and I went to Dora's house. We told her that Jeannie Orloff had been murdered and that we were asking for information. Did she know anyone Orloff had problems with, or anyone who might want to harm her? The only person she mentioned was Vittorio, Orloff's former boyfriend."

Phillips recalled the visit. "Dora Green appeared surprised, but quite calm. She told us that she and her daughter had attended the funeral service for Jean." While Green mentioned that Orloff had been dating a man named Vittorio for a long time, she did not mention that her neighbor, Myra Davis, had been murdered ten years earlier. Nor did she mention that her son and son-in-law were both on parole from unrelated crimes.

Phillips and Mounger thanked Green, gave her their cards, and asked her to call them if anything new developed.

With little to go on, they launched a search for

Orloff's former lover. Said Mounger, "Jean's family also mentioned her longtime boyfriend, Vittorio. He was a big guy, over six feet four inches. It took us a few days to find him. He was out of town at the time of the murder and showed us airline tickets. His alibi looked pretty good, but we still had questions about his involvement."

Dora Green, Mounger later learned, had reacted emotionally to the news of murder after they left her. Nervous and upset, she had called her son, George Green. Her panicky voice frightened him. He felt that she was so traumatized it might have a detrimental effect on her health. Fearing that she might suffer a heart attack, he rushed over to be with her. "I believe," recalled Mounger in retrospect, "she was worried that we might try to pin something on Sonny." He was still on parole, and if the officers inadvertently discovered an infraction of the conditions, he could be sent back to prison. "But, at that point, we had never heard of Kenneth 'Sonny' Hunt. We didn't even know he existed," said Mounger.

On the day before Detectives Mounger and Phillips interviewed Dora Green, Sonny Hunt violated his parole conditions. LAPD officers in the Rampart Division observed him acting suspiciously. When they found a small amount of rock cocaine on him, they arrested him for possession and being under the influence. A few hours later, he was released. He would later say that when he walked out of the police station, his drug supplier accosted him, robbed him, and beat him up. Of course, Hunt didn't bother to report the robbery to the police or to call his parole agent, John Widener.

He hadn't informed Widener of another problem. He'd been involved in a traffic accident on Saturday, April 4, shortly after four o'clock in the afternoon. While driving east on Washington Boulevard, less than two miles from his residence on Beverly Drive, Hunt slammed into the rear of another car at an intersection. He told traffic officers that he had seen a woman stopped at the light, but when it turned green, he expected her to move forward. When she didn't accelerate quickly enough, he realized he was moving too fast and hit his brakes, but they locked and he skidded into the back end of her car. The other driver's account was somewhat different. She stated the light hadn't yet turned green when the vehicle behind collided with hers. No arrests were made and Hunt returned home.

When his wife and mother-in-law noticed scratches on Hunt's hands, arms, and body, he explained they were the result of trying to fix the shower in their bathroom. And that he'd been manhandled by the guy who robbed him.

Hunt's employment had been sporadic in recent months. As a member of a labor union for pile-driver workers, he'd been hired to help build the Los Angeles Metro subway, the Red Line, under construction in North Hollywood, but quit after a short time. In March, the union had sent him to an Encino construction company, where he'd labored for a few weeks. But he hadn't reported to the job in the last days of March or the first week of April.

His behavior raised the ire of someone who knew him well, someone who picked up the phone and made a call that would alter the life of Kenneth Dean "Sonny" Hunt.

Nine

Near Lake Tahoe, a scenic body of crystalline water that sits astride the California-Nevada border in the Sierra Nevadas, a spirited, attractive young woman named Elyse Casebolt married Gordon Hunt, a former U.S. Navy seaman, in August 1965. One week later, she was pregnant. But her husband wouldn't be there to see her through it. She would later explain that he was serving time in a Milpitas, California, jail for failure to support a child born to his other wife.

Elyse Hunt gave birth to a healthy son during Memorial Day weekend, on Sunday, May 29, 1966, and named him Kenneth Dean Hunt. The father had been released from jail in time for the event. The new mother loved her baby, but had mixed feelings about her husband. "Our marriage was good and bad. He was not faithful and had numerous other women. While he was away, I found some papers that showed he had another wife." According to Elyse Hunt, she suffered both physical and emotional abuse at his hands. She called him "opinionated" and said "he always wanted everything his way."

The problem, she said, revolved around Gordon

Hunt's drinking problem and his unpleasant temper. "He was an alcoholic and he smoked pot."

During his two years of naval service, which began when he was seventeen years old, Hunt had been a medic, so he utilized those skills later in civilian life. While living with Elyse near San Jose, California, he worked as a medical aide in a hospital. To supplement their income, he labored part-time in a gas station. Elyse worked with her mother in a dry cleaning shop, and took the baby with her each day.

Restless and unhappy, chafing under friction with relatives, the couple moved to Kansas City, Missouri, where he found employment with a construction firm and she worked for the telephone company. Still unsettled after a year, they decided to start again, this time in Los Angeles.

"We lived in a duplex," Elyse Hunt recalled. "The neighbors grew marijuana in the backyard. I could smell the smoke when they used it, but I didn't know what it was. Gordon was friendly with them and I think he smoked their pot. I always suspected he was on something other than alcohol. I was so young and ignorant." She said that her husband was very moody, and wondered if "substance abuse" caused wide mood swings in him. "He would get more verbally abusive and demanding. His violent temper got worse."

Hunt, questioned about the allegations years later, admitted some of them, but rejected the notion that he used marijuana. He also said that he really wasn't an alcoholic. "I drank excessively," he said, "but I knew I could quit, and when I made up my mind to, I did quit."

Elyse Hunt expressed another complaint about her husband. Asked if he had "unusual" sex interests, she said, "I thought so. He liked me to dress in see-through blouses and took pictures of me wearing them. He took snapshots of me and my sister, both of us topless." During their stay in Kansas City, Elyse said, she thought her husband also had sex with a second sister, this one only eighteen years old. "He kept pornography around the house. And he was a very good artist, so he drew pictures of women." She later reported that Gordon Hunt had "kinky sexual desires and wanted other people to join [us] in sexual activities."

On Christmas Eve, 1972, Elyse Hunt checked into a hospital to give birth to her second child, a daughter she named Gina. "Little Kenny was so excited by the arrival of his new sister," recalled Elyse, "that he wouldn't open his Christmas presents until I brought her home." She was concerned, though, about her son's tendency to play with matches. "I thought it was just curiosity. But it scared both of us when he set fire to the carpet." His father remembered little Kenneth as an unruly boy who "pushed it to the limits" and needed discipline, such as an occasional spanking or frequently being sent to his room. When someone accused Gordon Hunt of slapping the boy, he denied it. "I never hit him with an open hand or closed fist. If we hit him, it was on his butt."

In mid-1974, eighteen months after the birth of Gina, Elyse and Gordon separated. She explained, "I was fed up with his booze and women. He moved out to someplace in Hollywood. I kept both kids with me and worked to support them." Elyse packed her belongings and took her young son and daughter to Fremont, near San Jose, where all three of them could live with her mother.

Gordon Hunt felt cheated. He thought he deserved to have custody of a child. Nearly two years after the split, he decided to act on it. "I wanted at least one of my kids with me," he said. The decision of which one to choose was helped by little Gina during a visit. "The reason I picked Kenneth is because my wife Elyse brought Gina to me and asked the little girl if she knew who I was. She said no. So I didn't want to take her away from her mother. . . . Elyse was already living with another man and Gina was calling him 'Dad.' It hurt." So Hunt decided he couldn't take his daughter.

Instead, he drove from Los Angeles to San Jose ostensibly to spend a few hours with his son. Clear, windy weather helped him form a plan. He told Elyse that he would like to take the child to a nearby school yard and teach him to fly a kite. It made sense to the mother, so she gave permission. Hunt and the boy climbed into the car, waved good-bye, and drove away. They didn't stop until they reached Hunt's house in Los Angeles.

To avoid a panicky reaction from his ex-wife, and perhaps an unpleasant confrontation with the police, since he had no court order to retrieve his son, Hunt paid her the courtesy of a telephone call. "I've got Kenny with me in Los Angeles," he said. Hunt made it clear he planned to keep the lad, who was nearly nine years old.

The boy's new home in Hollywood, a two-bedroom one-bath unit in a fourplex, came complete with a substitute mother. Hunt's live-in partner, Barbara Brown, would soon marry him. The union with Elyse had ended with an annulment.

Brown had been married at least twice, and one of her previous husbands had mysteriously vanished. She had fallen into a severe depression and found solace in bars. One afternoon, en route to her favorite watering hole, she stopped for gas at a station on Franklin Avenue and found the attendant, Gordon Hunt, quite attractive. They began seeing each other regularly and the relationship seemed to infuse her with new life and changed behavior. Karen Lee, her adult daughter, would later describe it: "I was sixteen at the time, in the eleventh grade. Mom just wasn't there anymore. She was always with Gordon Hunt. Over a period of time, she started dressing differently with see-through tops. At least she did that only at home and didn't wear them to work."

When they moved in together, Lee said, life in the home changed, too. "He brought over his stuff, including a lot of soft-core porn. He posted his drawings of naked women throughout the house. Later he even put up pictures of my mom revealing her breasts."

Hard feelings developed between Lee and Brown, especially when Gordon Hunt listened to audiotapes in the living room that Lee regarded as pornography. "He put them on, even when we had company." Rebelling against the perceived vulgarity, Lee eventually voiced her criticisms and tore down photos she didn't approve of along with drawings Hunt had sketched. Her actions infuriated her mother, who yelled, "If you don't like it, you can just move out." Lee said she would do that very thing as soon as possible.

Hunt drank a great deal, said Karen Lee, and used foul language, which embarrassed her. At her high school graduation dinner, he made "disgusting, derogatory" comments that so enraged her, she ran out and walked several miles home.

At age eighteen, Lee was able to get out of the un-

comfortable environment by going away to college.
During the first summer, she returned and stayed a few
nights in the house. That's when Gordon Hunt brought
his son to live there. It bothered Lee that Hunt continued to drink heavily around the young boy.

Even more bothersome to her, Karen Lee later said,
were her feelings that Hunt was spying on her. "He
used a Polaroid instant camera and snapped a picture
of me in my underwear," she complained. It did no
good to tell her mother. When she complained, it just
brought on more arguments. "He used the excuse that
he was taking an amateur photography class," said Lee,
"and he wanted me to pose nude for him." Her face
turning red, Lee muttered, "My mother also pressured
me to pose, so I finally consented, gave in and did it."
In haste, she added, "But you can see by the expression
on my face in the pictures how upset I was."

Part of the ill feelings in Karen Lee stemmed from
Hunt's efforts to "establish a private relationship with
her." As she remembered it, "He would offer me
rides and try to have mutual secrets with me. He
would say, 'Now don't tell Mom.' He even put sexually
inappropriate gifts in my Christmas stocking."

Karen Lee felt that the home environment would
be just as unwholesome for young Kenneth, now
called Sonny, as it had been for her. She fretted about
the ultimate impression it would have on him. Before
she left again, she noticed that the boy seldom spoke
and always seemed to be scowling.

Scowling wasn't the only manifestation of something
going wrong with Sonny Hunt. For some reason, he
couldn't seem to control his bowels. He frequently
soiled his bed. His father found the problem not only
difficult to understand, but disgusting. Hopeful that it

might be controlled by medication, he took his son to
Cedars-Sinai Hospital for an examination. The medical
staff diagnosed it as a behavioral disorder and began
psychological treatments. Years later, a lawyer would say
that Hunt "decided that the boy was just too lazy to get
up and use the bathroom." The attorney also observed,
"The boy's dad reported that you could beat the hell
out of him or you could love him. It didn't make any
difference."

Nothing seemed to help. Adding to Hunt's conster-
nation, the boy began a pattern of vomiting unexpect-
edly. No matter how Hunt reacted, with punishment
or discussions, the repulsive habit continued. Since
hospital treatment seemed to have no positive effect,
the father discontinued it.

The problem reached a pinnacle when Sonny vom-
ited at the dinner table one night. Two conflicting accounts of the incident would emerge. Acquaintances
of the family reported that the boy's father, in rage and
frustration, grabbed him by the nape of the neck,
pushed his face down into the mess, and forced him
to eat his own vomitus. Gordon Hunt would deny re-
acting in a violent manner. He said he thought the vomiting was self-induced, used as a device to get attention.

Sonny, if he was seeking attention, found another
way to do it. He ran away. But, as with most young
boys who try such an escape, it was unsuccessful. The
police picked him up within hours. When they questioned him about his reason for fleeing, Sonny replied
that his father had been mercilessly beating him every
day. The answer is not uncommon, and unless obvious
physical injuries from beatings could be found, children who run away were often regarded as "delin-

quent" at that time and simply returned to the parents.

Back at home, Sonny again failed to control his bowels at night in his bed. His father reportedly "lost his temper, picked the boy up, and hurled him across the room into a metal bed frame," resulting in cuts and bruises.

Once more, on March 26, 1979, the now twelve-year-old Sonny sneaked out and ran away. This time, he found his way to a Hollywood radio station, broke into the closed building, and decided to do as much damage as possible. When the police caught him, they charged him with trespass and vandalism. During a brief stay in a juvenile facility, he was interviewed and given psychological testing. It was decided he should be committed to the mental ward of the Los Angeles County-University of Southern California Hospital.

Most children confined in the institution spend a week or ten days being classified, examined, and treated. Sonny Hunt wound up staying nine months. His astonishing behavior during the period shocked staff and doctors. First they found he liked to set fires, not an unusual trait in unstable young patients. Next they discovered that Sonny Hunt was forcing other children in the ward to perform oral sex on him. They recommended that the boy go into a structured twenty-four-hour closed supervision setting, and promptly sent him to juvenile hall.

His father denied ever being told of the sexual conduct by Sonny at the hospital. "They never said that. They said he was just a plain juvenile delinquent." He also asserted that he went to the juvenile hall once to pick up Sonny. "He didn't want to come home. So we left him there."

In Los Angeles County, when police or school officials recognize troublesome patterns in a child, they can refer the problem to the County Probation Department. When that happens, a deputy probation officer (DPO) is assigned to investigate the issues and recommend appropriate action. The case of Kenneth Dean "Sonny" Hunt fell into the hands of DPO Alex Ford, a soft-spoken, mild-mannered, bespectacled man of medium height. With a master's degree in correctional counseling, his use of multisyllabic words in long sentences reflected his pride in that education.

Ford's first duty was to build a dossier on the boy. That required interviewing a list of people knowledgeable about Hunt's social history, educational background, and his aberrant behavior, including emotional problems and arrests.

It alarmed Ford to learn that Hunt had been in ward 6B of the mental hospital for so long. Was the boy mentally retarded? That question was quickly discarded when Ford saw that Hunt's IQ was a superior 122, or as the psychological report on him read: "In the rapid learning range."

Trying to discover what might have driven the adolescent boy to coerce other children into sexual acts, Ford examined reports on him. Speaking later, he said, "I learned that Kenneth had been, according to the social workers, subject to a somewhat abusive upbringing by his natural mother, natural father, and stepmother when he was residing in their homes. There had been moves, oftentimes very rapid, back and forth between the homes. I also learned that the mother and father had a lot of discord in their marriage, specifically over Kenneth, almost from the time he was born." This harms the child's ability to get along with others, said Ford.

Both parents, he found, had complained about Kenneth's lying and stealing and odd behavior for many years. "If they wanted to go out to dinner, he would vomit. This behavior continued until the father, on one occasion, forced Kenneth to eat his own vomit." The bowel-control problem aggravated his father, who did everything he could think of to stop it. Finally, he threatened to tell Kenneth's peers about it. "The father reported this apparently had effect, that it caused Kenneth to stop doing this conduct." But it was only temporary, and the pattern soon started again in the mental ward. The problem, Ford said, is a manifestation of turmoil within the child. "It's a symbol of anger. It's a symbol of a child in a power struggle with his parents and with society at times." Thus, it becomes a "psychiatric problem."

One major function of the probation department is to determine suitable placement for a troubled child after release from hospital or juvenile hall. Four general options were available, said Ford, and all of them should include psychological therapy and counseling. The first choice would be to return the child to his home, under informal probation. The second would be another home, a place with no locked doors but careful supervision. A third would be a program that is called camp placement, consisting of nineteen rural camps offering varying degrees of security. Los Angles County administers those three options. The fourth choice, for more difficult offenders, would be incarceration in a California Youth Authority institution, which is operated by the state.

Placing Kenneth Hunt, Ford discovered, was not

going to be easy. His destructive nature and his behavioral pattern of fire setting and defecating in his bed presented serious obstacles to finding acceptance for him. "These particular three items," Ford explained, "are called a triad by some people. They are seen by heads of facilities and by intake social workers as reasons to reject persons with this background. They would not accept them in their particular facilities. . . . To some degree, even though the purpose of these facilities is to assist young people in changing their conduct, amazingly a number of these agencies want what they call potential successes. They want people they can see in advance can be turned around."

Ford, seeking optimum treatment for Hunt, suggested that he be sent to Camarillo State Hospital, a mental institution near Ventura, on the coast north of Los Angeles, where he could receive intensive care for his psychological problems. Of course, said Ford, "Kenneth did not want to go there." Neither did the hospital want him. Ford quoted their answer to his recommendation. "The hospital committee said Kenneth was not diagnosed as fulfilling the requirements necessary to place him in any program that Camarillo currently had available."

Seeking alternatives, Ford settled for a "Special Treatment Program" as the acceptable placement for Hunt. "It was designed at the time because there were kids that were falling through the cracks. They [had] a certain number of mental and behavioral disorders and problems for which there was no facility available to send them. They weren't appropriate for camp; they were perhaps too young for California Youth Authority; open placements wouldn't take them because they had a myriad of problems."

The special treatment program had been installed in a facility at Sylmar in the northern end of the San Fernando Valley. Staffed with psychologists and trained nurses, it was designed for young offenders like Kenneth Dean Hunt. He was sent there to see if a ninety-day program would put him on the right track. It seemed promising for the strange boy who had recently turned thirteen.

Dr. Sharon Sims, a psychologist, examined Hunt and recommended a long-term treatment program of concentrated therapy. When the ninety days had elapsed, a special extension allowed him to stay another month. He appeared to be improving.

Inexplicably, at the end of four months, a decision was made to remove Hunt from the program and place him in another facility for troubled juveniles. He was transferred to the Guadalupe Home for Boys, a minimum-security institution at Redlands, near San Bernardino. The program had been designed as residential quarters where the main form of treatment was the presence of positive male role models. It took Hunt only a few weeks to recognize lax controls and learn how to manipulate them. He watched for the opportunity and then simply walked out of the place. It didn't take long to bring him back.

Hunt's mother, Elyse, had remarried and settled into a comfortable home with her husband and her seven-year-old daughter, Gina, in Fremont, near San Jose. She received a telephone call from authorities at a southern California juvenile facility about her son. "They said he had been in trouble and needed a place to live." There was no mention, as she recalled it, of his sexual behavior, of his stay in a mental ward, or any specifics about his "trouble." Elyse and her husband, after a long discussion, agreed to provide a home for Sonny.

Speaking of it later, Elyse said, "I saw no reason to think he was bad. You have to give kids a chance, and not just throw the problems up in their faces." She also recalled having written letters to Sonny's father to ask what he knew about the difficulties, but she never received any response.

Hunt arrived in January 1980 and seemed to settle into the new environment with ease. He entered school and appeared to interact with other kids satisfactorily. Other than minor behavior matters common to all kids, he seemed to adapt well to home life with his mother and her husband. He seemed especially fond of his little sister, Gina. She recalled that "it was really cool to have a big brother." During an excursion to the zoo, he led her around and helped her feed the pigeons. A snapshot of them depicted Gina smiling and enchanted with the whole experience. Hunt, staring at the camera, appeared sober with no smile or expression of joy. His sister thought he looked "confused."

Both parents worked nine-to-five jobs. Prior to Hunt's arrival, they had arranged for Gina to stay in a day-care center after school. With his presence, though, it seemed foolish not to allow Gina to be cared for by her loving brother in the home. At age thirteen, he seemed capable of looking after the little girl. "I trusted him to baby-sit Gina," recalled Elyse. "I had no reason not to."

Gina loved the idea. "We would listen to AC/DC records. He let me dress up in military-style clothes like he wore. He taught me to blow bubbles with bubble gum. I heard him whistling and asked how to do it, so he taught me." She described their activities as "a typical brother-sister relationship."

One afternoon in April, though, when Elyse's husband arrived home a bit early, he discovered the relationship between the siblings was far from typical. The boy was forcing Gina to perform oral sex on him.

Years later, Gina painfully spoke of the incest. "It happened a handful of times, maybe three or four. It happened after school before Mom and Dad came home from work." She couldn't recall exactly how Hunt convinced her to do it, whether he cajoled or threatened her. "He forced me to do it. I don't remember why . . . what he used to force me, but at the time I was under the impression that I had to do as he said."

Hunt even worked out a method to prolong the act to his satisfaction. "He would turn on the microwave oven timer. It meant that I had to perform oral sex for a certain amount of time." The running clock provided the child a time limit, so she knew when she could stop. "I wasn't willing to this. I was being forced to, and I would complain. And, OK, you know, at least the timer, there was an end coming."

The end came for Hunt's residency in the family home at Fremont. The stepfather was furious and threatened to call the police.

Facing a threat of being returned to juvenile custody, Hunt resorted to his usual routine, trying to run away. He broke into the locked garage, grabbed his mother's bicycle, and then pedaled away. Needing money, he took a few dollars. Vague juvenile records were unclear as to whether he stole it from his mother or entered another home. Fremont police caught him within hours and brought him back to the house.

When southern California authorities had arranged

to send Hunt north, they had tried to wash their
hands of the problems with a proviso stating that any
further violations by the boy should be handled by
the San Jose juvenile justice system. The local authorities took over, charging him with burglary and placing
him temporarily in an Alameda County facility. But
Alameda County wanted no part of him and found a
way to send him south again.

Back in Los Angeles County, Kenneth Dean Hunt
was convicted of burglary and sent to yet another
lockup.

Ten

In Los Angeles County, Kenneth Hunt served his time at a facility called Camp Kilpatrick, near Malibu Beach. It was part of the project called "camp placement" considered earlier by Deputy Probation Officer Alex Ford. The goal was to place young offenders in environments other than prisons with the hope of avoiding experiences that might turn them into hardened criminals. With good behavior, the inmates could be released in just a few months. The plan was not entirely successful. Hunt went in at age thirteen. He was still there after his fifteenth birthday.

Still incarcerated after so much time, Hunt presented a problem to authorities. They contacted his father, now married to Barbara, and asked if the boy could be released to their custody. The father refused.

Instead of sending the youth home, he was placed in an institution called Pacific Lodge, located in the San Fernando Valley community of Woodland Hills. A program had been developed there for troubled teenagers who had few other alternatives. Called the Jonah Project, it primarily provided supervised housing. Most of the adolescents involved were on probation, so any violation of the rules would place them back in high-security custody.

Arriving at the Pacific Lodge in June 1981, Hunt linked up with another juvenile, Joe Cardenas. Before long, they hatched plans to escape. In late September, they slipped away.

Walking for miles, the pair headed in the direction of Canyon Country, a rural community in the foothills of northern Los Angeles County. They hoped they could find Jerry Peterson, a fellow resident of Pacific Lodge who had been released a few weeks earlier to live with his aunt.

As it grew dark and chilly, the young fugitives spotted a fifth-wheel trailer house parked near a home on Hardesty Street in a residential tract surrounded by hills. Needing shelter from the cold and a place to sleep, they crept alongside the unlit trailer, listened, and heard no sounds from inside. They pried a window open, crawled through, and found a bed. To make certain no one would discover and arrest them, the pair took turns, one sleeping while the other stood guard, until about midnight, when they both fell asleep.

Shortly after dawn, they left the sanctuary and wandered around for a few hours until hunger drove them back, at about nine-thirty the same morning. This time, they circled the house on the same lot as the trailer, scouting it to see if anyone was around. Satisfied that the residents were away, Cardenas pried the screen from a window and slipped inside. He unlocked a door to let Hunt in.

First they raided the kitchen, eating their fill and drinking beer. Then they both took leisurely showers, steaming up the bathroom and splattering water everywhere. Searching the rooms, they began grabbing loot. Cardenas found a ring topped by a diamond-studded miniature horseshoe; he also picked up a T-shirt imprinted in large letters with BUDWEISER and put it on along with a cowboy hat. Then he bagged some aftershave lotion, cigarettes, and beer. Hunt snatched a pellet rifle, a wallet, a carton of cigarettes, and a lighter. On a table, he found six silver dollars and pocketed them.

Back in the trailer house, they guzzled beer for a while, then left. At an elementary school across the street from the home they'd raided, the pair of burglars decided they shouldn't be carrying the stolen items with them. The roof of the school would make a good temporary hiding place for their plunder. They tossed the bag containing most of the material, along with the pellet rifle, onto the top of a rear building.

That Monday afternoon, September 28, Arlene Logan, fifteen, left Canyon High School tennis practice at about four o'clock. Wearing light blue terrycloth shorts and blouse, her blond hair in a ponytail, she headed toward home, taking a shortcut up a narrow, secluded trail through hills above the school.

About ten minutes later, she heard sounds of someone behind her. Glancing back, she saw two young men following a few yards to the rear. One of them had sandy brown collar-length hair, hazel eyes, stood about five-eight, and wore black corduroy pants with a white T-shirt. The other one, a little shorter, had olive skin, black hair, brown eyes, a fuzzy mustache with a goatee, and wore a T-shirt emblazoned with BUDWEISER. They seemed to be about her age, and might have been Can-

yon High students, so she thought nothing of it. Logan
had walked about 200 yards up the hill when the pair
caught up with her. She stepped aside to let them pass.

The sandy-haired youth suddenly grabbed Logan
from behind around the waist. As she started to
scream, he wrestled her to the ground. Lying on her
back, she flailed at him and tried kicking her way
loose, but he pinned her down. He held her with one
hand while groping at her chest with the other. He
managed to hook his fingers into the top of her
blouse and jerk it down, exposing her breasts. She
wailed and screamed, which seemed to do nothing
but energize her assailant. He tore her blouse loose
and roughly fondled her, then tried to cover her
mouth. Failing to stop her from screaming, he
shouted, "Shut up, bitch."

Certain the youth was going to rape her, Logan felt
a rush of great relief when he loosened his grasp,
stood up, and sprinted away. His partner loomed over
her. She screamed, "Don't you touch me!"

It surprised her when he replied, "Don't worry. I
don't do that shit." He turned and loped off in the
direction the assailant had taken. Arlene Logan did her
best to cover herself with the torn blouse and ran back
to the high school. A teacher first made certain the girl
hadn't been injured, then gave her a ride home. Her
parents called 911, but said Arlene was too emotionally
distressed to answer questions that day. Los Angeles
County Sheriff's deputies agreed to meet with her on
Tuesday.

Trembling and trying not to cry during the interview, Arlene Logan told the deputies what had happened and described the two youths. Her story was
corroborated in interviews with school officials who

said they had seen two young strangers who answered those descriptions hanging around near the campus earlier Monday afternoon. A maintenance supervisor reported he had noticed the same pair in a nearby park following girls as they left the school.

Two hours after the report was taken, the maintenance supervisor again spotted the two youths loitering around the corner of Nadal and Camp Plenty Streets, close to the park, and only a block from the high school. He called the sheriff's office. Deputy George Ewing rushed to the intersection and surveyed a group of young men sitting on a block wall. Two of them matched the fugitives' descriptions.

Stepping out of his cruiser, Ewing approached the two boys and asked for identification. They said they didn't have any. The sandy-haired youth told Ewing his name was Joseph Russo, while the olive-complected youth said he was John Simmers. Ewing asked if they were students at Canyon High School. "Yes," they both replied, and claimed they were in the tenth grade.

The maintenance supervisor, who had watched the whole thing from his vantage point in the park, approached. He told Ewing that these two were the boys he'd seen the day before. Another man came forward, identified himself as the dean of Canyon High School, and stated he'd seen the pair loitering around the campus on Monday. "They are not students here," he asserted.

While Ewing kept the two suspects at the intersection, Deputy Jim Kellaris drove to Arlene Logan's home and brought her to the scene. She looked carefully at the one who called himself John Simmers and said, "It looks like the boy, but I'm not sure." Studying the other youth, who had said his name was Russo, Logan said, "His hair is exactly like the one who attacked me and the features are the same." But she fell short of a positive identification.

Deputy Ewing, in his report based on several witnesses' comments, expressed strong confidence that these were the assailants suspected of attempted rape. He placed them under arrest and transported them to the Santa Clarita Valley station.

In the booking room, Ewing asked the suspects to empty their pockets. The sandy-haired one placed six silver dollars on the counter.

At two-thirty that afternoon, Deputies George Johnson and Bill Wood faced the two youths in an interview room and read them their Miranda rights. It took the officers only a few minutes to learn their real names. After separating the pair, they asked Joe Cardenas what he'd been doing in the past twenty-four hours. The street-smart adolescent said that he knew his rights and had nothing to say. Then he blurted out that he had stood right behind Kenneth Hunt during the incident with the teenage girl, but hadn't seen anything.

Fifteen minutes later, they confronted Hunt. He agreed to speak without a lawyer present. Asked what he and Cardenas were doing in the area, Hunt said they had traveled the previous day from the San Fernando Valley to visit his "cousin" Jerry Peterson, who lived on the hill above Canyon High School.

Pressed for more details, Hunt soon caved in and admitted they had run away from Pacific Lodge boys' home.

"Why did you lie about your name to Deputy Ewing?" Wood asked. Hunt replied that he thought if they didn't know who he was, the officers might set him free.

"How did those six silver dollars come into your possession?"

Clearing his throat, scratching his head, and staring at the tabletop, Hunt said, "A counselor at the boys' home gave them to me."

After a short break, Wood resumed the interrogation, asking about what happened with the high school girl on the hill.

"We saw that girl climbing the hill behind the school," Hunt said, then proceeded to blame the whole thing on his partner, Cardenas. According to Hunt, Cardenas had said, "Let's rape her just for the fun of it." Hunt, of course, had replied, "No." To which Cardenas had insisted, "Come on. Don't be a pussy, it ain't going to hurt you." So, said Hunt, they had followed the girl up the trail, but Cardenas had fallen behind. As Hunt caught up with the victim, and playfully reached for her, she fell to the ground and started screaming. He placed his hands over her mouth to shut her up, but she broke loose. "I must have grabbed her blouse and breast accidentally," he claimed. When she continued screaming, he "got scared" and ran away through the hills to Jerry Peterson's house.

Perhaps realizing how phony his story sounded, he changed his tune. Deputy Wood asked Hunt if he intentionally planned to rape the victim as he was struggling with her. He replied with a simple "Yes."

"What was Cardenas's participation in this act?"

"He only suggested we do it. But he never took part in it."

Terminating the interview, Deputy Wood started preparations to transport Hunt and Cardenas to the Syl-

mar Juvenile Hall. In the midst of the paperwork, he
learned something else that changed the whole picture.
Deputy George Johnson told Wood that a burglary had
taken place and the missing loot included six silver dollars. Hunt had been carrying the same amount in his
pocket. This couldn't be a simple coincidence. His guilt
was sealed when Johnson mentioned that one of the
burglars had apparently left a school program card in
the victim's home. The card contained the name Kenneth D. Hunt.

Deputy Johnson made a quick run to the home of
Jerry Peterson, the boy Hunt and Cardenas had visited. His aunt, with whom he'd been living after leaving Pacific Lodge, told Johnson there had been two
boys there Saturday night who knew Jerry from
"camp." Jerry chimed in and admitted that Hunt and
Cardenas had confessed to him about doing a burglary, sleeping in the people's trailer, and drinking
their beer.

At the Santa Clarita Valley interview room, Deputy
Bill Wood had a few more questions for the boys suspected of attempted rape and now a burglary charge as
well. After advising Hunt of his rights again, Wood asked
if he knew anything about a burglary on Hardesty Street.
Hunt admitted he and Cardenas had been involved, and
gave Wood all the details.

In a separate room, when Cardenas learned that Hunt
blamed him for proposing the attempted rape, he decided to talk more about that. They had seen the girl
climbing up a hill, said Cardenas, but it was Hunt who
said, "Let's rape her." According to Cardenas, he had
refused, saying, "No, man, I'm not into that." Hunt, he
said, had started running after the girl while he followed

behind. "I was too far back to see what happened, but I saw her running down the hill, crying."

Wood asked Cardenas if he and Hunt had done any burglaries while in the area.

"No," the goateed youth replied.

Deputy Wood contacted administrators at Pacific Lodge to report the capture of Hunt and Cardenas. Since they had violated conditions of probation, neither of them would be eligible for return. Now they also faced felony charges of attempted rape and burglary.

Eleven

In the California juvenile justice system, a defendant under sixteen years of age may face trial much as an adult would, but with several significant differences. Adults have a choice to put their fate in the hands of a jury or let a judge arrive at the verdict. Juveniles have no choice. They are tried without a jury. Adults are generally tried in courts open to the public. Juvenile trials are ordinarily held behind closed doors, ostensibly for privacy protection. The privacy is carried a step further by the sealing of juvenile records so the offender is not burdened for a lifetime with transgression made during youth.

In October 1981, Kenneth Dean Hunt faced charges of assault to commit rape, burglary, and grand theft. A judge weighed the evidence, found him culpable, and sentenced him to serve time in the custody of the California Youth Authority (CYA). Hunt's previous confinement had been in hospitals or camps operated by Los Angeles County. CYA is operated and controlled by the state criminal justice system.

At the Southern Youth Correctional Reception Center and Clinic in Norwalk, Los Angeles County, Hunt was processed into the CYA. Within a short time, he was transferred to Stockton, in central California, to the O.H. Close Youth Correctional Facility. Four hundred other juveniles were housed at the site, which offered, according to CYA information, "programs for younger offenders."

Unlike adult prisoners, offenders committed to the CYA do not receive determinate sentences. CYA guidelines state, "In practice, the period of incarceration is determined by the severity of the commitment offense and the offender's progress toward parole readiness." CYA wards are subject to release when the Youthful Offender Parole Board finds they are ready for freedom. Most of them still must serve a period of time under conditions of parole. If offenders are still incarcerated when they reach the age of twenty-five, they must be transferred to adult prisons. Some are transferred sooner.

Serving time in CYA facilities is probably not as difficult as hard time in adult prisons, but it is certainly no picnic. More than 10,000 youthful offenders are confined within institutions and camps throughout the state. Conditions in some of the facilities are tougher than others. The CYA tries to separate various types and ages of offenders for maximum control and safety. The Stockton unit, for example, houses nearly 800 males and is restricted to young men ages eighteen to twenty-five. Ventura, on the other hand, provides accommodation for much younger inmates, both males (nearly 400) and females (about 340), while offering both work and college programs.

Alex Ford, Hunt's juvenile probation officer, spoke of the CYA. "I thought Kenneth should go there. CYA has available to it direct contact with mental hospitals and mental programs, more than any county agency.

The state has money, a number of diagnostic tools, and state hospitals available." Judges who commit juveniles to CYA, said Ford, "trust the state to do the right thing that they need."

Expressing confidence in CYA, Ford added, "A lot of people think the [California] Youth Authority is simply a housing place for long periods of time, with a parole at the end of it. That is not the truth. CYA has the greatest variety of mental programs and vocational rehabilitation programs of any agency in the state."

Author Stephen Lerner, who researches and writes about social issues, saw CYA in a completely different light. In the early 1980s, he conducted extensive research of the organization, visiting several facilities—interviewing inmates, guards, and administrators, to assess the effectiveness of the system. Said Lerner, "The original idea behind CYA, which was formed in 1941, was a model program to separate wayward youth from adults for treatment rather than punishment. Tragically, though, it was gradually drawn into the prison business." Overcrowding, obsolete housing, and violence within the facilities have undermined the original goals. Infestation of gangs among the population creates tension. Guards fear for their own safety. "Some facilities are worse than others," said Lerner. "But most of them had frequent outbursts of violence, up to two thousand incidents a year. A lot of fighting among the inmates took place, with twenty-five to thirty percent of the inmates being involved." Even these figures are underreported, he states, because the kids are afraid to snitch. "They will lie to cover up beatings to avoid being known as an informer, or in the parlance, getting a 'snitch jacket.' "

Newly arrived inmates are tested by the bullies. Said one observer, "Your things are stolen soon after you arrive. Then you walk through the dormitory and see your stuff on other boys' bunks. What do you do? If you do nothing, you get a reputation of being weak. If you report your losses, you are a snitch. If you have 'heart,' you stand up and fight. But if you are caught fighting by staff, you earn demerits that might prolong your stay. You can't win."

"Some of the smaller inmates," Lerner noted, "feel helpless and scared. They beg to be transferred to protective custody. That earns them a so-called 'p.c. jacket,' and makes them an even greater target for bullies."

A former employee of CYA agrees with Lerner's observations. Bob Lasseter recalled his alarming experiences with the staff at a central California facility. "We were called group supervisors, not guards. I was in charge of a unit housing from sixty to eighty boys, many of whom were certainly not kids. One hulking youth who stood well over six feet, and had the physique of a wrestler, needed to be handled with extreme care. And he wasn't in there for singing too loud in church. He'd killed three people. He was OK as long as you talked softly to him, but if you raised your voice, he exploded into a violent rage. Another inmate worked in metal shop where he managed to secretly solder razor blades along a length of metal pipe. He attacked a staff member and sent him to the hospital with severe lacerations. I didn't mind graveyard shift [midnight to eight o'clock in the morning] just patrolling the bunks and calling the tower each hour to report. It was relatively quiet then. But day shift in the yard was terrible. Fights all day long. Most of our time was used breaking them up and sending the boys to protective custody, a nice term for solitary confinement. I worked there about six months before I made the mistake of speaking loudly to the hulk. In a frothing fit, he lunged at me. I held him off with a size-thirteen boot in his stomach until help arrived. Soon after that, I found more peaceful employment. No, at that time certainly, the CYA was no country club."

These were the conditions faced by Kenneth Hunt at age fifteen. Typical of other inmates, he was challenged by the tough guys in his dormitory. He had to show "heart" and fight. He took several serious beatings. So he learned to hit first and hit hard.

Years later, Hunt would report that he couldn't recall receiving any type of psychological treatment during his stay. Experts say that Hunt's record as a sex offender should have signaled the need for counseling or clinical therapy. But since his records were later shredded, it's impossible to verify whether it took place or not.

Hunt would also claim he was severely beaten by a guard and forced to stay in a damp, isolated cell until he "promised to be good." Released after ten days, he said, he was angry and got in more trouble, which cost him a month "in the hole." That meant staying in a cell alone, unable to have any contact with other inmates. "It was no hassle, though," he said, "and was more comfortable than my regular bed."

Administrators decided Hunt should be transferred. They sent him to DeWitt Nelson Youth Correctional Facility, on the other side of Stockton. CYA says DeWitt offers an "extensive job-training program" at the site, plus "a youth conservation camp within the institution." One expert labeled DeWitt as "more violent and heavy-duty." To Hunt, it meant facing the same initiation, fighting and showing "heart."

A big problem, Hunt complained, was that gangs "ran the place." One gang leader allegedly ordered him to "make a hit on someone." During a baseball game, he said, he followed orders to slug the guy with a bat. When he did it, it resulted in "race riots." Certainly, there were racial tensions at DeWitt, with its diverse ethnic population. Hunt said the majority of the inmates were African-American. Whites, he said, were a small minority, so he aligned himself with a Hispanic gang.

Eventually, Hunt found himself transferred again, this time to Chino in southern California. According to CYA, the Herman G. Stark Youth Correctional Facility at Chino is "an institution for one thousand two hundred twenty-five males. It includes special counseling, precamp, extensive vocational, and job training." To Hunt, it meant "big-time fights." He later complained that he been "gassed" there, in his cell.

The record on Kenneth Hunt reflects that he was moved, near the time of his eighteenth birthday, from the CYA facility to a California Department of Corrections institution. Reasons for his transfer aren't clearly stated. It may have been related to his behavior, or possibly to provide vocational training in preparation for reentering free society. His new home, Deuel Vocational Institution, suggests the latter by its very name. Near Tracy, just south of Stockton, the facility was expanded in 1981, and claimed to offer "educational and vocational programming geared toward providing inmates with skills and education which would allow them to find jobs upon release."

By the time Hunt was paroled, on April 25, 1986, he was almost twenty years old. He had learned a great deal during nearly five years in the lockup. Most of it bad. Had he received counseling, treatment, therapy, or vocational training while incarcerated? If so, none of it seemed to have much effect.

Seventeen days after leaving prison, Hunt was seen attempting a burglary. He entered a residential yard in West Los Angeles, walked to a side window, and tried to slide it up while glancing around in all directions. Unsuccessful, he left. The resident who nervously watched the whole thing called the police. Minutes later, patrol officers arrested Hunt a short distance away. He had a pocketknife in his possession, which could be considered a weapon.

Convicted in Santa Monica Superior Court of attempted burglary, he was sentenced to serve 210 days in jail. Already on parole, his probation was extended to three years.

Free again by October, he was accused of another burglary attempt, but the district attorney found insufficient evidence to convict him. Instead, he was found guilty of theft and sent to jail for a week.

Perhaps to stay out of trouble, Hunt joined the U.S. Army in 1987, but was discharged due to the criminal record he had failed to disclose. That same year, he met Betty Green, the woman he would marry.

His life seemed to take an encouraging turn. Living in Dora Green's home, he worked when he could, had a fine relationship with Betty and Dora, and reported regularly to his energetic, strict parole agent, John Widener. However, in early July 1988, Hunt's next-door neighbor, former body double Myra Davis, was murdered. Over the next few months, the community suffered additionally, when a mysterious series of bizarre sexual assaults in which the assailant grabbed and fondled women on sidewalks in broad daylight erupted around Cheviot Hills.

Trouble came calling again for Hunt. While walking his dog in March 1992, he was offended by comments an older couple made. Yielding to furious impulse, Hunt struck the husband. When the man died, Hunt wound up in prison again, until 1995. A violent argument with his secret girlfriend cost him another year behind bars.

In midsummer 1997, he rejoined his wife in Dora Green's home.

Twelve

Detective Francene Mounger and her boss, Detective Ron Phillips, along with Bradford Roberts, still working on the murder of Jean Orloff nine days after the discovery of her body, felt like they were running out of leads. Vittorio Amati, the victim's ex-boyfriend, seemed to be in the clear. The crime scene had been compromised because of some mistakes by personnel who assumed she had died of natural causes, so there were no usable fingerprints, fibers, hairs, blood, or any other forensic clues that might help. They had interviewed Dora Green, Orloff's manicurist, on Tuesday, April 7, in the early afternoon in her home. The discussion turned up nothing important, although she appeared to be in serious distress.

The investigators hadn't given up, but hope was rapidly fading. When the phone rang on Mounger's desk at six o'clock that same evening, she felt tired and a little edgy. But her mood changed in a hurry.

She heard the familiar voice of Parole Agent John Widener, who sounded excited. "Francene, I just got a call from George Green, the brother-in-law of one of my parolees, Kenneth Dean Hunt. From what I heard, you might want to take a look at this guy Hunt."

"Be glad to," she answered. "Can you come over and tell me about it?"

"You bet," said Widener. "Be there in a few minutes."

A half hour later, Widener sat in a meeting room with Mounger, accompanied by Detectives Ron Phillips and Brad Roberts. The parole book Widener had brought, containing the history of Kenneth Hunt, lay open on the table between them. It included his rap sheet and an assortment of reports telling his life story, nearly everything except his juvenile history. The law keeps that hidden. But the sexual battery incidents were there, along with the manslaughter case for causing the death of Bernard Davis.

Widener spoke. "Until recently, George Green lived for quite a while over on Beverly Drive with his mother, his sister, and her husband. He'd been in some trouble, forgery charges, and I supervised his parole until it ended. He's been doing OK. You met the mother, Dora Green, and her daughter, Betty. Betty's husband is Kenneth Dean Hunt, better known as Sonny. Green doesn't like him. This afternoon, after you guys left Dora's house, she called her son and told him the details of how Jean Orloff was killed. George thinks he knows who might have done it. He told me that we should have a look at Sonny Hunt."

Hunt, Green had explained to Widener, has a violent, explosive personality and a long rap sheet, including quite a few sex-related crimes. Furthermore, Hunt had been doing repair work in Jean Orloff's apartment and delivering Avon products to her from his wife. Alone, that didn't mean much. But the next comment from Widener sent chills up Mounger's spine. According to George Green, Hunt had also done handy work for their next-door neighbor, Myra Davis, who had been murdered ten years earlier. The case had never been solved. Both women had been raped and strangled by ligature.

Phillips and Mounger made a mad scramble to a metal cabinet in another room. It held all the old, unsolved homicide cases. They pulled the file on Myra Davis, sprinted back to the meeting room, and spread papers over the table. Mounger couldn't restrain herself. "Bingo!" she said. Later speaking of the moment, she recalled, "I had a good feeling that we were onto something really important, on the right path at least. I felt really good about it." Everyone in the room had agreed that "you don't have two women end up dead with a violent parolee working in their houses unless there is a strong connection. This is not coincidence."

Widener wasn't finished. Green had also revealed that Hunt had been in a motor vehicle accident the previous Saturday. Hunt also was using drugs, breaking the conditions of his parole. He'd been beaten up by his drug supplier in the Rampart Division. "I'm going to violate him," announced Widener. With a grin, he asked, "You guys want to go along?"

In recalling the events, Mounger said, "We gathered up seven or eight officers and went to Beverly Drive. John Widener telephoned Sonny on the way, using a cell phone, and said, 'I'm coming to see you.' He just wanted to make certain Hunt was at the house."

At Dora Green's home, Widener approached the front door, flanked by two uniformed officers, while the others waited. When he knocked, Hunt answered the door. Widener told him he was taking him into custody for violating parole. Hunt surrendered with no fuss or resistance.

With Hunt on the way to jail, Mounger, Phillips, and Roberts talked to Dora and Betty again. "Betty was hysterical. We were sitting in the kitchen asking questions, trying to pinpoint Sonny's activities that weekend. The victim, Jean Orloff, had been seen alive on Saturday, March twenty-eighth, and was dead on Sunday. We wanted to know where Sonny had been both of those days, and on the weekend of April fourth and fifth."

Sobbing and trembling, Betty Hunt told the officers, "He was with me all the time."

Mounger shook her head. "We knew he'd been in a traffic accident and was alone when it happened on Saturday, April fourth. And he'd been alone when he ran into the drug pusher."

Mounger mentioned to the women that Hunt looked like he had some scratches on him. Did they know how he got them? The answers were vague.

Working overtime at their office, Mounger and Roberts brought Sonny Hunt into an interview room one hour before midnight on Wednesday, April 8. No more than eighteen square feet, the diminutive cubicle had mustard-yellow walls, a small table topped with black walnut veneer, and three chairs. On the wall, someone had mounted a framed message in needlepoint: NO MAN HAS A GOOD ENOUGH MEMORY TO BE A SUCCESSFUL LIAR.

As soon as they sat down, Hunt asked, "Can you tell me what this is about?" As far as he knew, he was being detained for parole violations and nothing else.

Brad Roberts spoke softly, in even tones. "All right,

Ken, I'm Detective Roberts. This is Detective Mounger, my partner. Basically, we want to talk to you. There's some things that we're investigating. We work homicide, OK?"

Nodding almost imperceptibly, showing no alarm, Hunt grunted. "Uh-huh."

Roberts, deliberately staring directly into Hunt's eyes and pausing, said, "That gal who was friends with your mother-in-law?" Hunt nodded again. "OK, we know you did some work for her. We're just trying to peel off some . . ." Roberts avoided saying the victim's name, but Hunt seemed to know who he was talking about.

"Yeah, I did some work for her. I still have her box." He referred to a decorative cubelike stand he'd taken from Orloff's apartment to sand and paint for her.

"I know," said Roberts. He really didn't, but he just wanted to probe and test to see how Hunt would react. "You delivered that box, I guess, huh?"

"No, I never delivered the box. I picked it up before I left. Her mom called . . . It needed one more coat. Still does."

"Is that when you painted her . . . What did you do inside her place?"

"Well, the mirror above the piano . . . I painted. She had it reframed. It fell during the earthquake or something. I repainted it and hung it for her and I looked at some other things. She wanted the mirror— there's a mirror and shelf next to the doorway, in the hallway or something. She wanted that painted and I was gonna do the box and that mirror, put another long mirror over her bedroom and do the—hang the

mirror on the bathroom door." Hunt spoke falter-
ingly, and seemed to be getting nervous.

"So you still had more work to do on her place?"

"Oh, yeah. Oh, yeah. Yeah, I was gonna do one
thing at a time. And she said there was a hole in her
roof and the manager had some guys fixing it. They
screwed it up and she wanted me to look at it."

Roberts shifted the subject. Using the age-old technique of asking open-ended questions, and avoiding
direct accusation, the detective maneuvered to keep
Hunt talking. "OK. How long you been living down
there on Beverly Drive? I know you been in and out
of prison a couple of times."

Knitting his heavy brows as if calculating the
amount of time he'd lived in Green's home, Hunt
said, "Since a couple of years before I'm married. Got
married in eighty-eight."

Ready to bore in a little tighter, Roberts said, "OK,
I'm gonna get into some very particular questions
about the [woman] who got murdered out there. So
because you are in custody here, I'm gonna ask you
some questions and I have to advise you of your rights
first."

His hazel eyes widening, Hunt shot back, "Am I
under arrest?"

"You are under arrest, but for the parole violation.
Not for murder."

"Do I need a lawyer? I mean . . ." Hunt's words
trailed off, replaced by humorless laughter.

For Roberts, it was a difficult moment. Any police
interrogator dreads the instant when the suspect asks
for a lawyer. It means either the interview ends and
the opportunity to obtain valuable statements is gone,
or if the questioning continues, there is strong risk

that anything the suspect says will not be allowed as evidence in a courtroom. Roberts said, "Well, you're in jail right now on the parole officer's—"

Hunt butted in just to grunt his assent.

"—and your parole violation. And that is it. OK?"

Hunt did not ask for a lawyer. Roberts felt safe in continuing. "Basically, I'm just talking to you about this because I know you did some work for her and I want to try to see if you can maybe help me on this thing."

"Can I ask a question?"

"Go ahead."

"Last time I got arrested for parole violation, my wife was about to kill herself. And that's got me stressed out right now. Is there any chance you could . . . I don't know if she's here . . . She told me she might be coming."

"We talked to her for quite a while. She's calmed down now."

"Is there any chance I could talk to her real fast? I mean, it's got me real stressed."

An interruption could wreck chances for learning anything, so Roberts chose to forestall an answer. "It won't take much longer. Let me get this part done. . . ." He read Hunt the Miranda warning just to get it on the record. The last sentence is always the tricky one. "Do you wish to give up the right to remain silent?"

Hunt answered, "No." It appeared to be the end.

Disappointed, Roberts replied, "In other words, you don't want to talk to us?"

Apparently, Hunt had misspoken. "No, I'll talk to you. I'll talk to you. Yeah."

Relieved, Roberts made his tone friendly. "That's

what I meant. You really want to talk to me right now?"

"Yeah, I wanna talk to you right now." His statement dripped with cocky confidence.

Roberts asked, "OK. When did you first meet . . . Do you know that lady's name?"

"Jean."

"Yeah, Jean. When did you first meet her?"

"Uh, it was after I got out the last time."

"Which was . . . When did you get out?"

"In ninety-five."

"You been out for three years?"

"No. I went back on a violation."

"Where and when did you first meet her?"

"When I first got out, shortly after November, ninety-five."

"Oh. So you've known her for quite some time now?"

"Yeah. She's my mother-in-law's customer."

"And she comes to the house to have her nails done?"

"No. She came to the house for, like, uh, Halloween. They had a party and she came. Her and her other friend. I forget her friend's name. I did work for her, too. She lives on the next block over in the same area."

"When did you first go up to [Jean's] place?"

Hunt struggled with his answer. He thought it had been perhaps two months ago, but couldn't be certain. "My wife was with me," he said, suggesting that Betty might be able to provide the exact date.

Hoping to hear something more specific, Roberts asked, "When was the last time you were there?"

"When I picked up the box. Three or four weeks ago, I guess."

"And you just picked up the box?"

Hunt faltered again. "Well, I . . . Oh, no, I dropped off Avon for my wife. My wife sold her Avon. I took the order up there and dropped it off. I sat and read the ingredients to some eye-makeup shit, and we went through the order. She made sure it was what she ordered. She went through the books to make sure they were the right sizes. And I picked up the box and left." He'd rambled without answering the question.

"OK. That was the last time you were there? Three or four weeks ago." Orloff had been murdered eleven days ago.

"Yes. I . . . I don't know the exact date."

"Did you go inside at all?"

"Yeah. I was sitting on the couch with her. . . ."

"Do you remember . . . actually when you worked on hanging a mirror by the piano?"

"Yes. Yeah, it's a big gray mirror."

"What else did you do there?"

"Uh, I took, took off the shelf that . . . under that mirror I was talking about in the little hallway right there between the living room and the bedroom, the bathroom thing." Roberts's expression turned sour. Hunt saw it and continued. "Do you know what I'm talking about? There's a gray shelf right there. I took that off because she wanted to know how come it was so loose and I was just explaining to her about the molly [bolts] and I loosened up the bathroom mirror to show her what was wrong with that . . . why she couldn't fill the holes with toothpaste. That's what I mean, it's a lotta work I did in there. I mean—"

The long answer had grown tedious. Roberts cut in. "You didn't do any painting or anything like that?"

"No. Oh, yeah. Oh, yeah! I painted the mirror and did that at her house."

"Were you ever in the house when she wasn't home?"

"No."

"Was it daytime or nighttime?"

"The last time? It was at night. About five, six, seven o'clock."

"You were up there by yourself?"

"Yeah. My wife was sick that day."

Roberts wanted to know when Hunt had first heard of Orloff's death. Hunt thought it had been about a week ago. "I'm not too sure. I was getting a haircut and my wife paged me and told me that Jeannie had a heart attack."

"A week ago Sunday?"

"I believe it was then." But he couldn't be certain.

"OK. And when did you find out something else happened to her besides a heart attack?"

"The other day." Still waffling and avoiding any specific time frames.

"What other day?" Roberts refused to let it slide.

"When you guys went and talked to my mother-in-law. I heard her and my wife talking about it. They said [you] would probably want to talk to everybody. And then I didn't know if I should call or wait for you guys to come see me, you know."

Hunt seemed to be indicating that he'd heard about Orloff's death on the same weekend her body was discovered. Roberts wanted more. "OK, can you tell me what you did that whole weekend, that whole Saturday and Sunday?"

"I worked on the bathroom." He didn't make it clear whose bathroom or where it was. Perhaps, he said, his wife could help with the exact dates and places. "I mean, my curfew starts at eight-thirty, so I have to be in the house by then." Pushed by Roberts, he still kept his answer vague while shifting back and forth in his chair.

"Are you nervous?"

"No, I'm worried about my wife."

"Did you like Jeannie?"

"Yeah, she was cool."

"Did she flirt with you?"

"Yeah."

"How did she do that?"

As if sharing some sexual adventures with locker-room buddies, Hunt relaxed a bit. "She talked about, uh, she couldn't believe channel three, or something like that. It has Conan . . . *Live with Conan,* or something, and she couldn't believe that television was showing naked people in the hot tub with him and all that. Because she used to tease me and complain about how they always show the women [in] full nudity and never the men. And stuff like that."

Incredulous, Roberts had a tough time concealing his skepticism. "And how, how is that flirting with you?"

"Well, she was just, you know, it was the way she said it. She'd smile and wink at me and stuff. It was just, we'd. . . ." His voice faded.

"Did you ever hit on her?"

"No." Hunt made it emphatic and unequivocal.

"Did you want to?"

"No."

"Did she hit on you?"

"No." Not quite so strong, with a hint that a gentleman wouldn't say so even if she did.

Gambling that Hunt may have known about Orloff's younger boyfriend, Vittorio Amati, Roberts asked, "You know she had kind of an attraction for younger guys?"

Nodding, Hunt agreed. "I heard that, yeah."

"Kinda like hope that she had an attraction for you?"

"No."

"Do you like older women?"

"I like my wife."

"Yeah, I know that, but . . ." Roberts let it drop. "OK, I'm gonna bounce away from that for a couple of seconds here, and jump back to 1988. OK? Do you remember your next-door neighbor, the one that got killed?"

If the sudden allusion to the murder of Myra Davis jarred Hunt, he didn't let it show. He simply commented, "Myra? Yeah."

"Do you remember what happened to her?"

"They said her nephew or somebody raped her and killed her. Strangled her or something?" He made the last part a question. After Roberts nodded and grunted assent, Hunt added a peculiar admission. "Yeah, I was there when that guy came to the house. I was trying to help him get in."

"Who?"

"The grandson or somebody. He was a burly guy."

"You helped him get in?"

"Well, he was trying. . . . He didn't have his key."

"Was this before or after she was killed?"

"I guess it was after. It was the day she was found."

Recalling that Myra Davis had probably been killed

at least a day or two before her body was discovered, it didn't make sense that someone was trying to get in the house on the same day Sherry Davis found her grandmother. Hunt's story might be a feeble attempt to convince the detectives that he was unaware at the time that Myra had been murdered. "Were you home all that week?"

"I was working for an ambulance service then. I really don't know."

Returning to the Orloff case, Roberts asked, "Do you know how Jeannie was killed?"

"Yes. Well, first they told me she had a heart attack, and then said she was strangled."

"Kind of a coincidence, huh?"

"I guess. I don't know."

"No? You don't know?"

"No."

Roberts felt it was time to push a little harder. "Would you believe we're sitting here looking at you for that?"

His eyebrows arching, brow wrinkling, Hunt could manage nothing more than "Huh?" Roberts repeated the question. Hunt seemed momentarily to deflate, then took a defensive tack. "Because of my past record, or what?"

"That has a lot to do with it. Sure."

"I think it's time to get a lawyer, right?"

By putting his comment in the form of a question, Hunt allowed Roberts some wiggle room. It was an appeal for advice, not a request for a lawyer. The fine difference might become a point of argument in a court, but Roberts felt comfortable with continuing the interrogation. "Well, let me throw this at you. The day that Jeannie got killed, when you came back home, you were seen with some scratches on you?"

Snapping his answer back, perhaps a little too fast, Hunt practically growled. "If I had scratches at all, they were on my hands from working on that damn shower in the bathroom and doing the tile. I still got cuts and shit on my hands from that day."

Cutting a little slack, not wanting Hunt to retreat in anger, Roberts sympathized. "Yeah, I've done that, too."

Calmer, Hunt added, "And shit. You nip your fingers and all kinds of shit." His knee had started to bounce up and down.

Roberts, staring at the pumping knee, asked, "What are you doing there?"

"What am I doing?"

"Yeah, the way you are bouncing around in your seat."

Reddening, Hunt said, "Just moving my . . . moving my leg."

"Why? Are you nervous?"

"I'm worried about my wife. I told you that to begin with." He paused, then asked, "Was she calm when you left the house?"

"Oh, yeah. She's fine." Roberts was not about to describe her near-hysterical behavior. "When we talked to her, she was fine. So you really don't know what you did on March twenty-eighth in evening hours? You might have gone out?"

"To the best of my recollection, I stayed home. Like I said, my wife could answer that a lot better than I could. She keeps better track of what I do than I do."

"Even when you take off on your own?"

"If I leave the house, if I . . . say go to the store

or something, she's more apt to remember it than I am. I really don't remember."

Roberts decided to aim directly at the center of the target. "OK. So if I asked you if you killed Jeannie, what would you say?"

"I'd say no."

"If I asked you who killed Myra—"

"I'd tell you no."

"All right. If I said I wanted to give you a polygraph . . . you'd take it? No problem?"

"If my lawyer advised that, yeah. When I was in Y.A. [Youth Authority] . . ." Hunt paused, collecting his thoughts. "I don't smoke marijuana. Don't like it. OK? They gave me a polygraph [asking] if I smoked marijuana and it came back positive. It came back that I was lying. I mean, I don't know, man, I don't know. I don't know what to do. I didn't kill Myra. I didn't kill Jeannie. I liked Jeannie. She was cool as hell. I didn't kill her. I didn't kill her."

"Well, your record kinda indicates that you do like older ladies. I mean, it speaks for itself, doesn't it?" It was a taunting gambit, making reference to an event that took place shortly after his release from CYA. An elderly woman was the victim of an attempted rape in the laundry room of her apartment. A sheriff's deputy spotted Hunt strolling in the area and noted that he matched the suspect's description. Hunt increased his pace and disappeared through a doorway. The officer sped around to the rear of the building just in time to see Hunt emerge and arrested him. Hunt denied everything. The victim could not positively identify him, so Hunt was never charged with the crime.

"No, not really." Anger flashed across Hunt's face.

"I was never charged with that. I was picked up and never taken to court for that. Why is it even on my record?"

Ignoring his protests, Roberts charged forward. "What about the one you did go to prison for?"

Assuming that Roberts meant the attempted rape of Arlene Logan in Canyon Country, when he was fifteen, Hunt launched into a heated explanation. "That was about being a kid, being high, running away from boys' home. I forget the name of the home. And we tried to rob some girl, and the guy I was with snatched her shirt off and she started screaming. Next thing I know, we're being jacked up for attempted rape, and burglary, and everything else."

"What about the manslaughter?"

Shaking his head as if to minimize the death of Bernard Davis, Hunt said, "That manslaughter. Wow. Uh, that was about my temper. It was about . . . Here's the fuckin' deal. I hit the guy. I saw him make a move and I hit him. I shouldn't have done it, but I did."

Roberts couldn't quite picture tiny Bernard Davis "making a move" on the husky youth. "So you still have a pretty hot temper, I guess, huh?"

Trying to brush off the appearance of anger, Hunt answered, "Not like that, no."

"Not like what?"

"No. I don't just hit at random. I mean, you know . . . Sure, everybody gets mad, but no. I'm a lot calmer than I was."

"Yeah?" Roberts suppressed a disbelieving smile. "You're being violated right now for, I guess, because you were doing coke or speed again."

With a sigh, Hunt agreed. "Fucked up, yeah."

"How do you get when you're stoned on coke or speed?"

Frowning, Hunt showed discomfort with the subject. "I only did it yesterday."

"First and only time you did it?"

"I've done it before in my life, but since I've been out, yeah, that's it."

Francene Mounger had been quietly listening. Roberts nodded in her direction, a signal to take over the questioning. She asked, "What happened yesterday?"

Turning toward her, Hunt said, "Everything came to a head and I saw the right person."

"What's everything?"

Hunt whined his answer. "It was . . . me and my wife, my feelings inside me, and dealing with me. It all came to a head and I saw . . . I saw the right person. I was offered the dope, I took it, fucked up that one."

"You were arguing with your wife?"

"Not arguing, but we go through little periods where we don't really see eye to eye on a lotta things."

"What were you not seeing eye to eye about?"

Apparently lulled by Mounger's gentle, easygoing style, Hunt opened up. "Just her family basically. All the yelling and screaming that her sister and her kids do. And I . . . when I work, which I haven't been the last week or so, but when I do work, I wake up at three-thirty, four o'clock in the morning to leave the house at five. And I'm tired when it comes nine, ten o'clock at night. When you got some kid, and his mother is screaming at him at ten o'clock at night right outside your door . . . I'm gonna tell 'em to shut the fuck up. It's just little things."

Calm and precise, Mounger kept the pace casual. "Where were you going to work?"

Hunt named an Encino construction company in the San Fernando Valley, but couldn't recall exactly how long he'd been employed there. Six or seven weeks, he estimated. Regarding the previous job, he said, "I was laid off." Reconsidering for a moment, he retracted that. "I wasn't laid off. . . . I quit actually. From the North Hollywood Metro Line. They're building the Lankershim Station and I was working steady for them."

"Who were you working for when you dropped off the Avon stuff at Jeannie's house?"

Hunt said he thought it was the construction company.

Mounger wanted it clarified. "Obviously, you didn't drop off that Avon at five o'clock in the morning, before you went to work?"

"No. It was probably during a weekend. I, really, I don't know. It was probably on a weekend after I did the shower, you know. I did that stuff in the bathroom and took a shower and everything else, but I really don't remember the dates. Sorry, I don't remember."

"You said you were sitting in the living room with her, watching television?"

"No, we were looking at her Avon order."

"Is that the time she was talking about channel three?"

"Nah. That was just . . . It was off and on. I mean, I'd go up there with my wife and she just talks. I see her at the beauty salon and she talks."

"How many times did you go to Jeannie's with your wife?"

"Two or three, probably."

"Do you think you might have dropped off the Avon one weekend?"

"I imagine that was a weekend. My wife would have a receipt with the date."

"Did Jeannie give you money or a check?"

"She paid me, but I don't remember how. I think maybe it was cash. I would have taken that home to my wife. That was her Avon money."

For the next few minutes, Mounger shot questions at Hunt about the interior of Orloff's apartment and what work he did there, testing his memory, watching for conflicting statements that would indicate his need to lie about any part of his activities in Orloff's presence.

"Do you remember how long you were in the house that evening?"

"It might have been an hour or so." Hunt thought it was after he'd eaten his dinner. "I called her and told her I was coming over. She said, 'Come on.' "

Remembering the chicken parts draining in Orloff's sink, Mounger hoped she might hear Hunt say something connecting him to that. "Was Jean eating dinner, or maybe cooking dinner?"

Hunt said he couldn't remember. "There's a security guard. You have to call before you come up, so I don't know what she was doing before I got up to her apartment."

"I mean when you walked in. I realize you don't know what she was doing when you are standing in the lobby."

"When I walked in, she was just standing there. Anytime I ever went up there, even with my wife, she never really seemed to be doing anything." He kept it noncommittal, nullifying any chance of conflict in his statements.

"What was she wearing?"

"I have no idea."

"You don't remember if it was a dress, or pants, or . . . ?"

"I don't think I've ever seen her in a dress. I couldn't tell you what she was wearing."

Mounger wanted to know where he was in the apartment while going over the Avon order. On the couch, he said, and described how Orloff scrutinized the bottles of lotion and creams he'd brought.

"And she didn't hit on you that night?"

"No. No."

"How was it that you were aware she liked younger men?"

"Through my wife and her mother. My wife would make comments and stuff to me. She'd say, 'Jeannie might get you,' and stuff like that. It was just like a joke. I guess it's a joke around the beauty shop. I really don't know, you know, but that's what I heard from my wife and her mother."

After chatting a bit about the establishment where Dora Green ran her manicure business, Mounger returned to Hunt's presence in Orloff's apartment. "How long were you there that night?"

"I'd say about an hour, probably."

"That's quite a while just to go over a—"

Hunt interrupted. "I was dealing with Jeannie and her money. To her four dollars and ninety-nine cents is four dollars and ninety-nine cents. She wants as much as she can get and she was digging everywhere to see where the hell that big bottle was that cost four ninety-nine." Mounger noticed that Hunt kept referring to Orloff in the present tense, as if in denial the woman was deceased. And, each time a question hinted of challenge to his story, he spoke faster and used more profanity.

Mounger dug a little more for details in Hunt's memory of the interior of Orloff's apartment and the work he had completed in there; then she made a quick switch back to the frequency of his visits to the victim. It's an interrogation technique to throw the suspect off balance. "How often did you take Avon products to her?"

"I usually went with my wife to deliver that stuff. But that day, she wasn't feeling good, and was getting backed up on deliveries, so I helped her out. That was it. Jeannie was one person I knew. I delivered to her. There's a couple of people I delivered to on my own." He mentioned the name and location of another female customer to whom he would make deliveries.

"Did you go to work the day after you were at Jeannie's apartment?"

"Uh, I might have. I really don't know. We've been off . . . What's today, the seventh? I'd have to look at a calendar to tell you." He definitely needed a calendar. It was the eighth of April.

"How many scratches do you have on you, Ken? I see you have one nick on your forearm there."

Glancing at his arm, Hunt had a ready explanation. "No, that's not. . . . I picked that. That's like some kind of mole or scar tissue or something. I pick at it; even in my sleep and shit, I pick at it. I go my . . . hands, I got a scratch from last night right there." The subject of scratches seemed to upset him.

Mounger sensed she found a touchy issue. She repeated the question. "How many scratches do you have on you?"

"I really don't know."

She pointed to another scab. "How did you get that one?"

Hesitating and fidgeting, Hunt said, "When I came outta the police station last night, the guy that was supposed to get me my dope and his fucking buddy robbed me."

"Hmm, you had a bad night, didn't you?"

"Yeah. Real bad night."

"Is that scratch the only one you have from the robbery?"

"Yeah. If there was a fight. I really don't know." His answer didn't make sense. Was he starting to panic?

"Did you report the robbery and assault to the police?"

"No," Hunt snapped, "I got the hell out of that part of town."

"Now this past weekend, you had an accident. Is that correct?"

Hunt replied in the affirmative, and volunteered that it had happened on Saturday evening. Mounger redirected him to the previous weekend, when Orloff had died. "So you believe you delivered the Avon products the weekend of the twenty-eighth and twenty-ninth?"

"No," he suddenly blurted. "It was before that. It was like, because I picked up that box from here, like . . . it was before the twenty-ninth."

"Well, the twenty-eighth and twenty-ninth would have been a week and a half ago."

Stammering and halting again, Hunt replied,

"Yeah. I guess. But I said a week before I heard . . . when her mother called my mother-in-law. They said they had just found Jeannie and that . . . she had died of a heart attack. But I—I had already had the box because I was getting ready to do the last coat and take it back to her."

"So your mother-in-law notified you of that?"

"My wife notified me when my mother-in-law told her."

"And you were at work?"

"I was somewhere. Might have been getting my hair cut." He could remember getting paged, but not when or where. It sounded lame to Mounger.

"So when do you think you delivered the Avon?"

"Around the thirteenth or fourteenth. Right in there somewhere." Again he said his wife would be able to recall the date.

"You said earlier you were getting a haircut when you were told. But now you don't know?"

"I just had my hair cut about ten days ago. I don't remember. I'm sorry. I apologize but I just don't remember."

"That's not what you said originally. You said you were getting a haircut when your wife told you."

"If I said I was getting a haircut, I probably was. I just don't know. Really."

Mounger took him through the notification time and place again, but Hunt remained vague. Next she threw the catchall question interrogators nearly always use. "Is there anything you want to tell us that we haven't asked?"

"No."

"OK. Well, you're going to be going to jail for a while and we're going to be working on a few things.

By the way, we have someone who said they saw quite a few scratches on you a week ago." It was a bluff tossed out to see how he would react.

"On my hands?"

"No, not on your hands."

"My wife might have put some on my back. But, I mean, I don't know. I work construction. I don't know about my scratches."

"But you just said you hadn't worked for a week."

"That was last week when I didn't work."

"How about this week?"

"Only in the house."

"So you've not worked for a week and a half?"

Hunt nodded and gave another convoluted account of his sporadic employment. Brad Roberts glanced at Francene Mounger, rolled his eyes, then turned to Hunt. "You know, we don't know if you did this, but—"

Frowning, Hunt cut him off. "My question, check this out. . . . I been accused of a lotta fucking things—"

"I'm sure you have," said Roberts.

"—because of my record."

"No doubt."

"You're not going to turn me into a scapegoat just because of my record."

Roberts, deliberately calm, said, "We're not about to do that. All I can tell you is where we're going with this thing right now. If we find fingerprints in there, it might not mean a damn thing. But I'll tell you, we have a lot of DNA evidence."

Hunt could only manage an assenting grunt.

"You are a suspect, obviously. There are a couple of other people we are going to look at, too. Maybe we're going to get lucky, and maybe we're not. . . ."

Hunt's mind appeared to be troubled still by Mounger's mention of scratches someone had seen on him. Stammering rapidly again, he said, "As far as scratches and shit goes, as far as scratches—I don't—I mean, I work in construction. I don't know—I trample through bushes. I—you know . . ."

"Yeah, we know."

"I got scars, too, but I mean—"

Roberts didn't want to get Hunt too excited. "Well, maybe it's no big deal."

Apparently recognizing he was in serious trouble, Hunt expressed worry about mundane issues. "Who's gonna take me down? . . . Where are they gonna book me?"

"Over in Venice. There's no jail here anymore."

"Wow! Is my parole officer gonna get me tonight?"

Roberts said he doubted that Widener would be there. It was nearly midnight.

Hunt seemed rattled. "He told me this shit was all a fuckin' hit and run. He said that Culver City wanted me for a hit and run for that accident. It was no hit and run. It couldn't have been. I stayed there. I gave the cop my information. I don't know. . . ."

"Well," said Roberts, "we've turned over every stone on this thing. It's going to take some time to wind it up."

That interested Hunt. "How long does it take?"

"We're tracking down virtually everybody who has had contact with her in the last couple of months. Through her family, through her friends. Everybody's making a statement."

Hunt was curious about another aspect of the investigation. "You say you got the DNA and people are being submitted. How long does that take to come back?"

"Oh, not too long."

"A couple of months, or what?"

"Yeah. It could be quicker than that, I hope. It all depends on how backed up they are at the laboratory."

Realizing the interview was over, Hunt stood and muttered some comments about news reports criticizing the "unsanitary" handling of DNA by police.

Roberts gave him a glance and said, "We shall see."

With a hint of resignation in his voice as he was led out in handcuffs, Hunt said, "OK, you know where I'll be."

"Yeah, we do," said Roberts. "We sure do."

Thirteen

Convinced that Kenneth Hunt had killed both Myra Davis and Jean Orloff, the detectives still faced a mountain of work. They had no solid evidence that would stand up in court. In the marathon interview, he had admitted nothing, nor had he said anything that would pin the crimes on him. The search had just started.

Mounger recalled, "We were suspicious that Hunt might have been involved in other homicides, too. We sent flyers with information about him to other agencies. We scrutinized several other cases. One woman was murdered in a West Hollywood convalescent home and her body had been badly burned from the waist down, so there was no sperm available for DNA testing." The burned ruffles at the base of Jean Orloff's bed took on a whole new meaning.

Mounger noted an unusual aspect to the Hunt-Davis-Orloff cases. "It is typical for this type of offender to go from sexual battery, to rape, to murder. But this was somewhat of a reversal, with Myra Davis being killed in 1988, then several sexual-battery cases occurring after that."

Certainly, the circumstances pointed to Hunt. Without a doubt, the two murders were linked by similarities. Both victims were older women. Each of them had been strangled by ligature and raped. Both lived alone, were security conscious, and kept their doors locked. No sign of forced entry could be found in either case, which suggested they probably knew the person who killed them, a person with whom the victims felt comfortable allowing into their homes. And Kenneth Hunt, as a handyman, had worked in both of their homes.

Investigation of other cases took into consideration that Hunt had been out of prison a limited time, which narrowed time frames to be examined and limited the opportunities. While the officers remained suspicious, they found no positive links to other killings. For these two murders, though, circumstances pointed directly to Hunt. But none of these facts, by themselves, would be enough to convince a jury beyond any reasonable doubt.

One major avenue remained open. "Once Sonny was violated, we obtained a warrant for blood samples from him to be used in DNA testing," said Mounger. "A nurse at the Peter Pitchess Ranch, the jail up on I-five, took them. He was going back to prison anyway on parole violation, so we went up there. He wasn't going anywhere."

The samples were sent to Cellmark Diagnostics in Germantown, Maryland, a laboratory specializing in DNA testing and analysis. Included in the material sent were samples of sperm taken from the bodies of Jean Orloff and Myra Davis collected by Senior Criminalist Lloyd Mahamay. The Davis swabs had been kept frozen for ten years.

Now all they had to do was wait. It would take about a month to get the DNA tests back. Would the long-frozen samples from Myra still produce usable DNA? Would they match the samples taken from Kenneth Hunt? If not, there was nothing but the slim circumstantial evidence to link him to the murders.

Even if the DNA came back showing a match to Hunt, there was no guarantee that a jury would accept its veracity. Cellmark had processed the blood samples in the notorious O. J. Simpson murder trial, but the jury apparently accepted arguments by defense counsel that Los Angeles police personnel had mishandled or contaminated the samples. Skeptics circulated the comment that DNA stood for "Do Not Accept." Ironically, several of the same attorneys who had fought so hard against the use of deoxyribonucleic acid evidence against Simpson later used its reliability to exonerate several men convicted of murder, some of them sentenced to death.

While waiting for the DNA results to come back, the investigators heard of a startling setback. Cellmark Diagnostics called to report they had misplaced the semen sample taken from the body of Myra Davis. It had been kept in a freezer for ten years, and now it was gone.

So many mistakes had already been made in both cases. What else could happen? Now critical evidence had been lost.

The Los Angeles Police Department, though, came to the rescue. Severely criticized for mishandling DNA evidence on previous occasions, they had worked hard on improvements. As a precaution, they had sent only one-half of the semen sample from Myra Davis. At Cellmark's request, they were able to provide a replacement for the missing swabs of semen.

Of course, the slipup delayed the whole process. But finally, in early June, the results came back.

Both semen samples, from Myra Davis and Jean Orloff, genetically matched blood samples taken from Kenneth Dean Hunt to a high level of statistical probability.

Elated, Francene Mounger, Ron Phillips, and Brad Roberts decided it was time to tell the victims' families. Sherry Davis and her relatives had waited a full decade. Lois Bachrach and Debby McAllister, along with their kin, had been hoping for encouraging news since the last days of March. Of course, the investigators had to make it clear that Kenneth Hunt was presumed innocent, but they could identify him as the person who would face murder charges.

When Lois Bachrach heard that Kenneth Hunt was the probable killer, she felt a sense of relief, but also a deep sadness. Not only had she lost her sister to a gruesome death at the hands of a killer, but had virtually lost her mother as well. "The biggest fallout, in terms of my family, was my mother. She literally just took a dive after she found out Jeannie was murdered. For quite a while, she had continued to have her nails done by Dora Green, unaware of the suspicions about Hunt." Elizabeth's broken heart, though, took its toll. "She went from this really vibrant, driving eighty-seven-year-old who was like sixty, to a broken woman. It just destroyed her. Physically and mentally. She could still live in her home, but required twenty-four-hour care. It was so hard for me. A huge financial impact, too. Her money is all gone, so my husband and I take care of the expenses now. My mother sometimes calls me Jeannie. I can't say, 'No, Mom, I'm Lois. Jeannie's dead.' What do you say? It's really, really hard."

Sherry Davis was working on the set of a television series, *The Practice*, when someone paged her with a message to call home. Hoping it wasn't an emergency, she grabbed a phone and punched in her own number. Her nanny, caring for the children, answered and said some plainclothes police people were at the front gate asking to see Davis.

Recalling the time, Davis said, "Ron Phillips and Francene Mounger came to my house. I had never met either one of them before. The front gate was locked. Ever since my grandmother was killed, I've been kind of skittish about security. My nanny knows that she is not to buzz anyone through that gate unless she recognizes them. So she kept them waiting outside and paged me."

The nanny, who had never heard about Myra Davis, said, "It's something about your mother." But Sherry sensed that the police would be there for only one reason, to talk about her grandmother. "I don't know why, but I knew it wasn't about my mother. So I said, 'OK, let them in the house.' She did, and put them on the phone. They told me they had arrested the probable killer."

Astonished, Davis felt a flood of emotions. "Oh, my God. I went hysterical on the set. I couldn't stop crying. I had felt so betrayed by the police department. I'm crying like mad on the phone. They wanted to know if I could come and meet with them." Between choking sobs, Davis explained that she was in the middle of a scene and asked if they could meet at a different time.

"I was a mess. A crying female on the phone, so Phillips put Mounger on. I could hear him saying, 'You'd better handle this.' She spoke to me and said,

'When you come in to see us, we'll talk about it and explain more.' "

Grateful and relieved after an eternity of waiting, Davis expressed her thanks. "That happened to be my last day on *The Practice.* I was scheduled soon to do a show called *Seventh Heaven.* When I came home, I called them to set up a meeting between the acting jobs."

The next day, face-to-face with Mounger and Phillips, they discussed the investigation and its outcome in less emotional circumstances. "Phillips talked about how it had looked like my brother Corey might have done it, but there was never enough evidence to make an arrest. It was especially satisfying to learn that he wasn't involved. I said that I was glad it had been solved, and now my family could know it wasn't Corey. That issue had caused a lot of turmoil. I didn't even want him around my children." Davis said that Corey had never even been inside the new home she and her husband had purchased after Myra's death. "But knowing what I know now," said Davis, "I realize there was never any way my brother could have done it."

"Well, Sherry," said Phillips, "this leads us to a very important question. You haven't asked us who we are holding as the suspect." The name of Kenneth Hunt hadn't yet come up. Davis had long suspected George Green, but since no reference had been made to him, she figured it must be someone else.

To Phillips, she replied, "I just assumed that it was a stranger and I wouldn't even know the name."

"Oh, no," said the detective. "You know who did it."

Later speaking of the moment, Davis said, "I was confused and shocked, like being stabbed."

Davis looked at Phillips. "I do?"

"Yes."

"Well, who?"

"The guy next door."

My God, thought Davis. *It* was *George Green.* To Phillips, she said, "My grandmother was always afraid of him." She asked how they had put it all together. From her comments, it suddenly dawned on Phillips that Davis thought they had arrested Green. He asked her if that's who she meant.

"Yes," said Davis. "I never liked him."

"We arrested Sonny Hunt," Phillips announced.

It took a couple of minutes for the shock to register.

When Davis had time to digest the events, she felt a mixture of relief and resentment. "It gets me, now that I know everything, that if the original investigator had just listened and examined the facts, this might have been solved long ago. A lot of people lived in that house next door to my grandmother. There were three men in there. If the cop would have just looked up their records, he would have zeroed in on Kenneth Hunt. He'd been in prison; he had a record of sexual offenses. It's in the detective's notes that I said the man next door could have killed my grandmother, and he didn't even check up on Hunt. I'm still angry about them letting us think it was my brother for ten years."

Even while acknowledging that human beings can make errors, Davis still felt unsettled. "If the detective had just listened to me and put the pieces together, it might have saved Jeannie Orloff's life. A person just doesn't randomly kill two people in ten years. There were probably more victims that have gone unsolved, just as Jean's nearly did. It was such a quirk that when they asked me for possible suspects, I suggested the guy next door. And the people next door apparently pointed to my brother, who became the prime suspect. What a twist. My brother didn't have a record, but Kenneth Hunt did. I wish the police had focused on him a long time ago."

Fourteen

John Francis Gilligan, assistant head deputy district attorney, inherited the duties to prosecute the case against Kenneth Dean Hunt. A veteran attorney, Gilligan had worked for Los Angeles County since 1987.

The Irish in Gilligan showed in the mischievous sparkle of his blue eyes and insouciant sense of humor. Considering his shortly clipped brown hair lying in a casual forward sweep, a growth of stubbly beard decorating a youthful face, and the appearance of a laid-back temperament, it might be easy to underestimate the serious drive within him. That would be a mistake.

A native of New Rochelle, New York, Gilligan grew up as the middle child between two older siblings and two younger ones. "An ideal position," he called it. His father practiced civil law within a firm representing major hotels in the state, including the Hilton chain; he often worked directly with the head man, Conrad Hilton. "It was a unique challenge," said Gilligan, "dealing with construction labor contracts and liability issues when the hotels were sued for anything. My father was certainly a major influence on my decision to become a lawyer."

Gilligan's family moved, when he was a child, from New Rochelle to Larchmont, a tiny town on Long Island. He attended high school in Mamaroneck, where he knew an energetic young female student one year behind him. Years later, he would meet her again.

Asked if he was a scholar or an athlete in school, Gilligan said, "I wasn't much of either at that age." He earned grades, though, good enough to get him into college. At age seventeen, he moved to the southwestern desert, where he subsequently graduated from the University of New Mexico. With a degree in hand, he returned to New York to find work. As a paralegal, he labored one year in Albany, then another twelve months with a law firm in the Big Apple. The urge to go West hit once more, resulting in another relocation, this time to Los Angeles. While employed as a paralegal with the city attorney, his nights were dedicated to studying at Southwestern Law School. Gilligan passed the bar exam on his first attempt. After spending another two years with the city attorney, he joined the Los Angeles County District Attorney's Office in 1987.

"I worked the usual gambit of assignments," Gilligan recalled. While in the sex crimes and child abuse unit, he prosecuted a dozen homicides. The emotional impact of dealing with cases in which babies were tortured and children tormented, battered, or killed lingers with him. "I handled a lot of rape and child abuse cases that were stressful and traumatic. Child victims bothered me the most. Some of them made murder cases seem relatively simple."

Thinking of at least one pleasant aspect of the assignment, Gilligan said, "I met my wife on a high-profile child abuse case I prosecuted. She was a reporter.

The case involved a boy whose father had remarried, giving him two step-children. He treated both of them very nicely. But for some reason, he starved his own child and made the kid sleep in a cage in the back-yard. It was like one of those storage structures you get from Sears to store your lawn mower in. Inside that was a cage he locked the kid in at night. The child was six, and looked no more than three or four in development, and perhaps five inches too short and twenty pounds lighter than normal at that age. Up and down both arms and on the hands, there were healed fractures." Gilligan's face darkened as he described the horror.

The case made headlines and fodder for television news. "A friend of mine came back from Europe after I did the preliminary hearings, and she said, 'I know what you've been doing lately. I was watching. It was on CNN television while I was sitting in a café on the Left Bank in Paris.'

"So that was the case I met my wife on," said Gilligan. "Now she is the public affairs director for this office, the Los Angeles County District Attorney." At the time of the interview, their one child was in kindergarten, and Gilligan's son from a previous marriage was a sophomore in college.

Mark Windham, the man who would defend Kenneth Hunt, was no stranger to Gilligan. "I've known him fifteen years." While Gilligan headed up the West Los Angeles prosecutor's unit, with a staff of twenty people, Windham supervised an equal number reporting to the public defender's group, same sector. The two men came close to facing off in court on one case, but resolved it before it went to trial. Both were also well acquainted with the woman who would preside over the Hunt trial, Superior Court Judge Jacqueline Connor. Gilligan had already prosecuted several cases in Connor's court. In the courtroom directly adjacent to hers, familiar to millions of television watchers, Gilligan had prosecuted a rape case. It was there Judge Lance Ito had presided over the most publicized trial of the century.

Speaking of Judges Connor and Ito, along with Windham and several colleagues, Gilligan said, "We were among a group of people who knew each other and had strong professional regard for one another."

In preparing for the Hunt trial, Gilligan pondered two tough problems. First of all, DNA would be a central issue, since there was little else of any real substance to link Hunt to the murders. "My number one concern was making DNA understandable to the average juror." Enough DNA cases had been previously tried to amass a stack of transcripts for use as reference material. "Using them as a guide, we could avoid errors other lawyers had made. You don't want to give the jury too little and leave them with an inadequate understanding of genetic fingerprinting. On the other hand, you don't want to bore them to tears by presenting too much. You have to hit the right pace."

The second issue Gilligan faced lay in the several blunders made by investigators. "We wanted to be very honest about all the slipups and problems that led to Mr. Hunt escaping justice so long. Evidence lost, LAPD oversights, coroner's office misjudgments. You have to be honest, yet portray the fact that, despite the errors, we would have a solid case. You can't be an apologist, nor do you want to undermine your own case by appearing to have no confidence." Gilligan acknowl-

edged that the defense would have plenty to work with.
"You have to anticipate that and be ready."

An energetic young lawyer, Laura Jane Kessner
joined Gilligan to help prepare and present the evidence. Just a little over five feet tall, with dark blond
hair pulled back into a ponytail, deep blue eyes, and a
gentle, softspoken manner that would convince a jury
of her earnestness, Kessner had a reputation for dedication and hard work. A native of Kentucky, with no
hint of a drawl, she had known from early childhood
that she wanted to be a trial lawyer, and more specifically, a prosecutor. "I'm not certain exactly why," she
explained with a laugh, "but it might have had something to do with arguments I gave my parents. They
would roll their eyes and say, 'You'd make a good lawyer.' " Following graduation from the University of Kentucky, Kessner migrated to California and worked to
earn enough for law school before entering Loyola. She
earned a degree and passed the bar exam in 1994. Join-
ing the L.A. County DA, she specialized in sexual assault
cases. DNA is exceptionally important in dealing with
sexual crimes, so Kessner became an expert on the subject. Her skill in both disciplines made her a natural to
team with John Gilligan on the Hunt case.

Another veteran member of the DA's office made
important contributions during the trial preparation
stage. Lisa Kahn had immersed herself in DNA study
when it first became recognized as forensic evidence
in the late 1980s. Prosecuting a defendant accused of
raping two women, Kahn successfully argued for a
warrant to obtain blood samples, submitted them to
a lab for genetic profiling, and for the first time ever
in California, called DNA experts to testify before the
jury. The defendant was convicted. She played an im-

portant role in the O. J. Simpson case as well, and earned recognition as the most knowledgeable attorney in the county about forensic use of DNA. When John Gilligan encountered Lisa Kahn, he was stunned to learn her background. She was the same young girl who had been a year behind him a long time ago at Mamaroneck High School in New York.

In the Hunt case, Kahn not only helped Laura Jane Kessner enhance her understanding of DNA, but she also argued before a judge in a Kelly-Frye motion, a court hearing to show the reliability of evidence and its general acceptance in the scientific community. The hearing was necessitated by the prosecutor's plan to use a new type of DNA analysis in the Hunt case. Kahn had spent several months boning up on the more sophisticated profiling technique called Short Tandem Repeat (STR) Polymerase Chain Reaction (PCR) testing, along with methods called "profiler plus and cofiler." She convinced the court that the science was fundamentally connected to preexisting technology and was admissible as evidence.

Armed with DNA as the foundation, along with less powerful circumstantial evidence, Gilligan and Kessner were ready to present their case to a jury.

Lawyers who defend suspects accused of horrendous crimes are sometimes misunderstood by the general public and categorized in unpleasant terms. Private attorneys are accused of doing it for fame and wealth. Public defenders, some say, are either ambitious, seeking promotions, or perhaps inviting notoriety in order to hang up their own shingles and become wealthy. Sometimes the criticisms are accurate, but for the most part, these defenders are people who truly want to protect rights guaranteed by the U.S. Constitution. One of those is a remarkably intelligent and spiritual man named Mark Windham, head deputy public defender.

A Californian born in April 1959, Windham grew up in the city of his birth, Van Nuys. In a high school named for the city, he was student body president and the debating champion of Los Angeles in 1976. It surprised no one that he became a lawyer. Like many other attorneys, he followed in the footsteps of his father, a civil rights litigator with a private firm. "My father," said Windham, "took a lot of pride in the large number of trials he participated in."

While still in high school, Mark attended a trial and found it riveting, which sealed his decision. He completed four years at the University of California, Berkeley, and followed it up at Hastings Law School in San Francisco. He aced the bar exam in 1980. But he wasn't quite ready to launch his career.

"I wanted to see the world first," he said. "So I strapped on a backpack and set out for India. I wanted to learn as much as I could." Deeply interested in religion and spiritualism, particularly Buddhism, he observed its influence while trekking through the East—India, China, and Nepal. He wound up spending some time in Paris before returning to Southern California.

His deep interest in theology and spiritualism remains a part of his life. "I read voraciously, particularly text that grapples with issues of life and death." But he doesn't want people to get the wrong idea that he is fanatically religious. "I've recently turned toward Christianity," he explains, "and I'm becoming a Catholic."

Harboring a strong opposition to the death penalty, he also doesn't want that misunderstood. "I'm not a pacifist and I certainly believe in self-defense."

In the Bay Area, he freelanced as a lawyer for some time, then joined a firm dealing in civil rights. "While those stints provided valuable experience, taking endless depositions wasn't exactly fulfilling for me. A friend of mine had joined the Los Angeles Public Defenders Office, so I decided to give it a try." The organization happily took him aboard in 1985.

By the time the case of Kenneth Hunt crossed Windham's desk, he had defended more than one hundred people accused of various crimes. With a certain glint in his expressive brown eyes, he said, "That's more trials than my father did." Thirteen of those defendants were facing the possibility of a death sentence. Through Windham's efforts, the DA "abandoned eight, dropping capital charges. Four were resolved by plea bargains. Only three went to trial." Hunt would be the fourteenth defendant on trial for his life.

In all trials, an important aspect is the attorney's rapport with the jury. Windham had no trouble in that area. Handsome, with a shock of thick black hair neatly styled, dark expressive eyes, a winning smile, and sartorial elegance, he had the image of a man one could like and trust. His emotions showed clearly on his face. He would tilt his head as if in deep thought before uttering a word. He would pause between sentences to let the impact of his words sink in. And it came off not as theatrical, but as honest sincerity. Juries listened and truly liked the man.

When not spending long hours researching or litigating a case, Windham relaxed by working out in a

gym near his Venice home. Or cooking Italian style
for friends, "preparing risotto with porcini." With an
understanding smile, he explains, "Porcini are flat little mushrooms."

With an ear for music, he likes to relax by playing
the piano, "but not in public."

Married to an Irish lass who is a film editor, Windham commented, "She knew John Gilligan before she
knew me." But when he met her at a birthday party,
fate took over.

Most of Windham's time is consumed by his dedication to the profession. "During the prolonged O.
J. Simpson trial," he said, "I completed *three* murder
cases! One was a triple homicide, finalized by the
defendant being found guilty of manslaughter. The
second was a double murder. It went to the jury and
he was acquitted. The third was a homicide during
a kidnapping. That defendant had been previously
convicted, twice! But both were reversed by appeals
courts." Windham had discovered "grievous errors
made by the LAPD, terrible mistakes at the crime
scene." He won an acquittal for the defendant. Recalling the hectic period of time, Windham said, "I
was so consumed with these cases, working right next
door to the Simpson trial, and wondering what took
place each day over there in Judge Ito's court, I
would have to call my mother each evening. She
watched it on television and kept me updated."

The Kenneth Hunt case was first assigned to Windham in December 1998, nine months after Orloff's
murder. It became a full-time project for him in January 1999, keeping thorough records of every step in
preparing for trial. At first, the documents related to
the case were easily manageable. As the trial date ap-

proached, the boxes of records nearly filled a work-room close to his office.

Just as John Gilligan realized the central issue would revolve around DNA evidence, so did Windham. He pondered the idea of attacking the validity of so-called genetic fingerprinting. "I spent three months in litigation hearings debating the admissibility of DNA. I talked to everyone I could find who is knowledgeable about it. And I took courses in it." It would all show up in the strategy and tactics he would use in the jury's presence.

In his meticulous examination of documents, including medical reports, witness statements, and police reports, Windham discovered an obscure notation that might just have considerable impact on the jury. It was an issue much like a cliche in a B movie. Windham saw a detective's note hinting that the ligature on Jean Orloff's throat appeared to have been twisted by a left-handed perpetrator. Kenneth Hunt was right-handed. He also had a witness who might turn everything around.

Kenneth Dean Hunt would face trial in Department 109, Los Angeles Superior Court, in early 2001.

The People of the State of California, plaintiff,
vs Kenneth Dean Hunt, (dob 5-29-66) aka "Sonny"
defendant, Case number SA034500

COUNT I
On or about June 28, 1988, in the county of Los Angeles, the crime of MURDER, in violation of PENAL CODE 187(a), a felony, was committed by KENNETH DEAN HUNT, who did unlawfully,

and with malice aforethought, murder MYRA
DAVIS, a human being.

COUNT II

On or about March 28, 1998, in the county of
Los Angeles, the crime of MURDER, in violation
of PENAL CODE 187 (a), a felony, was committed
by KENNETH DEAN HUNT, who did unlawfully,
and with malice aforethought, murder JEAN OR-
LOFF, a human being.

It is further alleged that the murders of MYRA
DAVIS and JEAN ORLOFF were committed by defendant KENNETH DEAN HUNT while engaged
in the commission of the crime of RESIDENTIAL
BURGLARY and FORCIBLE RAPE.

In California, a defendant charged with capital
murder faces a trial in two phases. Phase one is to
determine guilt of the crime, and if special circumstances are true or not true. Hunt faced the special
circumstances of committing residential burglary,
rape, and multiple murder, in the course of killing
the victims. If the defendant is found guilty, and the
jury finds any of the special circumstances true, the
same jury is reconvened a few days later to hear aggravating and mitigating circumstances, then deliver
a verdict of death or life in prison without the possibility of parole.

Fifteen

In Department 109, on the ninth floor of the downtown Los Angeles Criminal Courts Building (CCB), Kenneth Dean Hunt faced trial in a historic setting. The twenty-story building had been the site of numerous high-profile legal battles since its opening in 1971, providing endless fodder for books and movies. O. J. Simpson had been acquitted of murder charges in Judge Lance Ito's Department 110, next door to the room in which Hunt faced a jury. Down the hall, Richard Ramirez, L.A.'s notorious "Night Stalker," had been found guilty of thirteen savage killings. One of the state's longest and most expensive trials, the McMartin Preschool case, in which the day-care operators had been charged with sexual molestation of children, had played out its course in the CCB. And a few movie stars had waited nervously while Heidi Fleiss faced trial in the building, accused of running a call-girl business catering to the rich and famous.

Seven men and five women, plus six alternate jurors, filled Department 109's jury box at the right side of the courtroom. They settled into faux-wood swivel chairs with royal blue padding. In the gallery, observers crowded four rows of high-back benches, under the watchful eye of Bailiff Bond Maroj. Slim and athletic in his tan uniform, hair cut in short military style, Maroj occupied a booth on the left side, separated from the observers by two seven-foot glass panels, and within two steps of Kenneth Dean Hunt at the defense table.

Diffused lighting from the high ceiling softened the atmosphere and allowed a feeling of space in the compact, modern black-walnut-paneled chamber. On the other side of a yard-high divider between the gallery and the court, lawyers worked at three end-to-end counsel tables. Light blue carpet silenced their footsteps.

From her elevated, semicircular desk, under a five-foot wooden replica of California's great seal, Judge Jacqueline Connor commanded a view of the entire space. Much of the time, she focused on a computer screen mounted to her left, on which the rapidly scrolling words inputted by court reporters Donna Bennett and alternate Marianne Bracci appeared. Connor's clerk, Stacey Vickers, busied herself constantly with an endless flow of paper and whispered telephone calls, but always seemed ready to flash a warm smile.

Judges who have been elevated to the bench from the role of prosecutor are often perceived as slightly biased in favor of their former colleagues and against defense attorneys. In some cases, that may be true, but no one ever accused Superior Court Judge Jacqueline Connor of any prejudice. In her fifteen years presiding over a multitude of trials, she gained a reputation of being not only fair-minded but innovative as well.

Detroit, Michigan, was her birthplace on December

20, 1951, but she was reared in Tokyo, Japan, where her father ran an import/export business. A graduate of the University of Southern California Law School in 1976, she joined the Los Angeles District Attorney's Office the next year as a deputy DA specializing in sexual assault cases, as Laura Jane Kessner would do several years later. Connor cofounded and cochaired a special committee to prosecute sex crimes.

Most people encountering Connor would probably guess her to be in her early forties, with a smooth face somewhat resembling movie star Demi Moore, collar-length streaked blond hair in a casual style, tall erect posture, and quick, efficient movements. In her courtroom, she expects courtesy and adherence to the rules, but doesn't bother with many of the stuffy old formalities.

Connor accepted an appointment to a municipal court judgeship in October 1986. Governor George Deukmejian of California appointed her to the superior court in 1988, along with another jurist who would become well known, Judge Lance Ito. The new position came just nine weeks before the murder of Myra Davis.

Recognition for Connor as an innovative judge came as a result of her willingness to experiment with altering the roles of jurors. One of the major changes she pioneered permits jurors to submit written questions during a trial. Such procedures were unheard of in California courtrooms until 1998 when a state supreme court ruling paved the way for juror reform. Connor and a small cadre of her colleagues began testing the waters by providing jurors with notebooks containing written instructions, and by presenting opening statements to the entire panel so they would understand exactly what kind of a trial they were getting into.

The changes are not universally applauded, especially by defense attorneys. One lawyer commented that if jurors have to ask questions, then the prosecution has not proved its case. Another said, "I don't know where judges are coming up with this harebrained idea."

Connor rebuts this position. "It's a huge benefit to the attorneys," she says. Jurors who can ask questions will not need to speculate. In open court, when a trial starts, she tells the jury, "You are the judges. I am the referee. As judges, you do not do any investigation. But I do allow you to ask questions." If one of them needs to do so, they are told to write the query down and give it to the bailiff, who will deliver it to Connor. If she decides it can be answered within the rules of law, she reviews it with the attorneys and provides an answer to the entire jury.

If Judge Connor does harbor any prejudice at all, it might be against attorneys who prolong their arguments over long periods of time, turning short statements into ponderous speeches. With tongue slightly in cheek, she once mentioned a particular television program she watches, and gave the reason. "That's why I like *L.A. Law,* she said, "because arguments by the lawyers are cohesive and take only five minutes."

The guilt phase of Kenneth Hunt's trial for double murder would take only eight days of testimony and arguments. Then, seven men and five women would retire to weigh the evidence.

Bailiff Bond Maroj requested quiet in the courtroom shortly after 10:00 A.M. on Wednesday, February 28, 2001. Seated at the left end of the defense table,

Kenneth Hunt, clean shaven except for his bushy mustache, hair neatly combed, dressed in a dark suit and white shirt, slumped in his chair. Next to him, the paralegal Eric Johnson sorted papers. Mark Windham eyed the jury, wondering which ones he might convince to see his point of view. A few feet to his right, Francene Mounger, wearing a conservative dress, whispered to Laura Jane Kessner, seated next to her. In line with the standard procedure for the investigating officer to assist the prosecution, Mounger would be there for the duration of the trial.

Gilligan, at the far right end of the table, closest to the jury, looked up toward Judge Jacqueline Connor, waiting for her to give the green light for opening statements by the prosecutor.

"Mr. Gilligan, go ahead," she ordered.

Pacing himself with care and modulating his voice so that each juror would be able to hear every word, John Gilligan stood and spoke. Jurors reciprocated his greeting of "Good morning" with nervous smiles, nods, and barely audible words. For the first few moments, he commented on previous proceedings, paused, then jumped right to the point.

"Now, what we're going to do is to prove to you beyond any reasonable doubt that Kenneth Dean Hunt, the defendant, the gentleman sitting at the end of the table, committed these two brutal rape-murders." Gilligan leveled an accusing arm toward Hunt, who sat stone-faced looking into the distance. "I think what is going to be clear is that it's a very long strange road that brought us here, in 2001, to deal with these two murders, one of which was committed way back in 1988."

Striding back and forth in slow, measured steps, like

Gregory Peck in *To Kill a Mockingbird,* Gilligan's eyes
locked on the faces of each juror, one by one. "These
were murders, horrific rape-murders of two people
Mr. Hunt knew. One was his next-door neighbor and
the other was a woman who hired him to do some
handy work in her apartment."

The emotion-charged words "rape-murders" re-
sounded through the silent courtroom like fingernails
on a blackboard. And they stunned a beautiful woman
sitting in the gallery. Sherry Davis heard for the first
time that her grandmother had been raped.

Approaching an easel-mounted chart, Gilligan
pointed to a graphic map of Beverly Drive, showing
the location of Myra Davis's home and the house next
door. He told jurors that Sherry Davis would take the
stand and tell them about her grandmother and how,
in July, 1988, when Myra didn't answer the telephone,
Sherry drove to the house. "She sees newspapers and
mail stacked up. . . . She also sees a living-room light
on, even though it's broad daylight. This concerns
her. She goes to the door and knocks. There is no
answer. And this, she finds, is very curious."

Gilligan described the horror when Davis saw her
beloved grandmother lying dead in the bedroom. The
police are summoned, he said, and it's "very obvious
that Myra Davis has been murdered and there is the
circumstantial evidence of a rape." Taking the wide-
eyed jurors step by step through the grisly discoveries,
Gilligan defined "ligature" strangulation for them
and described the murder weapon, the handle of a
pot scrubber used to twist "undergarments" around
the victim's throat. "And the force you will hear about
is such that it actually broke muscles and bones in
her neck.

"A rape kit was used. I will have the technician explain its use in looking for evidence of sexual assault in various orifices of the body and on the skin. They take samples to test for semen. In this case, the rape kit turned up positive. There was, in fact, evidence that Myra Davis was sexually assaulted at the time she was murdered and her house was burglarized." The fluid evidence, he told the panel, was kept in a freezer for future use.

Detectives, said Gilligan, knocked on neighbors' doors, looking for information about the victim's activities and acquaintances. "One of the places they went was right next door . . . and who do they meet? Detective Rockwood will tell you he interviewed Kenneth Dean Hunt, who knew Myra Davis . . . but he hadn't seen her in approximately ten days. You will see that it turned out to be a very significant piece of evidence."

Making certain he had each juror's full attention, Gilligan said, "The case remained unsolved for ten years!"

Striding back and forth again, he said, "The second murder [victim] was Jean Orloff. She lived alone on Bentley Avenue, apartment 306." Placing a new poster on the easel, he showed them an aerial photo of the building. He informed the jurors they would hear from Orloff's friends, including the last person to see her alive. Another close companion would tell them how she had discovered the body. "Barbara Kappedal opens the door, goes into Jean's bedroom, and sees her lying down, naked. Jean's feet were blue and it was very obvious that she was, in fact, dead." Gilligan listed Kappedal's observations, the smell of smoke, burns on the bed skirt, and chicken in the sink. "It was an odd thing . . . her friend would be naked, cooking, and end up on the bed. It just didn't add up."

The police, paramedics, and a coroner's investigator arrived, said Gilligan. They see cigarettes and heart medicine, and conclude she died of a heart attack. "And they are wrong!" The family is notified and arrived on the scene. Told erroneously that it was a natural death, they make arrangements for cremation and a funeral. "At this point, two things happen that prevent the destruction of evidence in this case and ultimately lead to Mr. Hunt's sitting in that chair, facing justice."

The expressions on jurors' faces signaled to Gilligan their intense interest. The first thing that happened, he said, was the problem with getting a signature on the document certifying natural death. That led to the arrival, a few days later, of a coroner's investigator to view the body. "When he gets there, a man named Sherwood Dixon, he sees a distinct red furrow on her neck. He looks at this and says this is a classic sign of a strangulation murder. Based on that, he calls the police. Detective Francene Mounger and several others from the West L.A. Homicide Division get involved . . . and the body is taken for an autopsy."

Describing the examination by Dr. Pena, Gilligan promised the expert would testify. "He will tell you that just like in the Myra Davis case, what you have is the rape-murder of an elderly female, again with the use of a ligature."

Several people in the gallery who knew Jean Orloff, and remembered her tenacious struggle to remain

young, thought how she would have resented the
word "elderly" to describe her.

"The ligature was not found on the neck as it was
in the earlier scene, but it's an identical cause of
death. Some kind of an object was twisted around
Jean Orloff's neck way beyond what was necessary to
kill her, to the point where bones and muscles are
fractured. She is murdered.

"Again they do the rape kit as I described earlier
on the Myra Davis case, and lo and behold, it's positive for semen.

"Now what have we got? At this point, the detectives are just working the 1998 case. They are just
working on Jean Orloff. They have found out that this
is, in fact, a homicide and not a natural death. There
is no connection yet to the 1988 case.

"At this point, the second big break occurs that
puts Mr. Hunt in that chair."

Mentioning that Hunt had been on parole for voluntary manslaughter, Gilligan avoided spelling out
any details. Previous crimes are not allowed to be introduced into the guilt phase of a trial unless a judge
allows it on a limited basis for a specific purpose. If,
at the end of the penalty phase, the jury delivers a
guilty verdict and finds the special circumstances are
true (rape, burglary, and multiple murder in the
Hunt case), full details of the defendant's criminal
record can be presented in the penalty phase. So Gilligan brought up the manslaughter record only to introduce his plan to call Hunt's parole officer, John
Widener, as a witness.

"Mr. Hunt's parole officer received some information that Hunt may be connected to both homicides.
Mr. Widener takes this information to the West L.A.

Homicide Division. . . . At this point, they look at two
cases. The 1988 case is reopened. What have you got?
Two older white females found raped, strangled with
a ligature, found nude, lying in their beds. A lot of
basic similarities."

Experienced trial watchers recognized the time-
honored technique most trial lawyers use in speaking—describing an action, interjecting a question,
then answering it. Gilligan had already used it several
times. Windham would probably do the same.

"What else do they do? Well, they develop witnesses
who tell them the following: Mr. Hunt was the neighbor in the 1988 case. He lived on Beverly Drive next
to Myra Davis. And they find out, in the Orloff case,
that Mr. Hunt was in her apartment doing handy
work." Witnesses, said Gilligan, would testify to that.

"Based on this information, putting together the
M.O. [modus operandi], the connections, Mr. Hunt
being the commonality in both cases, detectives bring
this information to a judge and a search warrant is
issued for a sample of Mr. Hunt's blood." It would
be used to make a genetic comparison to body fluids
found on the victims. "Detective Mounger will tell you
that blood samples were taken. Now, we have the rape
kit from Myra Davis still on ice. We have the rape kit
from Jean Orloff. What happens at that point? The
blood sample from Mr. Hunt is compared to two separately analyzed sperm samples that were taken from
the bodies of Myra Davis and Jean Orloff at their
autopsies."

Mark Windham sat quietly on the right side of his
client, giving his full attention to Gilligan's riveting
presentation. He knew his colleague's skill with juries,
and realized the jurors would probably be ready to

come back with a guilty verdict immediately if they were allowed to deliberate right after Gilligan had finished his opening remarks. But Windham also felt confident in his own abilities. He scribbled notes as the prosecutor spoke of the blood samples. Here was a major point of attack where Windham planned to wage an aggressive battle.

To Gilligan as well, the blood and semen samples were going to be the pivotal point in the whole trial, and the trickiest for him. It was critically important to educate the jurors about DNA testing without boring them to death. They must understand it and accept its reliability. He needed to walk a fine line and begin laying groundwork for presentation of the complicated evidence.

"The Orloff sample is sent off to be analyzed by Cellmark Laboratories, and you will hear a representative from Cellmark telling you about the work they do. You will hear about them, and the fact that they are one of the most well-known, well-respected labs that do DNA analysis. So the Orloff samples are sent out. Mr. Hunt's blood is *separately* sent out." Gilligan emphasized the word "separately," anticipating that Windham would make an issue of that.

Bringing up another blunder that had to be admitted, Gilligan covered it with frank brevity. "Then the Davis sample is sent out. But Cellmark calls and says, 'We lost that sample. Do you have another one?' And the LAPD says, 'Yes, we do.' They send the second sample from Myra Davis." Gilligan hoped the jurors would see the error as innocuous. It would certainly be a point of vulnerability for Windham to attack.

"What is the result of the testing? Using the DNA technology that has been used by law enforcement

and by private labs all over the country for purposes
of convicting defendants, *and* exonerating the wrong-
fully accused; using that technology, Cellmark reported that the Caucasian database, which is obviously
the right database for Mr. Hunt, that the person providing the blood sample, Mr. Hunt, is a match to the
sample of semen found in the body of Myra Davis
and the semen found in Jean Orloff's body." Only
one in 2.4 million persons in the population would
match, Gilligan said, and Hunt is that one.

If that number didn't convince the jury of Hunt's
statistical culpability, Gilligan had another more impressive one. "Now, we have a great deal more [of a]
sample in the Orloff case. Cellmark, using a groundbreaking new technology that is being installed or is
already in use in labs all over the country . . . I'm
not going to go through it now. You will hear the
expert who can tell you in a much cleaner way than
I can. They will tell you, based on this new technology,
they are able to get a result in the Orloff case that
once again is a match to the blood sample from Mr.
Hunt to the semen that is found inside Jean Orloff's
body, and the match is one in 1.7 quintillion!"

The number boggled minds in the gallery, and
probably among jurors. One in 1.7 *quintillion!* The human brain seems incapable of coping with such a figure.

Gilligan made a stab at clarifying it. "We'll explain
to you how astronomical that is. It is one in 1.7 times
ten to the eighteenth power. That is a frequency with
which you would have that person. That is how rare it
is. That is how specific it is. And that specificity is to
Mr. Hunt." Math majors would be satisfied with that.
For most people, it didn't help much.

There are 6 billion people in the world. If each planet in the solar system had the same population as earth, Hunt would be the only one in all the planets whose blood sample matched the semen samples. And that is still only a portion of 1.7 quintillion.

There is more, said Gilligan. "We have the DNA matches. We also have the fact that we can connect Kenneth Hunt to both crime scenes with circumstantial evidence, even though there is no evidence these two women knew each other. We also have virtually identical crimes in many ways, ten years apart. Two older women, white females, found raped, strangled with ligatures, found in their own bedrooms in their own homes.

"In addition to the direct evidence, the astronomical numbers that you have heard, and that you will hear a great deal about, you will also have the testimony from a number of women who were attacked by Mr. Hunt in broad daylight. They were able to get away from him. You will hear all their stories. We will prove to you what occurred in those events. Should you find this evidence true, you will be able to take this evidence as showing character traits for misconduct, sexual misconduct on the part of Mr. Hunt.

"Ladies and gentlemen, at the conclusion of this case, you will be convinced beyond any reasonable doubt that Mr. Hunt is guilty of first-degree murder of Myra Davis and Jean Orloff, and that in each of these cases, the special circumstances of rape and burglary are true. And because of the nature of these offenses, that the third special circumstance of multiple murder is also true.

"Thank you for your time and attention."

At the defense table, Mark Windham gathered a

sheaf of notes and stood to deliver his opening statement. From his graceful movements, he might have
been a prizefighter entering the ring for a champion-
ship bout. In an interview, he said, "Preparing for this
case, I trained physically, like a boxer might for a
fight. I lifted weights six days a week, did cardiovascular exercises, and became very strong. Also, I meditated and prayed to God for guidance."

The mental preparation was just as rigorous. "We
gathered an enormous amount of evidence. Left no
stone unturned. We talked to everyone we could find
who knew Mr. Hunt." Research of the defendant's juvenile records presented certain obstacles, since most
of them had been shredded according to California
law. But records of previous court hearings contained
enough information to piece together Hunt's history.
"We found hundreds of names in the documents, and
looked up most of them for interviews. We consulted
with experts in several fields—psychologists, juvenile
justice authorities, DNA experts, and others. We were
first assigned the case in December 1998, and went
to work on it in January 1999. Through every step,
we kept meticulous documentation and records. And,
of course, in a sense, I'd been preparing for this case
eleven years, in every law case I had handled and studied, and the seminars I've attended in capital-case defense. I really try to be a state-of-the-art attorney." No
one would argue with that assessment.

Sixteen

Wearing a stylish gray suit, white shirt, and red patterned tie, Mark Windham stood at the lectern to deliver his opening statement. His smooth face appearing relaxed, eyes friendly, he demonstrated the articulate skills he'd used as a debating champion in school.

"Long ago, about twenty years back, September 25, 1981, two boys ran away from their juvenile placement, a group home, a foster home known as the Pacific Lodge boys' home, over in Woodland Hills in the valley. And one of those children was a fifteen-year-old boy, about five foot eight inches tall, name Kenneth Dean Hunt. The other boy, also fifteen, was Joe Cardenas.

"After about four days of living on the streets in the valley, these boys had made it all the way across the San Fernando Valley to Canyon Country. And on September twenty-ninth, as these two boys sat on a grassy hilltop overlooking Canyon High School, they talked to each other."

John Gilligan's head jerked in the direction of the speaker. Where was Windham going with this? The speech didn't sound to Gilligan like a statement de-

scribing the evidence or witnesses he would present
to the jury, but more like a penalty phase argument,
presenting mitigating circumstances for Hunt's behavior. In the discovery exchange, in which prosecution
and defense teams provide one another with a list of
witnesses they may call, plus a summary of evidence
they will use, there had been no mention of bringing
up Hunt's early life. Gilligan grabbed a pen to make
notes on legal-sized yellow paper.

Windham, now letting his face express compassion
for two wayward boys, kept his narrative moving.
While he spoke in dramatic form, utilizing the repetition of key words, pausing for effect, and beginning
many sentences with "and" as a tool of continuity, no
one questioned his sincere belief in what he was saying.

"And Kenneth, fifteen-year-old Kenneth, was very,
very angry. Why was he angry? He was angry because
although he had a mother and a father, he could no
longer live with them. They had refused to take him
back from juvenile hall. So he had to live in this foster
home, this group boys' home known as Pacific Lodge.

"And all the time he was sitting in juvenile hall for
the crime of stealing his mother's bicycle from the
garage—there was an arrest, it was the reason he was
in juvenile hall. All that time, his mother had never
visited him. . . ."

Gilligan leaped to his feet. "Your Honor, I'm going
to object. May we approach?" Judge Connor nodded
permission. At one side of her raised, semicircular
desk away from the jury, the lawyers gathered and
spoke in whispers. Gilligan said, "I am very loath to
object and I apologize for this. I'm just very concerned. In terms of the guilt phase, we have received

[from the defense] a list of very few witnesses. They
are all scientists. They are all very technical. This
sounds like an opening argument for the penalty
phase. We have no discovery; we have no indication
about this being part of the guilt phase."

Connor, leaning over the table separating her from
the lawyers, said to Windham, "I am assuming you
are calling these witnesses. You had better turn the
names over and the information."

Frowning, Windham replied, "They know who Joe
Cardenas is."

Laura Jane Kessner spoke up. "This is material they
gave us for the penalty phase."

After a few moments of discussion, Connor made
the decision to allow the defender to proceed.

Resuming his presentation to the jury, Windham
took a deep breath, perhaps revealing a subtle hint
of exasperation at the interruption, and picked up his
narrative exactly where he'd left off. "He sat on the
hillside with Cardenas and explained why he was angry. He was angry with his mother because all the
time he sat in juvenile hall, she did not visit him. And
all the time he sat in juvenile hall, his father did not
visit him; although his father had promised to take
him back when he was released, he did not because
his stepmother had refused to let him come back.
And his dad never visited him but once.

"So on his birthday, no visit. On Christmas, when
the other boys got visits, he received none. No cards
when the other boys got cards. No mail. His anticipa-
tion rose when the mail arrived, but no letter from
his dad or from Mom. So everyone in juvenile hall
was bad, but they got visits and they got mail. So he
was worse. He felt worse.

"So he is angry at his daddy, and he is angry at his stepmother, and he is angry at his mother. And that is what he told Joe Cardenas up on that hillside on September 29, 1981, about twenty years ago."

Gallery observers noticed that Windham's description of Hunt's male parent went from "father" to "dad" to "daddy." The word "angry" surfaced repeatedly. More than a few made private bets that Windham wouldn't really risk putting the other boy, Joe Cardenas, on the stand.

"Anger" continued to be Windham's mantra as he spoke again. "As he told Joe Cardenas this story, his anger grew, and as he told this story, sitting up on the hill above Canyon High, a girl walked by, cutting through, taking a shortcut home from high school. Fifteen-year-old Arlene Logan took a shortcut onto that hill. And as Kenneth Hunt talked to Joe Cardenas about how angry he was, he saw that girl and [he] was like boiling over, like a forgotten pot on the stove, boiling over with anger.

"And he saw Arlene Logan; he said, 'Let's get her.' And the two boys ran down that hill. Kenneth grabbed Arlene Logan, pulled her down and pulled down her top and started grabbing at her breasts. He covered her mouth as she yelled. And then he stopped. Kenneth Hunt stopped and he ran away.

"Kenneth Hunt was apprehended, adjudicated, and sent to the California Youth Authority, where he spent the rest of his childhood. And from that time in 1981 . . . fifteen-year-old Kenneth Hunt was identified as a sex offender and became 'one of the usual suspects.'

"So in 1988, almost seven years later, Kenneth had been out of the Youth Authority for about a year and a half, living with his wife to be, Betty, who is here today."

Eyes in the courtroom turned toward Betty Hunt, sitting perfectly still in the back row of the gallery beside her mother, her face expressionless.

"And sometime during the week before July 4, 1988, Kenneth's neighbor, Myra Davis, was raped and killed. And Kenneth is questioned at that time, but he is not a suspect. He is not accused in this case until years and years later. There is no reason to suspect him. There is no connection except that he is a neighbor and he has one juvenile sex offense.

"In February of 1989, Kenneth Hunt is twenty-three years old, and he grabs a woman who is about the same age, Tina. Tina will come and testify to you about his conduct, grabbing hold of her in a sexual fashion, grabbing her buttocks and scaring her."

Windham employed an interesting strategy by discussing in a little more detail the sexual-battery cases in which the victims had identified Hunt as the perpetrator. The prosecution had, according to discovery rules, notified him of their intent to call each of the women as witnesses. By revealing the stories to the jury in advance, he hoped to soften the impact when they would hear it directly from the mouths of the victims.

"In May of 1989, there is another woman, named Mary, and he reaches between her legs from the rear and grabs her.

"In 1990, a woman named Susan says that Kenneth Hunt . . . had a knife, but he reached under her skirt and grabbed her. She is about the same age.

"In 1990, a woman named Elsa says that Kenneth

grabbed her and pushed her to the ground and made lewd comments to her.

"In 1991, a woman named Bonnie is walking on Beverly Drive. Kenneth makes a rude comment to her, grabbed her breast. I believe he grabbed her breast over her shirt.

"In 1992, a woman named Lana sees Kenneth approach her, makes comments about her breasts. He touches her vagina.

"Eventually, he is arrested for these offenses and goes to jail for misdemeanor sexual batteries. So he has a number of different charges involving sex on his record, all girls about the same age, not elderly."

Those in the gallery who knew Hunt's background knew what was coming next, and wondered just how Windham would handle the story of Bernard Davis.

"About the same time as that last incident, he is walking his dog down the street, gets into a quarrel with a man and woman. They don't like the way he is treating his dog. They confront him. There is an argument. He hits the man, Bernard Davis, an older man." It was interesting that both attorneys had sometimes referred to Myra Davis, seventy-one, and Jean Orloff, sixty, as "elderly." Yet Bernard Davis, who was approaching seventy, was "an older man."

"Kenneth hits him one time, knocked Mr. Davis down. He falls, he hits his head, and he dies. As a result of that, Kenneth is apprehended, put in prison with a six-year sentence for manslaughter, not a murder, but manslaughter. So he has a record.

"He is out of prison in 1998 and acquainted with Jean Orloff when her body is discovered, she is found killed. And the police make telephone calls to the numbers they found on cards in her purse. They want to know everybody connected with her. They talk to her manicurist, who is Kenneth's mother-in-law, and she becomes upset about this, that her friend Jean had been killed. She tells her son, Kenneth's brother-in-law, a guy named George Green, who is on parole. Green decides he is suspicious of Kenneth because he knows Kenneth has a record, and because Myra Davis lived next door and because Jean Orloff was an acquaintance. So he tells the parole officer, Mr. Widener.

"Widener gets in touch with the detectives in this case, including Detective Mounger seated here at the people's counsel table. So what do they do? They don't really have probable cause to believe that he did it, because there is really no evidence connecting him. There is only suspicion.

"But he is on parole. So they decide . . . the police officers and detectives get with the parole officer and they decide they are going to do a parole search. They go into the house where Kenneth lives with his wife, Betty, and Dora, his mother-in-law. They arrest him. They get a warrant for his blood. And they take a blood sample from him pursuant to the warrant. And then the LAPD decides to do some DNA testing."

Backtracking to emphasize something he wanted the jury to clearly understand, Windham said, "I took the time to lead up to this point because you are going to hear testimony from these young women, each of whom feels offended, who was touched, who was violated, and there is a reason for you to hear that, because it's useful to you possibly to determine whether or not Kenneth Hunt had some sort of a character [defect] for sexual misconduct.

"But as the judge will instruct you, you are going

to have to be very careful and cautious when you evaluate his sexual conduct toward women his own age when you are judging whether or not he committed murders or sexual offenses against elderly people.

"So it's proper for you to hear it, but keep in mind it's not proof of the crimes he's charged with, and that alone doesn't prove guilt. You will not hear any evidence that anybody saw the crimes. You will not hear any evidence that Kenneth Hunt was observed entering or leaving any of those places. You will hear evidence that there was property stolen, but you will not hear any evidence that he has stolen any property.

"What you will hear is DNA evidence. The police suspected Kenneth Hunt and arrested him because of his record. But the DNA evidence is really the only evidence of guilt that you will hear, the only evidence about something physical that shows guilt. And when you look at the DNA evidence in this case, you will see there are more questions than answers.

"I think it's important that when the Cellmark representative comes in here to talk with you about their tests and how good they think their tests are, I think it's important for you to know in advance what it is that they are talking about." DNA evidence, said Windham, can be difficult to understand and misleading. "You might be nodding your head, you know, the understanding evaporates sometimes." He expressed hope that the jurors would not only see the "wonderful promise" of it, but would also recognize the important "limitations of DNA evidence."

Not only is DNA used in "attempts to show that a person committed a crime," Windham pointed out, but it is conversely an important tool to "exonerate innocent people. You know that every person has unique

DNA, except identical twins . . . but we all share some DNA. That is what makes us human. That is why we look alike, because we have a lot of the same DNA, each of us. But we also have differences in our DNA. Every one of us is unique, except for identical twins." Even they, he explained, can be different due to environmental or cultural influences. "But their DNA is the same.

"So we have in every one of our cells the same DNA that makes us unique, our hair color and eye color, and everything about us that is unique. There is the same DNA in every one of our cells. These cells are sometimes left behind at crime scenes, whether it's semen, or blood, or traces of skin, or the material on the follicle of a hair. All of that can be tested for DNA."

Observers wondered if Windham was really trying to help jurors understand the nature of DNA or to deliberately inure them to it. Was he engaging in repetitious use of the term to make them weary of it so early?

"So what are they accomplishing when they say they are doing a DNA test? They are comparing DNA from the crime scene to DNA from the suspect. In every cell, we have a lot of DNA. What is DNA? DNA is just chemical bases. You might have heard of a double helix, where chemicals [exist] that are labeled A, T, G, and C. It's adenine, thymine, guanine, and cytosine.

"And they always pair up in a special way. The A is always with A T; the G is always with A C. So these chemicals go together in a strand and they're in every cell.

"And how much DNA is there? Well, there are

Victim Myra Davis, 71. *(Photo courtesy Sherry Davis)*

Photos of Davis
(who used the stage name
Myra Jones), taken by
John E. Reed, Hollywood.
(Photo courtesy Sherry Davis)

Victim Jean Orloff, 60. *(Photo courtesy Lois Bachrach)*

Orloff with close friend Barbara Kappedal *(right)*,
who found her body. *(Photo courtesy Debby McAllister)*

Orloff with grandson
Andy McAllister.
*(Photo courtesy
Lois Bachrach)*

Myra Davis was found by her granddaughter in 1988.
(Photo courtesy L.A. Superior Court Records)

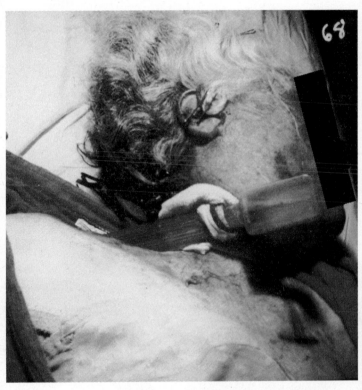

Panties and a pot scrubber handle were used to strangle Davis.
(Photo courtesy L.A. Superior Court Records)

Davis's chest of drawers had been rifled through.
(Photo courtesy L.A. Superior Court Records)

Davis's home on Beverly Drive.
(Photo courtesy L.A. Superior Court Records)

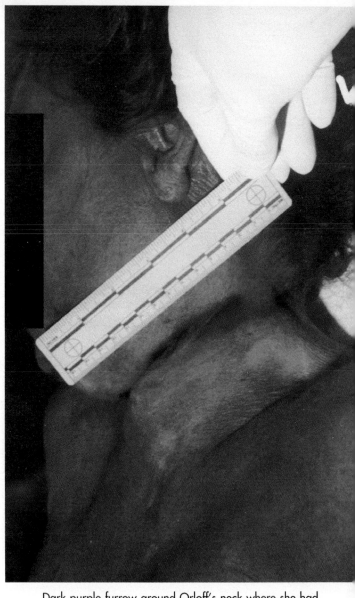

Dark purple furrow around Orloff's neck where she had
been strangled. *(Photo courtesy L.A. Superior Court Records)*

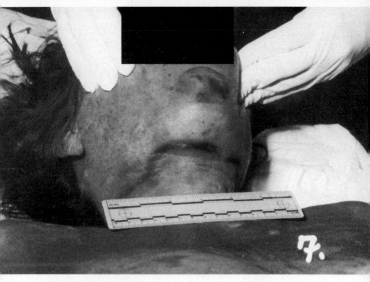

Abrasions on Orloff's face indicated she had struggled
with her killer. *(Photo courtesy L.A. Superior Court Records)*

Orloff was murdered in her apartment in West Los Angeles.

Kenneth Dean Hunt at age 25 with dog Ginger.
(Photo courtesy L.A. Superior Court Records)

Hunt was sentenced to six years for manslaughter in the death of
Bernard Davis, 67. *(Photo courtesy L.A. Superior Court Records)*

Hunt, 33, was charged with the deaths of Davis and Orloff.
(Photo courtesy L.A. Superior Court Records)

Hunt's attorneys assembled a room full of records
while preparing his defense.

Sherry Davis,
granddaughter
of Myra Davis.
(Photo courtesy Sherry Davis)

Orloff's mother
Elizabeth and stepfather
Myron Davis.
(Photo courtesy Lois Bachrach)

Lois Bachrach,
Orloff's sister.
*(Photo courtesy
Lois Bachrach)*

Debby McAllister,
daughter of Jean
Orloff. *(Photo courtesy
Lois Bachrach)*

Detectives Ron Phillips
and Francene Mounger.

Prosecutor
John Gilligan.

Prosecutor Laura Jane Kessner.

Public Defender Mark Windham.

three billion of these pairs. Three billion in every cell. DNA scientists compare the crime scene to the suspect. But when they do this, they don't compare the whole thing. That is three billion pairs. They can't do it; it's too big."

Using a felt-tip pen, Windham made marks on a graphic chart to illustrate his point. "So they are only testing one small bit.

"Where do we get our DNA? Where does it come from? It comes from our moms and dads. Mom has got two types and Dad has got two types. And just by the luck of the draw, randomly, you get one from Mom and one from Dad and this is you. At every gene, you have two types. So if there are ten kinds of genes, you might be type one and type five, type three and type nine, type ten and type ten. You might have gotten the same thing from both Mom and Dad.

"Why is this important? Because at those DNA tests, they are only looking at genes. The scientists called it 'loci,' or locations. They only look at, say, ten or twenty locations. And at those ten or twenty locations, there are two results. So you might be a one, two; one, three; one, four type. Let's say that's what you are. And let's say they compare you to a sample to see if you match. Let's say a one, two. Let's say the sample is one, three; one, five. This is different from you. So you are excluded. These two people are different. That sample doesn't come from you.

"Well, they keep on testing those locations. If at any place, somebody is excluded, that person isn't the contributor. So when you hear about old cases where a person has been found guilty and they do tests, find there is no match, the person is set free.

"So what are we doing here? We are talking about

certain test results. Mr. Gilligan pointed out that in testing the sample from Myra Davis, that the rarity for Caucasians is one in 2.4 million." Of course, Windham agreed, Caucasian applies to Kenneth Davis. But were the tests fair? "It's kind of interesting. You know, these DNA tests don't tell you what race the person is that contributed the sample. You could do a DNA test for race; you can find the components that give us our racial composition, but they don't do that in these crime-scene tests. There is a reason they don't do it. They are looking for junk DNA. They are looking to test things that don't really have any effect on natural selection. And I will explain more about what the witness will tell you about this."

Realizing that the material was growing increasingly complex and beginning to sound like gibberish, Windham apologized. "Forgive me, this is so dense, I know. We will have a lunch break soon, and afterward I'll try to make it a lot more clear."

Probing the complications of breaking down DNA testing by categories of race, Windham moved on to technology problems. "I'm going to talk to you about what can go wrong with DNA testing, and why we think something went wrong in this case. I will show you that these numbers are not reliable. I will show you that there are problems with DNA evidence and the importance of how it is collected, how it is shipped, and that human beings at all times are looking at this. Human beings are the analysts looking at the tests, and they can make mistakes.

"You will hear about brand-new, groundbreaking technology that was used, not in the Davis samples, but in the Orloff case. And I mean this is really new. This is one of the first cases where it's been used.

And I am going to show you there are some things about this new test that raise questions about whether Kenneth Hunt is the guy who contributed this sample.

"You will hear in this trial he was a suspect because he did grab so many different women his own age. You are going to hear they suspect him because he lived next door to one of the victims and he was acquainted with the other victim. But what this trial really is going to be about is this DNA evidence, what the expert is going to tell you, and what the limitations are in DNA evidence."

Everyone in the courtroom needed a break, and the lunch period gave the welcome respite. Judge Connor cautioned the jurors not to discuss the case and to have a light lunch so they wouldn't be drowsy in the afternoon session.

At 1:30 P.M., Windham stood at the lectern again and greeted the jurors. "I hope you had a light lunch and I hope not to be too boring with this material, but I want you to know that DNA evidence is really the heart of the case. It's really the whole of the case the prosecution is presenting and will leave more questions than answers when you fully understand the testing."

Once again, he valiantly launched an attempt to clarify one of the most complex of sciences. He spoke of polymorphism, DNA fragments being tested by their lengths, and the double helix as a "twisted ladder" loaded with chemicals. Types of DNA testing, he explained, consist of RFLP, restriction fragment length polymorphism, and electrophoresis. He worked to make jurors understand variations and types of "locus which are genes." He mentioned alleles, pronouncing it "all-eels," defined as different types or variations of

locus, or loci. Taking the jurors through lab procedures, he spoke of applying electrical charges and the
speed with which DNA fragments move through gel.
Observers felt certain that if the jurors were given written examinations after Windham's lecture, all of them
would have failed it miserably. And so would the observers. Certainly, Windham possessed a remarkable
knowledge of the science and explained it in terms as
simple as possible. It just wasn't something that could
be simplified, or taught to laypeople in a few hours.
The lawyers on both sides had studied it for months.

The question was raised in some minds about the
necessity for trying to educate jurors in such great detail about an extraordinarily complex science. Couldn't
they simply hear experts testify to its reliability? Juries
are made up of average citizens who don't particularly
want to know every detail of how things work. They
trust airplanes to deliver them to destinations without
knowing how the jet engines or on-board computers
work. They trust automobiles to carry them hurtling
along on high-speed freeways without knowing how the
engine or transmission works. They trust their television sets to deliver entertainment without knowing the
internal mechanics of them. Couldn't they trust experts' testimony about the reliability of DNA without
knowing every detail of how it works? Both sides could
present examples and statistics to support or deny the
forensic use of DNA without delving into the incom-
prehensible scientific details. Do jurors really need to
know all about alleles, loci, electrophoresis, or polymorphism? Couldn't it be simplified so that ordinary people who happened to be selected to sit on a jury could
clearly understand the evidence?

Probably not.

Both John Gilligan and Mark Windham understood the problems in dealing with DNA presentation and would do their best to make it palatable.

Moving into criticism of the statistical analysis, Windham said, "When the prosecutor asks the expert how we get these numbers, she will say, 'Well, we multiplied locus one times locus two, times locus three, and this was a thirteen locus match, and this number, quintillion. . . . I know everybody knows what a zillion is, right? What is a quintillion? Let's begin with a million; then it's a billion, a trillion, quadrillion, quintillion. It's more people than there are on earth."

A big jump in technology, said Windham, was the advance to PCR, polymerase chain reaction. "Polymerase is an enzyme. Chain reaction is like, you know, atomic bombs or something. Chain reaction means it gets bigger and bigger. So a tiny, minuscule bit of DNA can be amplified. And I think the expert will admit this is where errors can occur." Windham spent the next ten minutes explaining the technological complexities of how errors might develop, and hammered home that such errors would make the test results unreliable.

"The next kind of test that scientists invented," said Windham, was a method involving STR, short tandem repeats, allowing huge amplification of tiny DNA samples for more detailed testing. "And the technology keeps evolving. In 1999, Cellmark decided to do some more testing using laser flourescent capillary electrophoresis" using the "robotic arm of a machine" and a laser that "fluoresces dye in the sample." Eventually, he said, the results end up in a computer that turns them into measurable numbers. "It's very, very complicated and very sophisticated, very new. . . . They get to these numbers that are bigger than the population of the earth."

Dragging red-eyed jurors through several more rigorous technical explanations, Windham reached the critical point he wanted to make. The important question, he said, revolves around the numbers that claim to match Hunt's DNA from blood samples to the DNA of semen samples taken from the victims. "Is that number right? Is it a match? That's what you need to determine. That's what this case is about. What we will show in this trial is reasons to *disbelieve* the results."

One of the reasons to reject the numbers, Windham said, is possible contamination of the samples. "You cannot sneeze over a sample. You can't contaminate it. If somehow, Mr. Hunt's blood sample comes into contact with the crime-scene sample, there's a chance it could be contaminated."

The second problem, he said, is the possibility of foreign matter getting into the sample. An "artifact" can spoil results, much like a speck of dust on a camera lens can spoil the photo.

Another issue, he said, is the possibility of errors made by the personnel who conduct the tests at the laboratories. Controls must be in place to detect potential for such errors and prevent them. "For a while, Cellmark had proficiency testing. They had people come into the lab, give them samples, and ask the technicians to type them. They did it for several years, but they don't do it anymore."

To be fair, the defender cited Cellmark's low-error rate. "Out of eight hundred thirty-three times they undertook these tests, there were two mistakes." But, he said, those took place when they knew they were being audited. "The results demonstrate a distinct possibility of human error."

Windham expressed doubt about the quantity of sperm on one of the samples. "You will hear, in the Davis case, that in 1988 a lab technician looked at the swab taken from the victim, sample number fifty-one . . . I do not believe she saw sperm on it. No DNA testing was done at that time."

Now, ten years later, he complained how "Mr. Hunt is apprehended. A fellow over at LAPD named Nick Sanchez said that he found sperm. After they have a suspect, he says he found an adequate amount of sperm. They send it to Cellmark. Cellmark undertakes a test in the Davis case. The test fails to produce any result. . . . Several weeks go by, and then Cellmark decides to try again." But the sample has been lost. "They say this has never happened before at Cellmark. But sample number fifty-one is lost. So they contact LAPD." The remaining portion retained in storage is sent to replace the lost sample. "Then Cellmark claims they matched the sample to a genotype in Mr. Hunt's blood sample."

The test in the Orloff case, said Windham, was also flawed by "artifacts. They don't get a clean result. They find some artifacts. That's why it's a problem. So they decide to do this brand-new test. Their report shows how, when there are results that they think are artifacts, they erase them. They edit them. They take them out of the report."

Finally, challenging the astronomical numbers cited, that the characteristics in Kenneth Hunt's DNA sample match only one in 1.7 quintillion, Windham questioned calculation techniques used by Cellmark.

Summarizing his case, the defender said, "So when

you are looking at this evidence, you will know it's about a person who is under a great deal of suspicion because so many people feel harmed by him. I mean there are [women] his own age he grabbed and fondled, and that's why he is under suspicion. But when you look at the DNA, you will see that's the only test, really the only evidence that is presented against Mr. Hunt. When you look at that, think of the care with which the evidence was handled, whether anything was lost, whether any mistakes were made. You will look at some ambiguities and ask if it was done enough times to give assurance that it's right. You will look at statistics to see whether they are valid. You will look at whether or not there's a problem of contamination." These subjects, he promised, would be the focal point in his questioning of the expert witness from Cellmark.

"That's what the evidence will be in this case. I apologize for not having state-of-the art visual aids for you. I appreciate your patience in listening to what I had to say before you hear it again when the witnesses hit the stand. Thank you."

Seventeen

When John Gilligan and Mark Windham completed their opening statements, Judge Connor signaled the prosecution team to bring in their first witness.

While waiting, reporters and observers familiar with the case weighed the possibilities. Was there enough evidence to convict Hunt of two capital murders? Would the jury accept DNA evidence? Next door, in the most widely publicized trial of the 1990s, jurors had completely rejected the complex, highly technical "genetic fingerprinting." How would Mark Windham attack DNA? Just what else would John Gilligan present to support the murder charges against Hunt?

It is felt by many crime watchers that if a defendant is truly not guilty, no one could keep him out of the witness chair. He would insist on shouting his innocence to the jury. If guilty, though, maybe the defendant would rather not take a chance on answering questions. Defense attorneys don't see it this way, generally advising clients accused of murder to avoid testifying. Too many things can go wrong. The question remained: would Kenneth Hunt take the stand or remain silent?

Some observers attend trials hoping to hear and

see sensational or titillating events. Certainly, that possibility existed in the Hunt case considering the long list of sexual-battery cases he had been accused of committing.

Other people in the gallery had far more at stake. Lois Bachrach would be there every day out of respect for her sister and to see it through to its conclusion. Sherry Davis appeared between movie and television assignments. Dora Green and her daughter Betty Hunt would also attend regularly, sitting in the back row. Green, experiencing lingering health problems, sat in a wheelchair.

Relatives of the victims dreaded one particular aspect of the trial, the showing of gruesome photographs picturing both women, naked on the autopsy table, and close-up shots of their dead bodies. It's always a sensitive matter to present such photos. But most prosecutors realize the importance of hitting the jurors early and hard with emotional impact. Defense attorneys usually file motions to disallow such evidence, often suggesting the terrible and inflammatory effect it might have on unsuspecting jurors. Gilligan had answered Windham's motion with a powerful and frankly stated argument. He wrote: "Crime scene and autopsy photographs of murder victims are admissible to illustrate testimony of witnesses and enhance the jury's understanding of the prosecution's case." He pointed out that higher courts, in answer to appeals, have consistently upheld the use of such evidence. Citing a typical case, he noted, "We have two observations. . . . First, we subscribe to [the judge's] wise perception; (1) murder is seldom pretty, and pictures, testimony, and physical evidence in such a case are always unpleasant; and (2) many attorneys tend to underestimate the stability of the jury. A juror is not some kind of a dithering nincompoop, brought in from never-never land and exposed to the harsh realities of life for the first time in the jury box. There is nothing magic about being a member of the bench or bar which makes these individuals capable of dispassionately evaluating gruesome testimony which, it is often contended, will throw jurors into a paroxysm of hysteria. Jurors are peers, often well educated, as well balanced, as stable, as experienced in the realities of life as the holders of law degrees. The average juror is well able to stomach the unpleasantness of exposure to the facts of a murder without being unduly influenced. The supposed influence on jurors of allegedly gruesome or inflammatory pictures exists more in the imagination of judges and lawyers than in reality. Second, a defendant has no right to transform the facts of a gruesome real-life murder into an anesthetized exercise where only the defendant, not the victim, appears human. Jurors are not, and should not be, computers for whom a victim is just an 'element' to be proved, a 'component' of a crime. A cardboard victim plus a flesh-and-blood defendant are likely to equal an unjust verdict."

Judge Connor ruled the autopsy photographs would be allowed into evidence.

Gilligan chose to open the parade of witnesses by reaching back to 1981 when Kenneth Hunt, at age fifteen, and his pal Joe Cardenas had been accused of burglarizing a house and attempting to rape fifteen-year-old Arlene Logan. Bill Wood, who had been an L.A. County sheriff's deputy in Canyon Country at the time, took the stand to answer questions about that episode. Wood gave a summary of the events in brief terms, using copspeak much as Jack Webb had done in the old *Dragnet* television show when he played Sergeant Joe Friday.

The victim, Arlene Logan, came next. Now a thirty-five-year-old bespectacled woman, standing five-seven, she still seemed young with long blond hair and a pretty face. To Gilligan's questions, she told of leaving Canyon Country High School on September 28, 1981, after tennis practice. "I took a shortcut up the hill. About a quarter of the way home, I noticed two boys on the trail behind me." Suddenly, Logan said, one of them grabbed her. "The first thing I knew, I was thrown to the ground by the light-skinned boy with light hair. He's the one who did it. I was screaming and it seemed like a thousand hands on me. On my chest, groping and grabbing at me. He had one hand over my mouth, and I kept turning my head trying to get loose. I tried to hit him with my tennis racquet, but he took it away from me and threw it down the hill. He grabbed me around the waist. And he touched me all over, including my backside." Blushing and obviously embarrassed, Logan told how the assailant had pulled her blouse open and stroked her breasts before rushing away. Kenneth Hunt had been identified as the boy who physically attacked her.

Windham's cross-examination seemed perfunctory, establishing only that there had been two boys at the scene, not just one. Logan stepped down after only fifteen minutes.

If anyone in the gallery was there to hear the stories of young women who had been sexually groped, they were not disappointed on that first day. In addition to Arlene Logan, four other victims stepped up to tell how they had been victims of battery on the streets near Cheviot Hills.

As a general rule, episodes of previous criminal conduct not directly related to the crimes for which the defendant is being tried are not allowed in evidence for the guilt phase. But a penal code, PC1108, provides certain exceptions. In pretrial hearings, the prosecution requested permission for the victims of sexual battery who had identified Hunt as the assailant to testify regarding those attacks. The purpose was to prove he possessed a character trait for sexual misconduct to show that he could have raped the two murder victims. Over defense objections, the judge ruled the women would be allowed to testify.

Mary Lotolo took the stand after Arlene Logan. Questioned by Laura Jane Kessner, Lotolo spoke in whispers due to a sore throat. Short and stocky, with red hair and brown eyes, she kept her eyes focused on Kessner's face. In May 1989, she said, she had been walking on Roxbury, west of Pico, when she was accosted. She had caught a glimpse of a parked tow truck. A few moments later, she had heard footsteps, moved aside, then felt two hands on her, one touching her back and another groping between her legs. "He touched me through my clothing. I screamed. He ran away." Lotolo later identified Kenneth Hunt as the perpetrator. Kessner asked her if the man who touched her was now in the courtroom. The witness said yes and pointed to Hunt, who stared stonily back at her.

Mark Windham's strategy began taking form when he asked exactly what the attacker did. Lotolo said, "He touched my vagina through my underwear and grabbed at me." Windham wanted to know if it was broad daylight where anyone could see what happened. Lotolo said it took place about three-thirty in the afternoon on a public street. She seemed relieved when the questioning ended, and virtually fled the courtroom.

Observers recognized the defense attorney wanted to make it clear that these were not well-planned sex acts, but impulsive, spur-of-the-moment incidents. Could such behavior be carried out by anyone who possessed any shred of self-control?

Tina Joye was next in line. She said she had been taking care of two small children, walking with them on Castle Heights Avenue. "I felt a hand between my legs. I turned and yelled, 'Stupid!' He got very angry like he was going to hit me. I was very scared. He raised his fist and was a very nasty man. He kept yelling obscenities at me and walked away." She pointed to Kenneth Hunt at the defense table, and said he was the man who had attacked her.

"Was he laughing?" asked Windham.

"No."

"Did he appear to be happy?"

"No. He seemed very angry."

Joye's testimony took seven minutes.

Elsa Beebe, tall, with short red hair, bore some facial resemblance to movie personality Drew Barrymore, enhanced by full, bow-shaped lips and large eyes. Nervous, she told of her experience on November 1, 1990, when she was eighteen. Like the previous witness, Beebe had been walking on Castle Heights Avenue, which paralleled Beverly Drive, the street where Kenneth Hunt lived. Said Beebe, "I was coming home from school and was attacked. He grabbed me

from behind and forced me to the ground on my
knees. I fought to get up. But he grabbed me by my
neck with one hand, and my ass with [the] other
hand. He was so rude. He asked for sex and said if I
wouldn't give it up, could he buy it? I elbowed him
and said, 'How dare you touch me that way.' " When
Beebe finally freed herself from the assailant's grasp
and ran, he yelled, "Don't bother to run away. I know
where you live."

Afterward, Beebe said, a stream of lewd telephone
calls had disrupted her life. The caller made obscene
comments and said he was masturbating. He threatened to kill her cat. She later found the pet locked in
a closet and realized someone had been in her home.
Frightened, she locked herself in the bathroom at night
and slept on the floor. The terror made it impossible
to stay in the vicinity, so she moved to San Francisco to
escape it. In the following years, she required intensive
counseling. She had finally put her life back together
and now worked as a commercial artist. As her prede-
cessors in the witness chair had done, Beebe pointed
at Kenneth Hunt and said he was the man who had
assaulted her.

On cross, Windham established that the incident
had happened in broad daylight, between noon and
one o'clock. Also, he made the point that the assailant
had touched her buttocks, but not grabbed her
breasts or vagina.

One more victim of sexual battery came forward.
Lana Martin, now forty, had gained a few pounds in
the nine years since she had been attacked. She wore
a blue suit, white blouse, and red beret. In mid-March
1992, as she returned home from work, walking near
a bus stop, she had rounded a corner. "I heard some-

one comment about my breasts. The man came at me
and touched my vagina. I screamed. He jumped into
a car. I started running and twisted my ankle. He
drove the car up on the sidewalk and it was coming
in my direction. I thought he was going to run over
me. But he swerved off and drove away. Someone
came out of an apartment and helped me." She had
identified Kenneth Hunt from a six-pack of photographs. But she couldn't identify him in court.

Windham asked if the assailant had said anything.
No, the witness replied. Did he touch you through
your clothing? Yes, he had. Martin stepped down after
ten minutes of testimony.

Sherry Davis had waited patiently to testify about
finding her grandmother's body. Usually, witnesses are
asked to remain in the hallway until they are called.
But, with the agreement of both attorneys, Davis had
been allowed to sit in the gallery. Wearing a stylish,
conservative blue skirt and white blouse, she swore to
tell the whole truth and nothing but the truth.

John Gilligan questioned her, eliciting her recital
of events leading to the discovery of Myra Davis lying
in her bedroom. Francene Mounger, sitting at the
prosecution table, listened in awe of Davis's speaking
skills and the heartbreaking testimony about Myra.
Mounger would later say, "It was quite dramatic when
Sherry testified. It left a vivid impression when she
told of finding her grandmother dead."

At four-thirty, Judge Connor advised the jury not to
discuss the case with anyone and to refrain from reading newspapers about it or watching television cover-
age, then excused them until nine the next morning.

Eighteen

Murder trials might be compared to a movie set where it takes eight hours of technical work to film two minutes of drama and action.

To impatient observers, and often to the jurors involved, trials seem to be fraught with needless delays, wasted time, and inefficiency. To a certain extent, this is true. But the legal process cannot be executed with corporate efficiency. In business or other government structures, an absentee's duties can usually be carried out by a substitute. It's a different matter if the judge, one of the attorneys, or a juror is late. The whole proceeding must be delayed. Or, if the defendant is delayed in transit or ill, everyone else must wait. Especially puzzling to jurors are the long hours marking time in their room, or in hallways, without explanation. Usually, delays are unavoidable. For the most part, Judge Jacqueline Connor kept the trial of Kenneth Hunt moving expeditiously, managing to complete the guilt phase in only eight working days.

On the morning of Thursday, March 1, former detective Gary Fullerton took the witness stand. Observers were anxious to hear if he would be able to cast any light on reasons that it took ten years to solve the murder of Myra Davis, which he had investigated in 1988. Wearing a black suit, goatee, and mustache, the red complected, portly, retired detective answered Gilligan's questions in short bursts.

From the prosecutor's table, Gilligan lifted a brown paper bag. Slipping on a pair of thin latex gloves, he carefully opened the container and pulled out four items. Several faces in the audience appeared to wince when they saw the tan underpants and the pot-scrubber handle, which had been combined to make a ligature, the device used to savagely choke the life from Myra Davis. Her eyeglasses and the attached neck strap were still tangled in the twisted lethal weapon. Fullerton confirmed he had seen the items wrapped around the throat of Davis. Gilligan turned, stepped four paces to a ledge at the front of the jury box, and displayed them for each member of the panel.

Fullerton gave a perfunctory description of the crime scene, but was spared facing any embarrassing questions. There really wasn't much he could say. He had suspected the wrong person, focusing instead on Myra Davis's grandson Corey and his buddy. Sherry Davis felt that if Fullerton had listened more carefully to her, the crime might have been solved years earlier, and perhaps Jean Orloff's life would have been saved. But no mention of that could be aired in the trial.

Another sexual-battery victim replaced Fullerton in the chair. Susan Deane told how she had been chanting prayers on her way to a temple when she felt someone thrusting a hand between her legs from behind. "I turned around," she said, "and the man had a knife in his right hand. He held it at hip level. He was unshaven and his hair was unkempt as if he had just woken up. His clothes were wrinkled and his eyes were wild."

Gilligan asked if she had noticed anything else. Deane hesitated, then said the assailant's zipper was open and "his penis was outside his pants." The man spoke, she said, saying "vicious and nasty things." She had fled, but saw him again the next day driving past her, screaming crude comments. Yet a third time, a few days later, he passed her and yelled "vulgar insults and threats."

Kenneth Hunt, motionless, leveled a frigid, steely-eyed stare at the witness while she identified him as the man who had made her life miserable in October 1990.

The last person to see Jean Orloff alive, a trim middle-aged woman, entered the courtroom and settled in to answer questions. John Gilligan asked Doris Boesky, "In 1998 and before that, were you a friend of a woman named Jean Orloff?"

"Yes, I was."

"And prior to 1998, how long had you known her?"

"Approximately fifteen years."

"And were you familiar with Ms. Orloff's residence?"

"Yes. I lived right in the next building to hers and we went back and forth quite a bit to each other's apartment."

On a tripod, Gilligan placed a set of aerial photographs, depicting the apartment buildings on Bentley Avenue. Boesky pointed to the ones she had mentioned.

"Now," he said, "I want to bring your attention to March 26, 1998. Did you have some contact with Jean Orloff that day?"

"Yes, I did." Boesky said she had contacted Orloff. "I called her on the telephone. . . . I needed a favor. I had a flat tire and I needed to get a letter mailed. It was a Saturday." She thought the last pickup from a drop box outside the post office would be at four o'clock and it was already past three-thirty.

"Did Ms. Orloff agree to give you a ride?"

"Yes, she did . . . to the post office on Veteran Avenue, about five minutes away."

"So you dropped off the letter?"

"Yes. We didn't have to park. We just dropped it in the slot."

"Where did you go afterward?"

"Immediately back. We went back to her apartment, parked the car, walked to the sidewalk, and just visited. My building is right next door."

"For how long?"

"Approximately fifteen or twenty minutes."

"How was Jean dressed at that time?"

"She was wearing her sweats and she didn't have any makeup on. And I had told her on the phone, I said, 'You don't have to get out of the car, just drop it in the slot, so just come the way you are.' And that was the way she was dressed."

"If you were going out with Jean to a movie or a restaurant, something where you were going to be out in public, would that be a normal way in which she would be dressed, no makeup, wearing sweats?"

"No. She was pretty much of a perfectionist with her makeup and she liked to dress modern."

"So she took care with her personal appearance?"

"Very much so." Boesky agreed that it would be most unusual for Orloff to go out without makeup or fixing her hair.

"When you were standing outside the apartment chatting on Saturday afternoon, when you returned, did she indicate anything to you about any plans for that evening?"

"No, she did not."

"What time was it approximately that you went your separate ways?"

"I would estimate between four-fifteen and four-thirty."

"Did you ever see your friend Jean Orloff again?"

"No, I did not."

Mark Windham had no questions for the witness. After Boesky was excused, Judge Connor announced the lunch break.

Full, dark, wavy hair beginning to gray gave Dr. Louis Pena a distinguished appearance. With his strong voice and articulate clarity in speaking, he might have been a successful actor. He had been a forensic pathologist in the position of deputy medical examiner with the L.A. County Coroner's Office for five years, having practiced previously elsewhere.

Gilligan had arranged for Dr. Pena to review records containing details of the Myra Davis autopsy, performed in 1988 by a Dr. Swalwell. This would enable Pena to testify about the procedures related to both victims. On an easel, Gilligan placed close-up photos of both victims, along with two diagrams of bodies, and asked Pena to point out the "exterior" injuries on the body of Myra Davis.

The witness, using his pen for a pointer, brought attention to Davis's neck. "There is what we call a furrow mark, or indentation that is circumferential, meaning it goes all the way around the neck, completely in Ms. Davis's case. It's a dark brown abrasion. You can see the pattern. . . . When I use the term 'abrasion,' that simply means whatever object, whether rope, scarf, belt—you can think of most anything—that rubs the skin and peels off the superficial layers of our skin, that's an abrasion by definition."

"Is this something that is typically seen in a situation where a victim has been strangled with a ligature?"

"Yes."

"Could you explain to the jury what difference is between a manual strangulation and strangulation with a ligature?"

After informing the jury that manual strangulation means using the hands to choke a victim and ligature means using a device such as a cord or twisted cloth, Pena said, "In the use of a ligature, there is usually a sharp imprint pattern left around the neck. It's quite distinct. Nothing else looks like it. And that is known as a furrow. Manual strangulation entails a little more complication in the examination. Basically, with manual strangulation, you won't see imprints of hands on the victim. What you do see, though, are self-inflicted scratches. They are the result of the victim trying to get the perpetrator's hands off, trying to pry the hands away from the neck. In that process, the victim scratches their own neck, so they have a lot of curving lines and scratches under the chin, or abrasions. Sometimes, though, you won't see anything with manual strangulation."

It was also true that sometimes signs of ligature strangulation are difficult to see within the first few hours of death. That became evident in the Jean Orloff case.

Making certain the jury understood precisely what

had happened to Myra Davis, Gilligan asked a series of questions, which culminated in a revealing comment by Pena. "I've seen a lot of strangulation cases, and this is one of the few I've seen that the furrow goes completely around the neck. It's consistent with the perpetrator facing the victim while the ligature goes around."

Pointing to the photo of Davis taken shortly after she was found, Dr. Pena said, "You'll see the abrasion almost crosses itself at one point under the chin. The width of the injury tells me that perhaps another object, perhaps a stick of some sort, was used, perhaps with cloth or rope, a belt or whatever, and tightened to eventually close off her airway and blood supply, and cause her death."

According to Pena, considerably more force than necessary to result in death was exerted on Myra Davis.

Gilligan asked, "How would you know that this would be at the hands of another as opposed to, let's say, someone hanging themself?"

Pena, clearly an expert, warmed to the subject. "Well, the big clue here is that the ligatures are very distinct and they are horizontal both in the front and back. That's classic for another person involved in the strangulation. People that hang themselves, the noose or rope goes upward, and the person will squat down, or they'll hang from a rafter or beam. But the noose is going upward, not horizontal."

"What is petechia?"

"Petechia are little blood vessels in the white of the eye and the eyelids. When the blood flow is impeded trying to get back to the heart, from pressure to the carotid arteries at the sides of the neck and the jugular vein, the petechia engorge with blood. Much like a balloon filling up. The vessels are superficial, little veins. They begin to burst because the blood cannot make it back to the heart. Ms. Davis showed classic [petechial hemorrhaging] mainly on the left side. The vessels are also in the gums, and that was seen in her as well."

Next Gilligan inquired about the actual process of performing an autopsy and the internal injuries seen during the autopsy of Myra Davis by Dr. Swalwell.

A "Y-shaped" incision is made in the victim's body, said Pena. "I reflect all the tissue from the chest upward through the neck." In his usage, "Reflect," meant incise with a scalpel. "I also reflect the skin and fatty tissue over the rib cage. The chest is then open. We use a pruner, almost like you prune your trees, to take the chest plate off. The heart is then drained and removed, lungs are removed, and we move down to the abdominal cavity, remove the liver, and the rest of the organs are removed. We drain all the blood. Then the brain is removed. Then we proceed with what is called a neck dissection."

Illustrating with a chart again, Pena said, "Now, if you point with your own finger, you can feel your Adam's apple here. It is a bony structure. In men and women over thirty, it is going to calcify and get hard like a bone. Usually, it is cartilage when we are growing up as kids. Once you get over thirty, thirty-five, it turns brittle and is easier to break." Placing his own hands around his throat, Pena said, "With Ms. Davis, Dr. Swalwell noted, several of the little bones in the Adam's apple were fractured. There was also extensive hemorrhaging in the little muscles, we call them strap muscles, that are over the thyroid, the largest cartilage in the larynx, or over the voice box. So the fractures and the hemorrhaging indicate the excessive force used to compress her neck area. As a result of that, two things will happen."

Several faces in the gallery and the jury appeared to be a little more pale than they were just after lunch. It occurred to some that there was absolutely no dignity left for the poor murder victim. Not only was life taken away prematurely, but the mortal remains were suddenly no more than a specimen for probing, cutting, and examination.

Pena continued, "You cut off the blood supply and no oxygen can get to the brain. Normally, most of us in this courtroom, within ten or fifteen seconds, under that amount of pressure application, are going to pass out. So I can come up to any of you right now and press very hard. In terms of weight, I'll give you an idea. Our literature and books tell us ten, eleven pounds of pressure is all it takes to compress these. That's all it takes. Both sides together, hold it for ten, fifteen seconds, you would pass out. You release it; you come back to life. No problem." Some thought Pena appeared to relish his subject. He certainly made it clear.

"What happens with a ligature," he said, "it's very tight. It does not get released. The victim passes out, but the clock keeps ticking. The victim is unconscious. If they don't get help before between thirty seconds and a minute, they're at a point of no return and they'll die. Because there is no oxygen. The heart will keep beating, but the brain is not functioning. They can still be saved by a paramedic or a doctor up to six minutes later. But beyond that, there is irreversible brain damage."

There had been more damage found in Myra Davis, said Pena. "In strangulation, the tongue is often hemorrhagic, being bitten by the decedent. The reason for that is, when the neck is being compressed, either manually or with a ligature, compression of the voice box occurs, the tongue gets pushed up and outward, almost sticking out of the mouth, and the victim bites down on it."

"Would the victim be able to scream at that point?"

"No." Pena again placed his hands at his throat. "The muscles around the voice box are compressed. You can probably hear my voice changing as I squeeze myself right now. I sound like Mickey Mouse. Imagine pressing even harder. You are going to get no sound at all because the areas that articulate speech are disabled. The tongue is very critical to speech, and it is pushed out, making articulation or screaming impossible."

Gilligan pursued it a little further to leave no misunderstanding among jurors. "What would the symptoms or the experience be for the person who was going through this?"

"Well, they would become flaccid, meaning their muscles would relax. They would not respond to any command. Their eyes would close and they would go completely limp."

Satisfied that the desired impact had been made, Gilligan moved on. He established that blood samples had been taken from the body of Myra Davis. Inquiring about the condition of the body, he asked about rigor mortis and lividity.

Pena pointed out that the autopsy had been performed on July 5, 1988, after the body was discovered on July 3. "Rigor mortis, the stiffness of the body after death, had already passed. It is a chemical reaction and usually starts to form immediately after death.

Usually in the smaller muscles around the face and hands, and then it proceeds ultimately to all muscles. It is just a stiffness. Usually peaks around eighteen hours under a temperate environment and will break at about twenty-four to thirty-six hours later if someone is indoors with an average temperature. They become flaccid again about thirty-six hours after death."

In some murder investigations, the process of rigor mortis setting in, and then relaxing, becomes extremely important. More than one criminal has tripped himself up by not understanding the inevitable changes, lying about "discovering" a body two or three days after death and claiming it was in full rigor mortis. But that didn't apply in the Myra Davis case.

Gilligan asked about discoloration in the body. Pena explained that lividity occurs, meaning when the body lies still, blood pools in the lower portions. Myra Davis was found lying on her back atop the bed, with knees bent and feet on the floor, so her back and buttocks were a deep crimson or purple color as were her feet. That would indicate she died in that position and her body wasn't moved until discovered perhaps a day or two later.

Having thoroughly explored the autopsy of Myra Davis, Gilligan switched to the one of Jean Orloff. Because Pena had completed that autopsy himself, he could speak from firsthand knowledge, not from another pathologist's report. The furrows in her neck, Pena said, were different from those seen on Davis. "This one indicates to me that the perpetrator would be behind Ms. Orloff. The ligature didn't completely encircle her neck."

The abrasions on Orloff's neck created a vivid and horrifying mental image. "Ms. Orloff was trying to get this rope, or whatever was used, off her neck and [was] desperately scratching herself in doing it."

Pena also observed the classic indicator of strangulation, the petechial hemorrhages in her eyes and eyelids. In addition, he found injuries to her nose and lips. Gilligan asked him the significance of those. Pena said, "I have seen this associated commonly with people facedown on a carpet. I don't see any lacerations suggesting that she was struck."

"Would that be consistent with, say, while the ligature is on her, she is being forced, facedown, onto a hard surface and causing friction as she is being pushed into that surface?"

"Yes." She also had injuries to the neck, including fractured bones in the Adam's apple.

Gilligan wanted to clear up one misconception that had nearly shipwrecked the whole case. "In terms of Miss Orloff's heart, did you examine her heart and related vessels during the course of your autopsy?"

"Yes."

"And did you find anything in that area which would have contributed in any way to her death?"

"No." Jean Orloff had not died of a heart ailment as had been assumed in the initial investigation.

"How would you describe the health of her cardiovascular system?"

"For a sixty-year-old woman, she had the heart of a twenty- or thirty-year-old. She was in excellent shape."

Lois Bachrach, sitting in the audience, felt a flood of pride in her sister. The heart of a twenty-year-old. The term would stay with Lois for a long time.

The horror of Myra Davis's last moments were repeated in Pena's examination and description of Orloff's fate. The tongue being bitten, the inability to scream, the onslaught of unconsciousness, and finally death.

As Pena described additional injuries to the back of Orloff's rib cage, Gilligan seized on it to paint another mental picture. "Now, the fact that there was no furrow in the back of Jean Orloff's neck would indicate the person who was utilizing that ligature and strangling the life from her would have been behind her. Is that correct?"

"Yes."

"And the rib fracture in the back area, would that be consistent with someone who was holding the victim facedown and utilizing their knee to stabilize or hold the person in place while strangling her from behind?"

"Yes."

Even more injuries came to light as Pena spoke. Orloff had suffered bruises above her left collarbone, upper right arm, and on both of her legs below the knees. Gilligan asked for possible causes. Pena said, "It could have been blunt-force trauma while she was trying to ward off blows. It could have resulted from her putting up her legs and kicking at her assailant." Bruises on both of her hands, said Pena, might be from defensive reflexes, putting up her hands to protect herself from blows.

"Are you familiar with something called a sex kit that is used as part of the autopsy?"

"Yes. It is done by another technician, a criminalist."

After a few more technical questions, Gilligan turned the witness over to Mark Windham. So far in the trial, the defender had conducted very little cross-examination. But it would be a completely different tactic with Dr. Pena. Windham had an ace in the hole he had been waiting to play.

Using body language and interview techniques that appealed to jurors and spectators, such as tilting the head thoughtfully and apologizing for asking certain questions, Windham won a number of admirers. His words and actions seemed completely sincere and not theatrical.

Beginning slowly with Dr. Pena, the defender established that the witness used extreme care in performing his work. "And you are careful what you say to people about your analysis, aren't you?"

"Correct."

"You talked to detectives who investigated this case soon after you completed your autopsy, right?"

"I probably did, yes."

"And when you speak to detectives on such occasions, you are as careful with them as you are today when you speak to this jury, aren't you?"

"That's correct."

Approaching the topic of injuries to Jean Orloff's face, Windham elicited from Pena that the abrasions to her nose could have been caused by something other than having her face pushed into a carpet or bed surface. The fractured ribs came next. "There is no way, from looking at the fracture, to tell if it was caused by a knee being pushed into her back. While it's possible that during strangulation from behind, that a knee placed into the back could cause that, the injury is consistent with a great number of possible scenarios, right?"

Pena agreed. But he wouldn't concur with Windham's next suggestion, that the various injuries might have been inflicted hours or days apart. Said Pena, "These, in my opinion, all occurred at the same time, looking at the hemorrhages along the neck and in the back. They all have the same colors."

Gently, Windham persisted and elicited agreement from Pena that there is no positive way to tell, from looking at the injuries, whether they occurred simultaneously or hours apart.

Focusing on the furrows in Orloff's neck, Windham asked, "The marks were caused by something abrading her neck. This would be consistent with any number of objects used. You suggested a rope or a belt, right?"

"Yes."

"Would it also be consistent with an electric cord from a personal massager or vibrator?"

"Absolutely. Yes."

Turning to Pena's opinion about the health of Orloff's cardiovascular system, Windham established that she did, indeed, have atherosclerosis, loss of arterial elasticity and fatty deposits in the vessels. "Are you aware of the fact that this individual was receiving treatment for a heart ailment?"

Pena seemed surprised. "I'm sorry. I just heard about that today, actually before coming to court. I didn't know that before." But he still insisted the heart itself was healthy.

Shifting again, Windham said, "I want to ask you some questions about vaginal injuries. Now, you have examined persons who are deceased and who may have been raped, right?"

"Yes."

"And in those cases, you often see injuries to the vaginal area, don't you?"

"Not always."

"And when you see injuries to the vaginal area, that may be caused by the act of rape, right?"

"Sometimes."

"During a rape, a woman's vaginal muscles can constrict, can't they?"

"Not always."

"But they can?"

"They can."

"And when they do, and a rapist penetrates the victim, the result is an abrasion or laceration of the vaginal area?"

"That is incorrect. Not necessarily true. I have seen a lot of cases, even with children, the hymen is intact, penetrated by their own father, the stepfather, there is no tearing, no laceration. Even examination by a gynecologist, they have seen nothing. But the victim has been penetrated, so it's hard to tell."

Tilting his head and closing his eyes as if pondering for a moment, Windham said, "Doctor, I know it's hard to tell. I am not asking if it always happens. . . . My question is this: have you seen rape victims who have lacerations of the vaginal area as a result of the rape?"

Pena said he had.

"And that laceration is caused by a tightening of the vaginal muscle and the penetration nonetheless by the perpetrator?"

Pena hesitated and asked, "Meaning his penis?"

"His penis or a finger, or an object."

"OK, that's true."

Windham's next question came in faltering form, as if he wanted to ask it inoffensively, but struggled. "Now, an object could cause this because it is—even an erect penis can cause a laceration or some—even a soft object—I am saying an erect penis could cause a laceration because of this obstruction?"

Pena's answer also came in pauses. "I am—I don't deal with live patients, so it's very hard for me to comment on that to be honest with you." In the Orloff examination, he didn't know the circumstances of the rape.

"You saw no injury to Ms. Orloff?"

"That's true. No vaginal injury."

"Now, in the case of an elderly person, generally the skin tends to be more fragile than the skin of a younger person?"

"Depends on what area of the skin you are talking about." Windham said he meant the vaginal area. Pena agreed it could be true.

"So, for that reason, when an elderly person is sexually violated, you may expect to see an injury to the vaginal area, right?"

"You *may.*" Pena put emphasis on the word "may."

Windham wound up the topic by gaining agreement from Pena that no vaginal injuries had been found during the autopsies of Orloff or Davis.

Returning to the other injuries suffered by Jean Orloff, Windham set the stage for playing his ace in the hole. In the reams of discovery documents provided to him by the prosecution, he had found the note that Francene Mounger had written while observing the autopsy of Jean Orloff—that the perpetrator was "possibly left-handed."

Windham first posed several questions about fractures to Orloff's face, neck, and ribs, then asked, "You try to determine if the victim was assaulted from the front or the back, right?"

"Yes."

"And you are careful when you make that examination?"

"Yes."

"And you are careful when you describe that examination to the detectives, right?"

"Yes."

"And you discussed it with Detective Mounger, who is seated here today, right?" Another yes.

"And you made a determination on Ms. Orloff that because damage was mostly on the left side of the neck, that it was possibly a left-handed suspect who had inflicted the injury?"

Pena's face registered shock. "I would never say that. That is incorrect!"

"If I showed you a copy of her notes, could that change your opinion?"

"No. Because I would never—I would never, and I won't make that statement. I am asked that many times and it may be misconstrued, but I would not say that. That is incorrect."

At Windham's urging, Pena said he would examine the notes to see if they would "refresh his recollection." But upon scanning them, Pena said, "No. It does not. I'm sorry. It does not."

Windham had placed the issue before the jury. Although Dr. Pena had emphatically denied suggesting the perpetrator had been left-handed, the seed was planted, and Windham could bring it up again during Francene Mounger's pending testimony. Through her, he planned to show jurors that Kenneth Hunt was right-handed.

"No further questions," he announced.

John Gilligan dove headfirst into the notes made

by Francene Mounger. In redirect examination, he said to Dr. Pena, "You weren't able to comment on these notes. Is there something that you believe would be relevant for the jury to understand?"

"Yes. It's quite important. . . . Ms. Mounger writes here, 'Damage mostly on left-hand side of neck indicates possible left-handed suspect.' I am trying to interpret that."

"It's not your writing?"

"Oh, no."

"Did you make that statement?"

"No."

"Now, possibly is she interpreting the damage that you did note?"

"That's correct."

Satisfied the issue had been at least temporarily deflected, Gilligan wanted to reinforce the opinion about Orloff's heart. "Based on your expertise, is there any question in your mind that Jean Orloff did not die from heart disease?"

"It was not contributing, and she did not die from heart disease."

"Now, the statements about trauma in rape victims. Is it common, very consistent in cases where you have been told that a decedent was raped—and I'm talking about deceased women of all ages—to find no trauma whatsoever?"

"That's correct." Dr. Pena said he had performed at least twenty autopsies on rape victims. He added that scientific literature and his training also supported the opinion that vaginal trauma is not necessarily inflicted during a rape.

Gilligan pressed it just a little more. "Now, if someone is weakened by asphyxiation, or being strangled or held down, would they be less likely perhaps to resist or constrict their vaginal muscles to attempt to resist this phenomenon?"

Pena said, "To be honest with you, that is beyond my expertise."

It left an opening for Windham to pursue on recross. He asked Pena if most scientific literature on the subject stated that the majority of female rape victims do suffer vaginal trauma, but many of them don't. The witness wouldn't agree. After a volley of questions, he finally said, "From my cases where I have seen vaginal trauma, it's usually made with an object and not the penis."

"And that would cause more trauma than a penis, you would expect more trauma?"

"Well, yes."

"And . . . in an elderly person, whose skin may not be as supple or may be dryer, you would expect to be more vulnerable to an injury during rape, right?"

Pena refused to concede the point. "Well, there are a couple of ways to look at it. The skin is elastic as you get older. I don't know how many kids Ms. Orloff might have had. This tightening issue, I'm not quite sure. In a younger woman, perhaps, but I am not familiar with a living woman. I am dealing from a forensic standpoint, so I am thinking of elasticity, plus I see postmortem conditions, flaccid muscles in the vaginal area."

Realizing the jury had probably heard enough, and not wanting to lose their attention, Windham compromised. "In any event, neither Ms. Orloff or Ms. Davis suffered any injury to the vaginal area?"

"Grossly, no."

"Thank you."

The prosecutor stood again and asked if Pena had used the naked eye for the vaginal exam or a microscope. He had used a magnifying glass. "You are not telling us it's more likely than not that someone who has been raped would have trauma to the vagina, are you?"

"That's correct."

Dr. Louis Pena appeared relieved to finally step down.

The day concluded with the testimony of Barbara Kappedal, Jean Orloff's neighbor and close friend, taking the jury through her shocking discovery of Orloff's body and calling for emergency help.

Judge Connor had other matters scheduled for Friday, so admonished the jury not to talk about the case and to return on Monday morning, March 5. They would have three full days to digest what they had heard, and could speak of it to no one.

Nineteen

Monday morning, March 5, 2001, dawned gloomy and wet. Weather forecasts predicted a wind-driven storm that could drop from three to six inches of rain in the Los Angeles basin. Flooded intersections and snarled traffic on slick freeways made the commute miserable.

With wet umbrellas stowed, and stomachs full of hot coffee, lawyers, jurors, witnesses, and spectators crowded the first floor of the Criminal Courts Building, waiting for snail-paced elevators. They finally assembled again in Department 109, a windowless room that shut out the downpour outside.

Coroner's Investigator Sherwood Dixon led off the list of witnesses to tell jurors how he had been dispatched to a funeral home where Jean Orloff's body lay waiting for ultimate cremation. He had taken one look, realized from the furrow on her neck that she had not succumbed to natural causes, and called LAPD homicide detectives.

A close friend of Orloff replaced Dixon in the witness chair. Virginia Hauhuth had also employed Kenneth Hunt as a handyman. She told jurors that, while visiting Orloff, she learned a man named Sonny Hunt had repaired Jean's wall mirror. Needing some cabinet locks replaced, Hauhuth asked Orloff about Hunt, and subsequently hired him to work in her home. When news of his arrest as a murder suspect eventually reached her, she reeled in astonishment. Hauhuth couldn't say it to the jury, but she wondered if she had miraculously escaped a terrible fate.

Next came Chadwick Spargo, the L.A. Fire Department captain who had responded to the apartment from a 911 call by Orloff's friend Barbara Kappedal. When he saw Orloff's nude body lying facedown on the bed, he was immediately suspicious. "Her arms were splayed out," he said, "with the palms turned up. This was unusual. People ordinarily do not die of natural causes in that position." Most heart attack victims he'd seen were faceup.

Raw chicken pieces in the kitchen sink and burned sections on her bed had also set off alarms in his head. But, said Spargo, the LAPD detective at the scene didn't agree with his observations.

That detective, Christopher Giles, took the stand after Spargo. In his abbreviated testimony, he explained that he had seen heart medicine in the apartment, along with evidence of heavy cigarette usage, which led him to conclude that Jean Orloff had probably died of a heart attack. He had, though, allowed the coroner's deputy to make the final call, which was "death by natural causes."

Parole Agent John Widener settled his big frame into the chair and told the jury of a telephone call he had received from Kenneth Hunt's brother-in-law. George Green had connected Hunt not only to Orloff's murder, but also to the death of Myra Davis ten years earlier. Widener had notified LAPD homicide detectives and subsequently met with Ron Phillips and Francene Mounger. Together they had taken Hunt into custody for parole violations. Later the suspect was booked for murder.

Jurors and spectators had been waiting anxiously for Francene Mounger to take her turn as a witness. She stood up from the prosecution table and made a short walk to the witness chair midway through that rainy Monday morning.

John Gilligan first established that Mounger had begun working the Orloff case on April 2, 1998, at which time there was no known link to the Davis murder. The connection came six days later with a phone call by George Green to Parole Agent Widener.

Since DNA evidence would be crucial to his case, Gilligan opened the evidence trail by asking Mounger about observing a nurse use a hypodermic needle to take blood samples from Hunt, on April 14, in jail. He spent several minutes patiently developing the step-by-step procedures, demonstrating for jurors the care taken to prevent mishandling of samples that would wind up in a Maryland laboratory, Cellmark Diagnostics.

Years earlier, in Judge Lance Ito's court next door, the LAPD had been accused in the O. J. Simpson trial of "a rush to judgment," meaning the detectives had made up their minds early in the investigation that Simpson was the only suspect, and directed all their efforts toward pinning the murder on him. Gilligan had labored steadily to avoid any hint that Kenneth Hunt had been prejudged. Before asking Mounger any more questions, he requested a sidebar conference. In the whispered session with Judge Connor and the other attorneys, he said, "I don't want to run afoul of anything. My next question for Detective Mounger was going to ask if she was present when Hunt was taken into custody for parole violation and where it took place. Then I want to ask when he was actually charged with the murders to show that it didn't take place until almost nine months later."

Connor turned to Windham. "Any problem with that?"

Shrugging, he asked, "Why is it relevant?"

Gilligan answered, "It's relevant to show that, in fact, he was not charged until the investigation was completed."

The judge, recognizing instantly what Gilligan was trying to accomplish, said, "To counter the rush to judgment argument."

Quickly agreeing, Gilligan echoed her words. "And there's no rush to judgment."

"I see," said Windham. "Well, I'm not sure what to say. I'll just object, as irrelevant, and see what the court does."

It didn't take long for him to see. Connor said, "Overruled."

Questioning Mounger again, Gilligan spoke. "Now, on April 8, 1998, were you present when Mr. Hunt was taken into custody by Mr. Widener?"

"Yes."

"And what was the location where he was taken into custody?" Mounger gave him the address on Beverly Drive.

"Was Mr. Hunt actually charged with the murders of Jean Orloff and Myra Davis?"

Mounger shook her head. "I believe it was in December of '98 when a search warrant was actually served on him."

To wind up his interrogation of the detective, Gilligan asked about the smoke detector in Jean Orloff's apartment. Mounger told him it had been dismantled. "The wires were pulled out. There was no cover on the smoke detector. It appeared to be inoperative."

Satisfied, Gilligan turned her over to Mark Windham.

Informing Mounger that he would like to ask about events in Orloff's apartment, the defender inquired about items the police had taken during the investigation. "One of the items you retrieved was a personal massager or vibrator with an electric cord on it?"

"Yes."

"You took it from the vicinity of the bed, right?"

"Yes."

He asked if it had been examined by the Scientific Investigation Division (SID) to determine if the cord could have been used as a ligature. Mounger told him the coroner's office had, indeed, scrutinized it.

"Was it determined that the electric cord could have caused the mark on Ms. Orloff's neck?"

"It was a possibility."

To his next line of questioning, Orloff agreed that no usable fingerprints had been found in the apartment.

Observers had been waiting for him to get to the issue of a left-handed killer. Windham approached it by asking if she had discussed the injuries to Jean Orloff with Dr. Pena. Mounger said she had, at the autopsy and later by telephone.

"And you took notes when you spoke to him?"

"I took notes, yes."

"From that conversation, you got the impression that the perpetrator may have been left-handed, right?"

"I think that was a possibility."

After a few queries about taking Hunt into custody, Windham asked, "And at that time, you also determined that Kenneth Hunt was right-handed, did you not?"

"No."

"Have you since learned that he is right-handed?"

"No."

"You never inquired whether or not he was right-handed?"

"Not that I recall."

"You don't recall watching him sign any forms?"

"No. No, I didn't." To Mounger, the issue had been only speculative anyway. If DNA connected Hunt to the murders, it didn't matter if he was left-handed, right-handed, or ambidextrous.

Veering away from the subject, Windham pursued more details about taking the blood sample from Hunt while he was in custody at a sheriff's department facility. He wanted to know where Mounger obtained the empty vial, where she kept it, and how it was handled during and after a nurse filled it with blood from Hunt.

On redirect, Gilligan first dealt with the massager/vibrator cord. "The tests concluded that it couldn't be ruled out as the murder weapon, correct?"

"That's right. It couldn't be ruled out."

"But the report didn't say this was the murder weapon, did it?"

"No, it did not."

"OK, now, your notes about the damage to Jean Orloff's neck indicated that most of the damage was on the left side. Is that correct?"

"Yes."

"And you wrote, 'possibly left-handed suspect'?"

"That's correct."

"Was that supposition based on the location of the injuries you observed?"

"Yes, it was. I also thought that Dr. Pena had said something along those lines, but it's always difficult to understand what the doctors are saying during the autopsy because they do have the mask on that's muffling their voice somewhat. And we're also wearing protective gear."

"All right. But this does not say, '*is* a left-handed suspect,' does it? Or 'the murderer *is* left-handed'?"

"It says 'possibly.' "

With a few more questions about the arrest, Gilligan released Francene Mounger back to Windham, who spent only a few additional minutes with her before announcing, "I have no more questions for this witness at this time."

Witness Joe Murillo's full thatch of hair had turned white during his nineteen years as an evidence custodian for the coroner's office. Speaking in a hoarse voice, he answered Gilligan's questions about the processing, care, and storage of blood swatches. He had handled the samples from Myra Davis ten years ago.

Following Murillo as a witness, Mark Schuchardt, a slight, soft-spoken senior criminalist for the coroner's office, had created the blood swatch from Jean Orloff's sample.

Senior Criminalist Lloyd Mahamay, a twenty-one-year veteran of the coroner's office, came next to describe the use of sex kits for collecting samples. Arched eyebrows under his shaggy gray hair gave him a constant look of surprise. The lawyers asked him to explain how he had used the kits on Myra Davis and Jean Orloff. Mahamay spoke of the sealed sex-kit box and how it was necessary to break the seals for access to the contents. He used swabs to probe every orifice of the women's bodies plus skin surfaces of the breasts, nipples, and thighs. In addition, he did pubic hair combings and scraped the surface under the victims' fingernails to collect any hair, skin, or other evidence left by the perpetrator. Afterward, he resealed the boxes in which he had placed the material. Back in the lab, he said, the evidence was analyzed and preserved under refrigeration for future use.

The last witness of the day stepped forward to be sworn in. Nick Sanchez, resembling California's "Golden Boy" prizefighter, Oscar de la Hoya, said, "I work as a criminalist with the Los Angeles Police Department, Scientific Investigation Division. I am currently assigned to the serology unit. In our crime lab, we analyze and characterize body fluids such as blood, semen, and saliva." It was his job to examine the materials collected by Murillo and Mahamay.

If it had not been for Sanchez, evidence in the Myra Davis murder would have vanished, leaving the case in limbo.

Laura Jane Kessner, taking over questioning duties, asked Sanchez to tell what sex kits are. He said, "They consist mainly of what I'm going to call swabs. Those are sort of like big Q-Tips. And they are used for insertion into body cavities, like the oral cavity, vagina, and rectum. The person doing this is attempting to collect any sperm or semen evidence."

Not everyone understands the difference between

sperm and semen, so Kessner asked Sanchez to explain it.

"When I say sperm, I am specifically referring to the oval-shaped cells with the tails we all recognize as being sperm cells. Semen would be more specifically the enzymes and proteins and other fluids that would carry the sperm."

Step by step, under Kessner's questioning, Sanchez explained his processing of the blood, sperm, and semen evidence collected with the use of sex kits. He also detailed his preparation for sending the material to a laboratory for DNA testing. His testimony revealed meticulous safeguards to prevent loss, contamination, and mishandling of the evidence.

"Do you work on more than one sexual-assault kit at a time on your lab table?" asked Kessner.

"I do not. It would be against policy to have more than one item open and exposed on a workbench at any one time." The LAPD had once been accused of allowing different samples to contaminate one another. They had obviously learned from mistakes and installed effective controls to prevent errors.

"In the case involving Jean Orloff, did you use the sexual-assault kit to do a sperm-cell analysis?"

"Yes." Sanchez took the jury through each step of his tests. "I detected sperm cells on the external genital swab and on the vaginal aspirate swab."

"What was your conclusion? Specifically, did you think you had enough for DNA analysis?"

"I determined that—yes . . . There was enough to attempt DNA analysis." He said he sent portions of the samples to Cellmark Diagnostics on April 21, along with a swatch containing Kenneth Hunt's blood.

Over the next forty-five minutes, Kessner elicited

from Sanchez yet more assertions of care in processing and handling of the evidence. She realized nothing could be more important to the prosecution's case
than convincing the jury the lab results were valid.

"After you sent these items to Cellmark for DNA
testing, did you hear back from them?"

Yes, he said. He had received a response. To Kessner's next question, regarding a match in Hunt's
blood to the sperm samples found in the victim,
Sanchez started to reply, but Mark Windham objected.
At a sidebar conference, Judge Connor cautioned the
prosecution they could say if there was a match, but
give no details. That information would have to come
from a DNA expert from Cellmark.

Wording her inquiry with extreme care, Kessner
asked, "Did Cellmark tell you whether or not there
was a match between Kenneth Hunt's blood sample
and the swabs from Jean Orloff?"

"Yes, they did. There *was* a match."

With that important information established, Kessner went through the same process regarding the
swabs from the body of Myra Davis and Hunt's blood
sample.

But there was one major hitch.

"I detected sperm on the external genital swab, and
there was enough for a DNA analysis," said Sanchez,
referring to the Myra Davis samples. Barely enough.
"I sent a portion of that swab to Cellmark."

At least one juror, and possibly more, felt woozy
from the litany of blood, sperm, and semen testimony.
Or perhaps they just wanted to get an early start home
on the rain-soaked streets. Judge Connor interrupted
to say, "We have a note from a juror indicating it's
too much. How much longer will this witness take?"

Laura Jane Kessner guessed at least another hour.

It was agreed to recall Nick Sanchez on the following morning and excuse the jury for the remainder of the day. Windham anticipated his opportunity to cross-examine Sanchez and hope to punch holes in the armor of his care in serology processing.

One woman would also be questioned, not in the normal order. Ordinarily, defense witnesses are not called until the prosecution rests, but the availability of this person, from Windham's defense list, was limited, so she would also take the stand on Tuesday. If the defender's ace in the hole about a left-handed killer hadn't impacted the jury as much as he had anticipated, this witness would be an ace up his sleeve. Her story might just blast a crater in the prosecution's case.

Twenty

On another drizzly, gray day, Tuesday, Nick Sanchez
sat in the witness chair, radiating confidence. He knew
his job and didn't mind talking about it.

To provide overlap from the previous day's testimony, and to warm up the jury, Laura Jane Kessner
re-covered some of the same ground with Sanchez
about precautions taken with blood and semen samples before sending them to Cellmark. Having set the
stage, she opened the curtain on evidence related to
Myra Davis.

"Yesterday you were telling us that you sent some
evidence to Cellmark Diagnostics on August 31, 1998.
What were those?"

"That's correct. I sent an external genital swab
from Myra Davis's sexual-assault kit and a swatch
smeared with a sample of her blood." The swab had
been tiny, having been preserved for ten years under
refrigeration.

Emphasizing again the meticulous controls exercised to prevent contamination, Kessner spent another quarter of an hour leading Sanchez through
the procedures.

Then she came to grips with what could have been

one of the most disastrous bungles related to the
Davis case, on the part of a lab technician. Sanchez
had received a stunning notification from Cellmark.
"I spoke with one of their DNA analysts. He said he
had started testing the sample sent on August thirty-
first, the external genital swab, but he was unable to
extract enough DNA. He went back to try to reextract
DNA from that sample. And when he went back to
do that, he was not able to locate the sample!"

"How much of the swab did you send to Cellmark?"

Sanchez, with a hint of pride, told how, when preparing the external genital swab for shipment, he had
taken a special precaution. Because he had only one
precious swab available, he had used a sterile razor
blade to cut the cotton tip in half. He'd sent only
one-half of it to Cellmark. Upon receiving the shocking notification that it had been lost, along with a
request for more, Sanchez had sent the other half.
He knew he had rescued the entire Myra Davis case
for the prosecution by his cautionary action.

"So there was nothing left of the swabs at that
point?"

"That's correct. Nothing left."

"And did you get a report concerning the evidence
on Myra Davis?"

"Yes, I did. On November 29, 1998."

"Did Cellmark report a match between the DNA
types found in Kenneth Hunt's blood sample with the
types found in the swabs?"

"I cannot say the word match. But I can say the
DNA types that Cellmark detected off the external
genital swabs was the same as those DNA types detected in Kenneth Hunt's blood."

To the layperson, it sounded like different words meaning the same thing. But, to DNA experts, there was a big distinction. That issue would be handled soon by a representative from Cellmark.

Mark Windham began cross-examining Sanchez by attacking the chain of custody procedures used to safeguard evidence, but made little headway. He did seem to strike some pay dirt with revelation that a criminalist who had examined the Myra Davis swab ten years earlier had concluded there was not enough sperm present for DNA testing. But it would turn out to have little value.

At a sidebar to discuss another issue, Windham suggested he would like to bring up bias on the part of Sanchez as shown in documents the witness wrote. According to Windham, Sanchez had expressed the need to conduct testing for the purpose of "eliminating" other possible suspects in both murders. Blood samples had been taken from John Serpico, former boyfriend of Jean Orloff's daughter, and Corey Davis, Myra Davis's grandson. At the prosecution's request, Sanchez had conducted preliminary tests, and in his notes, he had written, "Elimination of victim's grandson . . . originally a suspect in 1988 . . . capital offense case." To Windham, that indicated Sanchez wished to "eliminate" other suspects in order to zero in on Hunt. Out of the jury's presence, a special hearing was conducted to question Sanchez on this point.

Windham asked, "So you came into this knowing that the prosecutor wanted to be able to rule out other males who were in contact with the victims?"

"No. When I took his request, it was my understanding that these people, John Serpico and Corey Davis, had been suspects at one time. And just to be complete with the entire analysis, we were going to look at their DNA samples and compare those to the external genital swabs." His use of the word "eliminate," said Sanchez, was nothing but a choice of terms. It could have been "compare" or "include-exclude."

Judge Connor sustained Kessner's objection, disallowing Windham from pursuing bias on the part of Sanchez.

With testimony from Nick Sanchez completed, Mark Windham was allowed to call a defense witness in the middle of the prosecution's case, even though Gilligan and Kessner had not completed their presentation.

Sworn in and seated, the woman said her name was Glenda Vale. Windham asked, "Ms. Vale, do you know Kenneth Hunt?"

"Yes, I do."

"What is your relationship to him?"

"He's married to my sister. He's my brother-in-law."

"In March of 1998, did you live in the same house with Kenneth Hunt?"

"Yes, I did."

"And did you know Jean Orloff?"

"Yes, I did. She's a customer of my mom's, and she was a friend of the family. She had come to our house for Halloween parties in the past."

"Do you remember the weekend, or specifically the date of March 28, 1998?"

"Yes, I do."

"And how is it that you remember that date?"

"I'm a Girl Scout leader of fourteen years and that just happened to be the final weekend of [the] Girl Scout's cookie sales." Spectators recalled something more important related to that date; it was the weekend of Jean Orloff's murder.

"On that particular day, March twenty-eighth, was Kenneth Hunt living in your home?"

"Yes, he was."

"And was he present in your home on March twenty-eighth?"

"Yes, he was."

A feeling of tension rippled through the court gallery. Had Mark Windham produced an alibi for Kenneth Hunt? Jean Orloff's apartment was about three miles from Dora Green's home, where Hunt and Vale had lived. It wouldn't have taken long to drive over there, commit the murder, and return. Would this witness cover for him the whole weekend?

Windham went directly to that question. "Do you recall what times you saw him arrive or leave on that day?"

"Kenneth was in and out of the house during the day, and then it was toward around dinnertime he left with his wife, Betty. And they went out to get some fast food, and they brought some movies back, and they went into their bedroom for the evening by themselves."

More questions ran through the minds of observers. Was this the first time this alibi had been mentioned? Had Glenda Vale told the detectives of Hunt's presence in the home that day? Or had she waited more than two years to tell this story?

"About what time was that?" Windham inquired.

"They must have been in about—it must have been about six-thirty, or sevenish, roughly around there, you know, give or take a half hour either way. But they were together."

"Did he ever leave that night?"

"No, he did not."

"Is there any way—could you tell if somebody were trying to sneak out of the house?"

"Yeah. Because my bedroom is right down the hallway, and my kids were sleeping in the living room with their sleeping bags. My daughter had a girlfriend over, who was participating in the cookie sales."

"When did you next see Kenneth Hunt?"

"I saw him on and off in the evening, you know, if they were to come out to go in the kitchen, and then we saw them Sunday morning."

"Thank you. No further questions."

John Gilligan nearly leaped from his chair. It was almost possible to feel the heat of his intensity in the room. But he spoke as if he were greeting folks in church.

"Good afternoon, ma'am."

"Good afternoon."

"Now, the date of March twenty-eighth, you said Mr. Hunt was in and out during the course of the day, is that correct?"

"Uh-huh."

"Is that a 'yes'?"

"Yes."

"The court reporter can't take down 'uh-huh.' "

"Sorry. Sorry about that."

"So he was alone, but in and out of the house during the course of the day. By alone, I mean he went out by himself, came back by himself, but then in the evening around six-thirty, you saw him come back with your sister?"

"Sonny was working—excuse me. Kenneth was working on a shower in our house. They had torn it out completely. When I say he was in and out, he was running to, say, the hardware store to get, you know, something he needed and then coming back."

Gilligan started to ask for clarification. "Predominately—"

Vale interrupted. "He was predominately home that day working on the shower. OK. When I say early evening, when he left, it was a matter of . . . He left with his wife because they were going out for the evening."

To court watchers, the witness seemed to be waffling.

Gilligan remained calm. "And what time was that? Six, six-thirty?"

"Like I said, it could have been six or six-thirty, maybe sevenish, but they left together. Kenneth never left the house after seven alone."

Gilligan started again. "He'd always go—" But was cut off by the witness.

"He always had somebody, and predominately he always went with Betty."

"But before that, before seven, he would go out by himself?"

"Yeah. Of course. He was working."

"Now, when did you find out that Jean Orloff had been murdered?"

"OK. The weekend of the cookie sale, that Sunday morning. We had gone off to the cookie sales. When we returned—my mom was watering a plant. And this was a plant Jeannie had given to my mom. And it broke. We thought that was really bizarre. We were cleaning it up and the phone rang. It was Jeannie's mother calling to tell my mom, because they were friends and she was her manicurist, that they found Jeannie had died."

Vale had not answered the question, but Gilligan said, "OK."

She continued her account. "And that was—could have been anywhere between three and four-thirty because we usually would tie up our cookie booths roughly around that time."

"So Sunday—"

She interrupted again. "So we got the phone call that Sunday afternoon."

Keeping his voice level without a hint of irritation, Gilligan asked, "Sunday, the twenty-ninth, sometime in the afternoon or early evening, you found out that Jean Orloff had been murdered, is that correct?"

"We were told she was found deceased in her home."

"OK. So you didn't know at that time she had been murdered?"

"No."

"The police later came and interviewed your mother?"

"Uh-huh."

Gilligan remained patient. "Is that correct?"

"Yes, yes."

"And that was on April seventh. Would that be the first time? Do you recall?"

"I'm trying to think."

"Well, if I told you that—"

"If I had a calendar, I can tell you exactly. It's in my backpack."

"Do you remember the night the police came to the house and that Mr. Hunt was arrested?"

"Yes. Definitely."

"OK. Assuming that is April eighth, did the police come to talk to anybody in the house before that date?"

"I believe briefly they—two investigators had come to the house and spoken with my mom because she was the manicurist of Jeannie. Like a person would go to a bar and speak to a bartender and divulge things, people would divulge things to a manicurist. So they were trying to get some more insight into Jeannie's actions."

"And that was on the seventh?"

"I don't know the date."

"All right. On the eighth, that was the date Mr. Hunt was arrested. You were present, is that correct?"

"Yes, I was."

"And that night the detective who is sitting here, Francene Mounger, the woman whose shoulder I am touching right now, she was one of the police officers who were there, is that correct?"

"Yes, she was."

"And you were there while she talked to your mom about the reasons they were arresting Kenneth and their suspicions about him?"

"No, they did not."

"OK. At what point did you realize, that day on the eighth, that they were looking at him for potentially being involved in the murder of Jean Orloff and of Myra Davis?"

"Actually, they were just searching the house erratically."

Still calm, but showing a slight crack in his patience, Gilligan said, "Just please try to answer my question."

"I'm sorry."

"My question is, on the eighth, did you know that

they were looking at Kenneth as a suspect in the murders? If the answer is no, then answer no. If it's yes, say yes."

Ignoring his request, Vale said, "I figured it out just by their actions."

"OK. So in your mind, you knew that Kenneth Hunt was a suspect, is that a fair statement?"

"After they barged in, yes."

"Did you tell them about Kenneth being home that night?"

"They refused to speak with me. I repeatedly offered to speak to any of the detectives. They said, 'Just a minute. You'll have your time. We'll take your deposition.' Nobody ever questioned me at all."

"OK. Now, later on, your husband was interviewed by the police, both the night of April eighth and the night of April sixteenth, isn't that correct?"

"I don't know what night for sure. On another day, I don't know the date. . . . I know he was questioned."

"Did you tell your husband, 'Make sure you tell the police that Kenneth was home that night'?"

"No."

"You thought it was important information, right?"

"Yes. It was."

"You wanted to get that information to the police, is that correct?"

"The police said that they would be in touch with me if they wanted to talk to me."

"All right. Now, did you ever tell your husband to make sure that he gave that information to the police any of the times he was interviewed?"

"No, I did not."

"Did you ever discuss with him any of the interviews he had, or inquire what they asked him?"

"I briefly asked what was going on. He just basically told me that they wanted to know about his relationship with Kenneth."

"So . . . Did you have any worries that they didn't know this important information, the information that Kenneth was home the night of the twenty-eighth? Were you concerned?"

"I wasn't concerned because there was no charges pressed immediately."

"What about when the charges were pressed?"

"I had said to my sister, is there anybody that we could speak with? And she told me that she would relay it to her attorney as the case went on . . . And I've always been open about this, trying to reach somebody."

"The interviews took place in January or February of this year where you gave some information to defense investigators, is that correct?"

"Yes."

"So for two years you had information about a murder that might clear your brother-in-law, and you never went down to the West L.A. station and said, 'You guys got to know this'?"

"They don't—they—I shouldn't say they don't. They didn't want to speak to me."

"Did you make a phone call to the station?" Gilligan's voice, while still courteous, began to show a hint of skepticism.

"No."

"Did you ever call Detective Mounger?"

"I talked to—I believe there was a gentleman involved, and he himself had told me that if they needed any questions asked, they would contact me."

"Did you ever call the station and say, 'I want to give some information to somebody regarding this case'?"

"No, I did not."

"Were you present when Betty, Mr. Hunt's wife, was interviewed the night of the arrest, April 8, 1998?"

"Yes, I was. I attempted on numerous occasions that evening to convey what I knew, and nobody wanted to listen to me. And this detective finally told me to be quiet and leave the room, OK, and had two officers stand near me and said, 'We don't want to hear from you at this moment.' OK. Nobody came forward after that to even question me."

"And you made no attempt at any time later on to contact this detective or anyone else at LAPD to say, 'I have some relevant information regarding this case'?"

Windham had been silent for the entire cross-examination, but finally said, "Objection. The question was asked and answered." He was correct and the judge sustained it.

Gilligan had made his point. "Nothing further."

Windham saw no need to prolong her testimony. The jury had heard it well, and would decide during deliberations if they believed Glenda Vale or disbelieved her.

Judge Connor dismissed the witness. "Thank you very much, Mrs. Vale. You are done." Connor then turned to the jury and said, "Tomorrow will be a full day. Rest up. Have fresh minds. Don't discuss the case. We'll see you at nine. Thank you."

Spectators could see possible loopholes in the alibi

Vale had provided. Hunt had been "in and out" during the day, and no clear-cut time frames had been confirmed. Was she acting out of loyalty to her family? Was her memory, two years later, precisely accurate? If her story was true, why hadn't she insisted on telling the police, or written a letter to the chief of police to protest being ignored by detectives? Those who wondered just how the prosecutor viewed Vale's story were eager to hear his arguments to the jury, which would be delivered just prior to their beginning deliberations. Of course, the defense attorney would have a chance to express his slant on Vale's testimony as well.

Only the jury, though, could make the final decision on how important her words had been. Only they could measure the weight of this surprising development.

Twenty-one

The rainstorm had tapered off by Wednesday morning when Judge Connor greeted the jurors and told them that Laura Jane Kessner would explain a little bit about the next witness and the subject to be presented.

Kessner, with a sunny smile and youthful enthusiasm, stepped to the lectern. "Good morning, ladies and gentlemen of the jury. I'm only going to take a few minutes of your time before I introduce our next witness. This is the final stage of our trial. I want to thank you for your attention and patience so far.

"You are going to be hearing from the director of Cellmark Diagnostics. Her name is Dr. Robin Cotton. She's going to be explaining generally the DNA process and the testing. She's going to be talking about Cellmark, a lab that's independent from the LAPD.

"This was the first accredited private lab. It does testing for both the prosecution and the defense.

"And in the course of her testimony, you are going to hear numbers. It's inevitable. But the important numbers I would urge to focus on relate to five big pieces of evidence." Placing a poster on an easel, Kessner drew attention to the listed points:

Swabs taken from Myra Davis
Swabs taken from Jean Orloff
Blood swatches taken from Davis
Blood swatches taken from Orloff
Blood sample taken from Kenneth Hunt

"Finally, ladies and gentlemen, you are going to hear about one common result, over and over again. Every result comes out to include the defendant, Kenneth Hunt. That, in addition to the fact that Hunt knew both of these victims, and has been placed inside their homes, is why the people, at the conclusion of this case, will ask you to convict him of all the crimes and allegations. Thank you for your attention."

When the prosecution speaks, the defense automatically gets a chance to counter. Mark Windham stepped forward and greeted the jury in an equally friendly tone. "We've gone through almost all of the people's case. We've heard from about twenty-four different witnesses. Yet, *you have not heard any evidence of guilt!*

"You have heard things that suggest Kenneth Hunt has a particular character. You have heard that he was acquainted with each of the women, the two women who were found killed. We have only heard evidence that he was *at home* on the night of the Orloff killing.

"We do not have any evidence connecting him to these crimes.

"The people's case will rely entirely upon the circumstantial evidence that will be presented from Cellmark Diagnostics from Dr. Robin Cotton.

"What I want you to keep in mind when you hear

her testimony is this: the results of the tests by Cellmark lab will be only as good as the material that is delivered to them for testing. Any mistake, confusion, contamination, degradation, or any problems with the evidence are something that Cellmark Diagnostics cannot change.

". . . They looked at what they received, and what they were told were swabs from these victims. And they will report to you that they have the same [characteristics] present that Kenneth Hunt had.

"That is the evidence the people will present as being very damning evidence. Keep in mind that these conclusions are subject to a couple of problems.

"First of all, the problem of *error*. The problem of mistake, not only in the material that gets to Cellmark. And keep in mind the loss of material by Cellmark; you already know about that. Keep in mind what that points to as far as how careful they are in the procedures they utilize.

"Second of all, you will see how this technology works, and you will learn there are multiple opportunities for error in this procedure. Error by people, error by technology.

"Also, please keep an open mind because when Dr. Cotton is done testifying and tells you that this genotype is rare, that you would only expect to find it in *one in a quintillion* people, or some number like that, keep in mind that the defense will rebut this. We will show you that those numbers are not good, that this testing is not as reliable as it is made out to be.

"So please keep an open mind during this: the opportunities for error, that all this testing depends entirely upon what was delivered to them, the quality of the work in gathering, storing, packaging, and transporting it to Cellmark Diagnostics.

"At the end of this, I think you will see that suspicion is there because of Kenneth Hunt's record, but the DNA testing will leave you with more questions than answers."

Dr. Robin Cotton raised her right hand, agreed to tell the truth, then took the stand. Her soft features topped by blond neck-length hair, rounded chin, rimless glasses, and dark pantsuit gave her a pleasant, nonthreatening look. Experts who testify in court generally present impressive credentials in their curriculum vitae, their brief biographical, career, and educational résumé. Cotton's was more than impressive. In addition to holding a Ph.D. in molecular biology and biochemistry, she had worked in the University of Iowa's biochemistry department and later for the National Institute of Health. Associated with Cellmark since 1988, she was in charge of all the lab work and involved in planning and research. In more than 160 court appearances as a DNA expert, for both prosecution and defense, few attorneys challenged her expertise.

With Laura Jane Kessner doing the questioning, Dr. Cotton first described the particular care taken at Cellmark to avoid contamination or errors.

Next she gave the jury a basic understanding of DNA, deoxyribonucleic acid. "DNA is what makes us unique as individuals. It is the physical molecule we inherit from our parents that carries all of the information that makes us individuals. It contains the information that allows our bodies to function and gives us our physical appearance. And it programs how our bodies grow as we develop from infants to adults, and as we age."

DNA testing, she said, is not only used in criminal forensics. It is also used in paternity determinations and for medical purposes. For example, "If you have a patient and a donor who is going to give bone marrow for a transplant, the success can be followed by using the same types of procedures that are used in DNA testing for criminal cases." It's used as well for identification of mutilated bodies in disasters or in unknown military personnel killed in action.

Judge Connor was a pioneer in allowing jurors to submit written questions during trials. Two queries came from the jury box for Dr. Cotton. The first asked if Cellmark had needed to correct any problems to renew their accreditation in the recent year. Even observers thought it was a remarkably perceptive and appropriate inquiry. Dr. Cotton said, "Yes, we did. If I'm remembering correctly, there were three items. One was related to how evidence is sealed." The problem was the absence of a written procedure, and it was corrected. Another procedural issue involved accounting for the amount of DNA in Cellmark's possession for any particular case, and the third was an in-house safety problem, an electrical outlet mounted too close to a shower head. The other juror note requested definitions of a few DNA terms. That would be answered during the course of Dr. Cotton's testimony.

Through questioning by Kessner, Cotton described a recent technological advance, labeled "profiler plus and cofiler" tests, which examine differences in DNA from person to person. Another important definition for the jury to understand, called PCR, was, in simplified terms, a way to "target a small location in the

DNA and make many, many copies, millions of copies which allow you to actually have enough DNA to measure in the lab." Cotton mentioned that the scientist who invented PCR won a Nobel Prize. The process, she said, could be compared to using a photocopy machine to make millions of copies from one original.

The body is made up of cells, said the doctor, and DNA is in the nucleus of those cells. It's contained in forty-six chromosomes inside the nucleus. "Each of those chromosomes is really a long strand of DNA. We inherit twenty-three of those from our mother, and twenty-three from our father."

What is DNA made of? "It is made up of four components, which have abbreviations: A, T, G, and C." Those are simply the first letters of the chemicals they represent.

Most everyone has heard of the spiral-shaped "double helix," the common image pictured to show what DNA looks like. "The molecule has the shape of a spiral staircase."

The next point Cotton made would be essential to understanding its use. "Now, one thing that's really important to know . . . The huge majority of our DNA, in all humans, would be the same. More than ninety-nine percent of our DNA is the same between all of us. A very small portion is different from person to person." That small portion, less than 1 percent, would be used for measuring and testing in criminal cases.

Two processes, she said, are used. One examines the sequence of the components. And if two samples show different sequences, they did not come from the same person. The other process measures the length of a chromosome. "It's sort of equivalent to looking

at the number of boxcars in a train. . . ." Length differences from two samples would show they did not
come from the same person. That was an oversimpli-
fied description, but would help the jury have a basic
grasp of the fundamentals.

Laura Jane Kessner spent considerable time allowing Dr. Cotton to explain procedures used in Cellmark's laboratories, with emphasis on controls to
prevent contamination, degradation, or other errors
that would invalidate the tests.

Another witness provided a brief break from the
complexities of DNA. Bonnie Rosen, one of the sexual-battery victims, had flown in from out of state to
testify about being victimized by Hunt. In February
1991, when she was thirty-four, she had been on Beverly Drive. "I was walking home from work, down the
sidewalk, and I saw someone coming toward me. I
looked away and didn't want to make eye contact. He
didn't look like he was from the neighborhood. As
we came upon one another, he grabbed my left breast
and said, 'Nice tit.' I just kept walking because I was
two buildings away from my apartment at the time.
He kept walking the other way. I ran in and called
the police."

Kessner asked, "Do you see that person in the
courtroom today?"

"Yep."

"Will you please point to the person, describe what
he is wearing, and where he is seated?"

Leveling an accusing finger at Kenneth Hunt, the
witness said, "Dark jacket, white shirt. The defendant."

Judge Connor interposed: "Mr. Hunt, for the record."

Kessner thanked Rosen. Windham declined cross-exam.

Resuming direct examination of Dr. Cotton, Kessner's questions took her through testing of the specific swabs and blood samples used in the two murder cases. In grueling, meticulous procedural and technological detail, Cotton explained every step. Next came a labyrinthian explanation of the process for statistical analysis and calculations.

In the Myra Davis case, the sperm sample received from the LAPD had been lost, Cotton candidly admitted. At Cellmark's request, another sample had been sent for testing.

In the early afternoon, Dr. Cotton's testimony culminated in these two conclusions. The tests on sperm found in the vaginal swabs of both Myra Davis and Jean Orloff showed that only one person out of 2.4 million Caucasians would have the DNA type found in the swabs, the type found in Kenneth Hunt's blood sample.

Additionally, more sophisticated testing in the Jean Orloff case produced astronomical numbers. The conclusion stated that the DNA profile, as seen in the sperm sample from Orloff's vaginal swab, would be seen in Caucasians in "one in 1.7 times ten to the eighteenth power. That is eighteen zeros." The single profile in that huge number belonged to Kenneth Hunt.

Mark Windham's cross-examination began with fundamentals, and gradually grew in complexity.

"When we are comparing blood or skin or sperm from a crime, comparing that to an individual, our underlying assumption is that a person has unique

DNA in every one of his cells, including the cells that he leaves behind at a crime scene, right?"

"Yes."

"Now, most of the human DNA is alike, which makes us alike, right?" Cotton agreed. Windham drew from her that each DNA strand in a human cell contains about 30,000 genes, which equals about 6 billion possibilities for an individual person to differ from another. Through more grilling, he elicited an estimate from Cotton that DNA testing looks at only nineteen out of 30,000 possible genes, or "loci." According to the doctor, the sample, even though it seemed tiny, produces reliable results. Windham's questions implied the contrary.

He used the remainder of the day probing, reinquiring, and subtly attacking Cellmark's procedures of handling, testing, and analyzing the DNA.

The next morning, Thursday, March 8, he picked up where he had left, then asked a protracted series of questions aimed at contamination issues. Cotton patiently explained each safeguard used to avoid such problems. Returning to the technical aspects, he pumped a barrage of questions exploring every aspect of the entire testing process. The aggressive pattern repeated itself all morning and into the late afternoon.

At last, Dr. Cotton's testimony ended. She had used nearly two days to inform jurors that, according to scientifically accepted technology, the DNA pointed to Kenneth Hunt as the man who had deposited semen in the bodies of two murder victims. Cotton's testimony filled nearly 300 pages of trial transcripts. It remained to be seen whether or not the jury had understood it to the extent they could say beyond a reasonable doubt that DNA had linked Hunt to the killings.

Laura Jane Kessner expressed confidence they would.

Having completed their case, John Gilligan announced, "The people rest."

Mark Windham hoped that he had exposed serious gaps in not only the credibility of Cellmark, but also how DNA samples had been handled and the conclusions arrived at by Dr. Robin Cotton. Now he would call only two expert witnesses in the defense segment. Through them, he hoped to further undermine the DNA testimony.

Dr. Lawrence Mueller told the jury he was a population geneticist who had written sixty articles in professional journals about how populations change, how they share traits, how they differ, and how calculations are made to draw inferences related to population distribution. In his testimony, he spoke of utilizing computer technology to make reliable comparisons in genes, going beyond the use of pairs in genetic strands, as Cellmark used, but expanded to trios, quads, and more. The projections in Cellmark's results, he suggested, were not valid. To illustrate, he offered an analogy using distribution of fruit flies, which he had studied, but left spectators wondering about the connection.

Windham asked Mueller questions about the reliability of statistical projections using just a few genes in the human makeup, and drew answers that such techniques would be suspect.

In Laura Jane Kessner's cross-exam of the expert witness, she asked how many other credentialed scientists in the field agreed with his assessments. Few did. One expert, Dr. Bruce Weir, had criticized and openly disagreed with him. Had Mueller ever personally conducted DNA tests to validate his arguments against technology used at Cellmark? No. Kessner wound up the cross by getting agreement that Mueller had been paid for his work with the defense. Experts are generally well compensated for testifying, including travel expenses.

Dr. Kenneth Berger, the second witness called by Windham, identified himself as a vice president of regulatory affairs with a company called Lifepoint Incorporated. "My occupation is the development of medical products." He had earned his Ph.D. in biochemistry at the University of Southern California. He was an expert in quality systems validation. "The importance about validation," he said, "is to understand what are the limits and boundaries within which your equipment or your process produces results or products. And the tests for determining that should be based on documentation."

After establishing Berger's extensive experience and understanding of validation processes, Windham asked if he had examined validation studies of a computerized machine used by Cellmark called an AB310 Genetic Analyzer, and associated profiler plus and cofiler kits. He said yes. Berger had also looked at Cellmark's quality assurance manual, standard operating procedure manual, and the company's validation of various DNA testing. To the defender's questions, Berger criticized the studies, results, and conclusions reached by Cellmark about their equipment and processes, citing inadequate controls and failure to set ranges of limits. The machine's manufacturer had not used reliable validation procedures, either.

Faces of jurors did not reflect enthralled excite-
ment. Two of them sent notes asking for a break.

Afterward Windham led Berger through additional
steps he'd taken to make his deductions, then turned
him over to Laura Jane Kessner. Her inquiries drew
admissions that Berger was neither a scientist nor a
DNA expert. He also acknowledged that validation
tests are not perfect. Eventually, he also agreed that
he "liked" Cellmark's standard operating procedures
manual, but not their validation of its use.

Kessner wanted to know if "human interaction"
with the machines and processes, especially humans
with extensive expertise, was appropriate. The witness
said, "Sounds right to me."

Windham, on redirect, finished by asking, "When
you actually examined the data that was provided by
Cellmark's validation study, did you see examples of
problems being uncovered by that testing?"

"I did. It shows they are not in the state of control,
and they should address these problems with correc-
tive action."

The prosecution declined the opportunity to recross.

Mark Windham rested the defense's case.

Twenty-two

One of the most illuminating parts of a murder trial is the argument by each side presented to the jurors before they retire to consider a verdict. The prosecutor takes the first turn, then the defender. Finally, because the burden of proof is with the people, the prosecutor is allowed to speak last. It provides the attorneys with an opportunity to put all of the puzzle pieces together to form a complete picture. During the trial, evidence and testimony are not necessarily presented in meaningful order, sometimes leaving jurors and spectators a bit confused about the importance of various parts.

The final argument is comparable to a detective in an old B movie calling all of the principals together in the parlor and revealing how he solved the crime.

John Gilligan opened by telling the jury it had been an honor for him and his cocounsel, Deputy DA Kessner, to present the case to them. "And now is the chance I get to argue the facts of the case. The defense will have their opportunity; then Ms. Kessner will get up and have the last word in rebuttal.

"What has been shown here, ladies and gentlemen, is that this man, here at the end of counsel table, Kenneth Dean Hunt, murdered and raped Myra Davis in 1988, and Jean Orloff in 1998. That is what has been proven, and that's what you are here for, to give justice to that."

Paying verbal tribute to the jurors for their close attention during the days of testimony, Gilligan promised to take them through the evidence presented. "There are three points I would like to make, things that I ask you to remember."

Point one: "There is no specific evidence of any problems with DNA testing in this case. . . . Such suggestions were nothing but speculation." He accused the defense of attacking DNA with witnesses who were not experts in forensics or in DNA technology.

Was there a "rush to judgment" by the investigators? Certainly not, said Gilligan. Hunt had a criminal record, which would naturally create suspicion. But to suggest that police had gone after him by planting evidence would be absurd. They took blood samples from him, but the evidence against him was in the sperm. To put Mr. Hunt's DNA in the sperm, it would be necessary to pour the blood on the swab containing sperm samples. Of course, that didn't happen.

The defense had tried to suggest contamination of the samples, which could have led to false DNA conclusions, said Gilligan. But if that had happened, there would be evidence of a third party in the DNA findings. "There is no third party. In each case, there is only Mr. Hunt and Ms. Davis, or Mr. Hunt and Ms. Orloff. No third party." Nor was there any evidence offered to show degradation of the samples.

"The second point I would like you to think about," said Gilligan, ". . . the defense would have you believe there is no real corroboration of the DNA testing in this case. I would point out that is simply not true." Other clues pointed directly at Hunt as the killer, backing up the DNA evidence. As examples, Gilligan brought up prior sexual misconduct and parallel characteristics of the murders. Two white older females, both found raped and murdered in their homes. Both lived alone, and both were strangled with ligatures and found in their beds, nude or partially nude. Both were security conscious. Neither case showed signs of forced entry. And both women knew Kenneth Hunt and invited him into their homes as a handyman. "So there is a tremendous amount of corroboration that only points in one direction, right there to Kenneth Hunt."

The third important issue, said Gilligan, was potentially the most powerful weapon the defense could have used. If there had been problems with the DNA, the defense could have asked for a retest at the lab of their choosing. "If they didn't like Cellmark, they could have taken it to private labs all over the country. It would have been paid for by the court, and that evidence would have been presented to you." They didn't do it.

Gilligan acknowledged that he, as a representative of the people, had the entire burden of proof on his shoulders. "Mr. Windham could have spent this entire trial with his feet up on the desk, saying nothing, doing nothing, making no objections, and then just stand up and say at the end, 'It's not good enough,' and then sit back down. That is the system of justice in America. The burden is ours.

"But does anyone here think that is the kind of lawyer Mr. Windham is? He has put on an aggressive defense. He has conceded nothing. He has fought tooth and nail. And I take my hat off to him. He is a fine lawyer." There was nothing pretentious about Gilligan's tribute. He truly did like and admire Mark Windham.

"But what has he *not* presented? The silence is deafening. There is no DNA evidence presented by the defense to counter the people's." If it had been re-tested, said Gilligan, it would have just "proved Mr. Hunt's guilt again."

"So those three things I would ask you to remember. No specific attack on our test results by any qualified DNA expert. Plenty of corroboration, and no defense action to retest the blood and sperm samples."

Gilligan spent the next several minutes recapitulating the series of sexual-battery cases against six women. The defense had put emphasis on the ages of these victims, pointing out they were not "elderly," as were the murdered women. Brushing that aside, Gilligan drew a different correlation. "These people were all outside, all in situations where they were able to fight, to yell, to scream, to get some help. The difference is that we had murder victims who are inside, and alone. They were older, weaker, more vulnerable, and in a position where no one could come to their help. It's not about the ages; it's about a situation where Mr. Hunt was able to do whatever he liked to these victims because they were in no position to run, to get help, to do anything.

"Does Mr. Hunt have a character trait for sexual misconduct? Well, of course he does . . . and you can consider this in your deliberations. It is powerful evidence of who Mr. Hunt is and what his attitudes are toward women."

A verdict of first-degree murder requires a finding

of premeditation and intent to kill, so Gilligan spoke
of that issue. Then he spent some time focusing on
the special circumstances charged: rape, burglary, and
multiple murder. The defense had questioned Dr.
Pena about the autopsy in which no signs of vaginal
injury could be found. So what evidence was there of
rape? Gilligan dealt with that by saying, "We know
there was sexual intercourse because Mr. Hunt's semen was found in the vagina by the use of rape kits
in both women. Certainly, Hunt was married to neither one of them. We know that he was married to
another woman. What is the evidence in this case?
Both of these women were murdered. Clearly, there
was nothing they did voluntarily. It was by brute force.
The act was accomplished by means of force, violence,
duress, menace, or fear of unlawful bodily injury. Well,
I don't think there is much question about any of
these elements, ladies and gentlemen."

During the next quarter of an hour, Gilligan walked
the jury through the sequence of both bodies being
discovered, the investigations, and the nearly bungled
case of Jean Orloff.

"Now," he said, "let me jump ahead a little bit and
talk about Glenda Vale, Mr. Hunt's sister-in-law. She
testified to what anybody who watches television
knows, what an alibi is. Of course, what is interesting
about this alibi is that Glenda gets on the stand and
tells you that Mr. Hunt was in and out all day, but
that at six-thirty or seven, he went out with his wife
and got some videos and then went back to his room
and they didn't come out the entire night.

"The problem with this alibi is that it was not two
years but closer to three years before this is reported
to law enforcement. Now, ask yourself if this makes

any sense. [When] you have an alibi that is known to the sister-in-law, it's going to be known certainly to the wife. She was with him in that room, reportedly, yet no one feels the need to bring that to the attention of law enforcement.

"If there was a problem with Detective Mounger, no one feels the need to call internal affairs, call her boss, or send a letter to Chief of Police Bernard Parks. It's not that hard to get an officer in trouble in today's political environment." If Detective Mounger had really refused to allow Vale to give information to police, had really ordered her to sit down and be restrained by two uniformed officers, said Gilligan, "that would have come to someone's attention." It did not seem reasonable, he added, that anyone with information to clear their brother-in-law of a brutal murder "would sit on it for two and one-half years."

Then to offset any possible weight jurors might give to the alibi, Gilligan commented further. "Let's just say it's true, or there is some truth in there somewhere. It doesn't matter. We know that Mr. Hunt's residence is only three miles from Orloff's apartment. If the last time Doris Boesky sees Jean Orloff alive is four-fifteen or so, and the next time we have a reference by Glenda Vale is six-thirty or seven, when Hunt goes out with his wife, that is two hours, give or take, two hours to go three miles, commit the rape-murder, and return."

Orloff, said Gilligan, was obviously preparing to cook dinner, as seen by raw chicken pieces in the kitchen sink, at the time Hunt interrupted her. "That corroborates the approximate time frame the murder took place. It was unlikely she would have been making dinner at two in the morning. She is preparing it around six, perhaps five, when people would normally be making dinner. At a time when there is no alibi for Mr. Hunt."

Referring to the dismantled smoke alarm and burned sections on the bed, Gilligan said, "It tells you that Mr. Hunt was trying to cover his tracks. Fortunately, the fires went out; the bed didn't burn." And the unlocked door showed that "the assailant was known to the victim, that Jean Orloff allowed her murderer into her house because she knew him."

Errors made during the initial investigation were covered next by the prosecutor. "It's frightening, but it's the truth, the state of the evidence."

Then, he said, "there is a turn of bad luck for Mr. Hunt." The misfortune came when another coroner's investigator decided Orloff had not died a natural death.

Step by step, Gilligan re-created the events leading to the incarceration of Kenneth Hunt, with emphasis on the care used in taking the blood sample from him. Getting to DNA evidence, he told the jury again what they had heard from Dr. Cotton, that for both victims, only one person in 2.4 million would have the same genotypes as Mr. Hunt. And in the Orloff case, new technology narrowed the frequency down to one in 1.7 quintillion.

Winding up, Gilligan spoke of the two defense witnesses who had criticized DNA results in their testimony, Dr. Lawrence Mueller and Dr. Kenneth Berger. "The first guy, who I like to call Dr. Fruit Fly, because that is what he knows. He gets up there and tells you that his numbers are the right numbers and Cellmark's are wrong. . . . Dr. Fruit Fly is the lone voice in the wilderness. You will notice that when Ms. Kessner crucified him on the stand, he had to admit that people with credentials don't agree with him. . . . Dr. Fruit Fly is a hired gun who can come in and testify for money because he is the only guy out there who is going to say the numbers are wrong. He doesn't have the qualifications. He has never run a DNA sample in his life. He is not a forensic scientist. . . . No one else in the field agrees with him."

Dr. Berger, the other defense witness, "told you he doesn't know about DNA technology. He doesn't know how DNA labs are accredited. . . . Again, another hired gun coming in here with no real expertise. You didn't have Mr. Windham calling a forensic DNA scientist to say Dr. Cotton did a lousy job. Nobody said that, ladies and gentlemen. Remember that.

"Justice has been delayed a long time in this case, but it's here now. I would ask you to do the right thing, to convict Mr. Hunt of two counts of first-degree murder, to multiple murder, the burglary, and the rape special circumstances.

"Thank you for your time."

Twenty-three

Mark Windham wasted no time getting to the point. "Ladies and gentlemen of the jury, try as they might, the prosecution did not prove Kenneth Dean Hunt guilty of these two homicides beyond a reasonable doubt."

Attacking the introduction of sexual-battery victims into evidence, Windham dismissed them as nothing more than an attempt to create bias against the defendant. "When you look at that conduct, unpleasant as it is, it proves nothing about these homicides. It doesn't involve elderly persons. It does not involve burglaries. While it's certainly unpleasant to the women, it did not involve substantial physical injury to them such as we saw in these homicides where Ms. Orloff and Ms. Davis were strangled and killed." He cautioned the jury to avoid getting caught up in bias, passion, and prejudice based on events completely unrelated to the murders.

"The only substantial evidence of guilt in this case is the DNA evidence," Windham admitted. "And as I told you, it has left us with more questions than answers."

A primary question, he suggested, involved integrity

of the blood and sperm samples. And the integrity would be destroyed if the samples were contaminated, or if Cellmark made errors in testing it.

Dealing first with contamination, Windham said it could be deliberate or accidental. He reminded the jurors to examine an exhibit, a pamphlet titled "What Every Law Enforcement Officer Should Know About DNA Evidence," produced by the National Institute of Justice. Windham read aloud from it:

> Because extremely small samples of DNA can be used as evidence, greater attention to contamination issues is necessary when identifying, collecting and preserving DNA evidence. DNA evidence can be contaminated when DNA from another source gets mixed with DNA relevant to the case. This can happen when someone sneezes or coughs over the evidence or touches his or her mouth, nose, or other parts of the face and then touches the area that may contain the DNA to be tested. Because a new DNA technology called PCR replicates or copies DNA in the evidence sample, the introduction of contaminants or other unintended DNA to an evidence sample can be problematic.

The prosecutor had ridiculed suggestions of contamination by saying a third person's DNA would have been found in the sample, which didn't happen. He had also commented that a deliberate planting of Hunt's DNA into the semen samples would have involved someone mixing his blood into the swatches. No evidence of that had been seen.

To squelch those points, Windham said, "Mr. Gilligan, I'm sorry, is confused about the contamination issue here." A sneeze or cough by the person handling the DNA could have blown "a flake of dry blood" from one sample to the other. So the handler's DNA wouldn't necessarily be the contaminant. And the risk of ruining integrity of the samples, said Windham, could happen during the collection process, the transportation, removal from packaging in the lab, or any of a number of places the swabs and slides are handled. "Contamination can be by officers at the crime scene, SID scientists, or the Cellmark scientists."

Regarding the possibility of Hunt's blood being used to insert his DNA into the semen sample, Windham said, "The blood was certainly in the custody of a number of people, [but] there is no evidence that any one of them put blood or DNA into the crime-scene sample." However, the prosecutor's scenario misses something, said Windham. DNA from a person's sperm, saliva, or skin cells is all the same. "You don't have to see a drop of blood on the swab. This stuff is microscopic. Just a few cells, or just one cell produces the material that is amplified millions of times by the testing process." The implication was clear, that the sperm samples might have been contaminated with something other than blood.

Another thing to consider, said Windham, was the finding by a lab technician in 1988 that no semen had shown up on the swabs. Then, ten years later, Criminalist Nick Sanchez finds semen on the swab. "How does this sample materialize for Nick Sanchez with the evidence that is so incriminating, only to be sent to Cellmark, and they lose it after it fails to produce a result? And Sanchez says he had yet another

sample at the end of a swab. He sends it off to Cellmark, where they test it and make it all the better by
getting the result they are looking for, which is the
inclusion of Mr. Hunt.

"What is going on here? This question needs to be
answered and answered clearly before you can say beyond a reasonable doubt that this evidence has integrity. Before you can say Kenneth Hunt is guilty. Before
you can give someone a death penalty." At this last
comment, Judge Connor glanced up and reached for
a pen to make a quick note.

Turning next to the technical explanations of DNA
testing given by Dr. Robin Cotton in her testimony,
Windham chipped away at it. He had the same problem John Gilligan had faced—trying to educate the
jury, yet avoid totally confusing them with technical
terms. Any attorney trying to cope with the subject of
DNA does his best, and watches jurors' faces for tell-
tale signs: yawning, eyes glazing over, brows wrinkled
with confusion, all signals that it is time to switch
channels.

Windham summarized by asserting that mistakes
can be made in the testing process that can lead to
reasonable doubt. "Unless you know it was mistake
free, unless you know that, you cannot be certain that
this is his DNA. And without that certainty, you cannot
convict him of murder. You cannot give him a death
penalty."

Again Judge Connor hurriedly scribbled a note to
herself.

Wishing to repair any damage Gilligan had done
to testimony from Windham's last two witnesses, Dr.
Mueller and Dr. Berger, he said, "You did hear from
two experts who negated this case in its entirety. Com-

pletely." Dr. Mueller, he said, was the only expert in the field of "population genetics" to testify. Gilligan had referred to Mueller as "Dr. Fruit Fly," called him "the lone voice in the wilderness," and said he was a "hired gun."

Unhappy with those comments, Windham worded a more flattering picture. "He is not only a notable authority, he is called a lone wolf. I guess, if anything, he is the lone voice of sanity." No one, he asserted, had come forward to say that Dr. Mueller was wrong. Regarding the "hired gun" slam, Windham pointed out that all expert witnesses get paid for their work, including those who testify for the prosecution. As a "population geneticist," said Windham, "Dr. Mueller had shown that the statistics projected by Cellmark were being abused."

To illustrate the potential error in statistical projections, Windham cited the U.S. presidential election that took place the previous November. "Think about those television networks. They get together to use state-of-the-art statistical techniques to project the outcome of the votes so you will know as soon as possible after the polls close who won each state. And what were the projections? They showed that Al Gore was the winner in Florida. And what happened a few hours later? It looks like George W. Bush was the winner. So the statistical projections are just that, projections. They are not always right. And the only population geneticist you hear from told you these projections are not right."

Mueller had also talked about error rates. One mistake, noted Windham, can be extremely important. Cellmark Diagnostics, he said, had made a couple of errors. In the Davis case, they had lost the sample. In a completely different case, tried in San Diego, California, they had transposed the labels on samples. "They made a mistake. Not only did it get past the analyst, and the Cellmark expert who signed off on it, it got past Dr. Robin Cotton, and it got past the director of Cellmark labs. . . . Through the grace of God, somebody found the error in time to prevent the conviction. . . . The experts didn't catch it, and I am doing my best to catch something in this case."

Cellmark, the defender said, "apparently wants to convict Mr. Hunt. They want to make a match. They are willing to stretch the rules a little bit in order to get the match."

His other expert witness, Dr. Kenneth Berger, had stated that Cellmark had failed to "follow strict test standards" and failed to demonstrate the ability to ascertain when the tests will fail.

Seeking to bolster the reputation of both witnesses, Windham pointed out their credentials. "Two doctors, a doctor of biochemistry and a doctor who is a population geneticist. They had the courage to testify to you about what is wrong with this system. The prosecution can make light of Dr. Mueller and call him the fruit-fly man to diminish him, but his study is unrefuted here." The numbers derived by Cellmark, said Windham, "are not right."

Tackling the issue of corroboration, on which Gilligan had expounded, Windham sought to derail it. Suggesting there was no corroboration at all, he told jurors they should demand its presence. "And what would be corroboration here? Well, how about an admission or confession? What else? If there were fingerprints at a crime scene. How about hair? Somebody is intimate, has violent contact with another individual, you don't think there is some hair shed, some pubic hair or head hair transferred from one person to the other? How about an eyewitness? Somebody seeing the perpetrator leaving the scene, or bragging in a bar, or saying something in jail. How about possession of stolen property? Were things taken from these ladies? Does Mr. Hunt have any stolen property? No. Is there hair there? No. Did anyone see him there? No. There is nothing substantial to corroborate this evidence, and while DNA is really a miracle in many ways, it's not infallible. It's a scientific test operated by humans, who make mistakes."

The morning had been filled with a staggering load of facts and opinions. Judge Connor called for the lunch break, which everyone welcomed. Mark Windham would resume his soliloquy at 1:30 P.M.

Opening the afternoon session with a reminder that DNA tests are subject to error, Windham said, "If a person has an alibi, and the alibi is true, the DNA evidence is wrong." Spectators had been wondering when he would get to the alibi offered by Glenda Vale.

"In this case," said Windham, "there is no corroboration. Well, what about the other side, contradiction? Is there something that, if true, negates the DNA evidence? And yes, we have that here in the testimony of Glenda Vale, Mr. Hunt's sister-in-law." She had recalled that Hunt was home at about six-thirty or seven on the evening that Orloff died.

"Mr. Gilligan has suggested that the killing was probably at or before dinnertime. That makes sense because there is chicken in the sink ready to be prepared. It is not certain, but it makes sense. But does it make sense that Kenneth Hunt could commit a rape and murder, and be home between six-thirty and seven, all fresh and nice, and nothing is awry? Does it really make any sense? It just challenges the imagination to think that the crime could be accomplished within that time frame set by Glenda Vale, whose memory is quite good."

Windham said he was troubled by other allegations revealed in Vale's testimony. According to her, Detective Mounger had blocked Vale's efforts to tell police what she knew. This hinted that Mounger was overzealous and biased. "Glenda Vale, on the other hand, is a very credible witness. . . . She has a good memory and can tell you when Kenneth came home. She's not lying to you. She's not saying he was home all weekend and never went out the door. That would be a lie. He did go out . . . and came back between six-thirty and seven. Does that give him time to commit the crime and get home after doing his errands? Not too likely. Not too likely." To Windham, the alibi presented reasonable doubt.

Seizing the opportunity to cast more doubt on Francene Mounger's objectivity, Windham said, "We know from the very beginning of this trial that her bias is clear. She has not acknowledged what everyone can see in this courtroom, that Kenneth Hunt is right-handed, even though she had an opportunity to see him write his name when he agreed to provide his blood for testing. Why is that? She had already talked with a coroner, and rightly or wrongly her understanding was that the assailant may have been left-handed." Admitting that Dr. Pena denied ever saying anything about the killer being left-handed, Windham noted, "The witnesses are in conflict. But then Detective Mounger tells you that, well, Dr. Pena had a covering over his mouth during the autopsy. Perhaps she didn't understand the words he spoke. So there is sort of a face-saving explanation for why the two stories don't jive." Perhaps, he said, Mounger was so close to the case it created a bias that interfered with her recollection of the events.

In Gilligan's argument, he had taken the defense to task for criticizing the DNA tests, yet failing to pursue an independent retest of the samples. Windham countered with a different logic. "If the samples were contaminated from day one, if this has Kenneth Hunt's DNA in it because a few molecules of his blood got into those [semen] samples, and I retest it with any method, and I get the same result, I am giving false confirmation of their tests. . . . As Mr. Hunt's lawyer, I refuse to be in the position of falsely confirming his guilt. The burden of proof is on the prosecutor."

After recapping salient points he'd already made, Windham moved on to the definition of reasonable doubt. "It is not a mere possible doubt because everything relating to human affairs is open to some possible or imaginary doubt. It is that state of the case which after the entire comparison and consideration of all the evidence leaves the minds of the jurors in that condition that they cannot say they feel an abiding conviction of the truth of the charge." One must ask, he said, "a week from today, a month from today, ten years from today, can you say that your conviction still abides?"

Windham paused, tilted his head, appearing to be pondering each word. "He's presumed innocent. No matter what you think of him for what he did in the past, he's presumed innocent. The contrary just hasn't been proved. This test is not reliable enough for a murder conviction, certainly not for the death penalty.

"Ladies and gentlemen, it is your duty under the law to acquit Kenneth Hunt. He is not proved guilty. He is not guilty. Thank you."

Judge Connor had made notes to herself several times. She added to them once more during the last moments of Windham's speech. She turned to the jurors and said, "To the extent that some references in Mr. Windham's argument—he made reference to the quality of the evidence and the death penalty. You are not deciding the death penalty right now. OK? That's irrelevant. Irrelevant. You are deciding the guilt, and that's all you are deciding." The prosecution had not objected to his mention of the death penalty, which didn't belong in arguments for the guilt phase, so Judge Connor had sustained her own objection.

She turned to Laura Jane Kessner and said, "Ms. Kessner, you're on."

Kessner took on the duty of rebutting Mark Windham's argument. In her soft, soprano voice, she exuded youthful vigor and honesty.

"Good afternoon, ladies and gentlemen of the jury. I know it's been a long day. I will try and be concise and to the point."

Mentioning again the burden of proof being with the prosecution, she thanked them and reiterated the judge's comments. "The court made the first point I was going to make, which is to remind you of the ground rules here. . . . This is *guilt*. We're not at penalty. And I know this may seem obvious to you, but there are certain things you can consider and certain things you cannot consider." She reminded them that this was the time to weigh testimony, evidence, witness credibility, and then enter their deliberations according to jury instructions. "You cannot consider penalty or punishment, nor can you be swayed by passion, sentiment, or sympathy for the defendant.''

After outlining a few more rules and guidelines, Kessner accused the defense of using generalities and loaded words to argue their case. "Words like 'contamination' and 'degradation.' Where is the specific evidence there were any real problems in this case? We're not talking hypotheticals here. We are talking about whether or not he killed Jean Orloff and Myra Davis.

"The defense brings up multiple issues. The DNA is bad . . . somehow the sample was contaminated, or there is an alibi, or everyone in the people's case is biased. The coroner's office is biased. Nick Sanchez is biased. Robin Cotton is biased. Everyone is biased against the defendant.

"The bottom line is, there is no evidence to refute any of our testing or any of our evidence in this case. About contamination, how is it possible in this case? Nick Sanchez said clearly that he examined the blood samples and the swabs on different days. They are packaged separately. You heard all about the steps he took in his lab to clean surfaces, to wear gloves. There is simply no possibility that could have happened.

"Cellmark analyzed the evidence, also at different times. When Mr. Hunt's blood was drawn, it wasn't even in the same physical location as when the swabs were taken from the victims. There is simply no chance for contamination.

"Mr. Windham talked about how Cellmark lost a sample. Big deal, ladies and gentlemen. We told you about that from the beginning. What does it really mean? If anything, it could have benefited the defendant. But fortunately, we had more of the sample left for testing.

"The defense implies that Cellmark somehow has a bias here, and brings up subjectivity like there is some way they could have changed the results to fit Mr. Hunt's profile. Both Mr. Sanchez and Dr. Cotton knew nothing about this case. They knew nothing about Mr. Hunt. What did they care? They are independent labs. Cellmark is completely independent. They would have been paid anyway."

Bringing up the allegation that a criminalist had found no sperm on the swabs in 1988, Kessner challenged the statement. "The technician did not even look at the swabs, and she wasn't looking for anything related to DNA analysis. In 1988, DNA technology was not the same as it is now. She was never looking at evidence for the purpose of determining whether or not there was the possibility of DNA testing."

Kessner refuted attacks Windham had made on the methods and means of DNA testing, as well as the statistical analysis. "The defense throws out a reference to the Florida election. That is designed to confuse and mislead. There is no relevance to what happened in Florida to what is here today in this case." The defense witnesses, Dr. Mueller and Dr. Berger, she said, were not experts about DNA. "Just because you have a Ph.D. doesn't mean you are an expert, and that is clear by their testimony." On the other hand, said Kessner, Dr. Cotton had provided valid, credible information about the entire process. "Whether it was bad for Cellmark or good . . . she just said it like it is.

"Ladies and gentlemen, let's talk about this alibi. Let's get real about this alibi. We have someone who is clearly biased, the sister-in-law of the defendant. She lived with Mr. Hunt and her sister, his wife. I mean if anyone has a bias, a motive, it's her, not Detective Mounger. And isn't it convenient that no one hears about this alibi until three years later? Is it believable that if a family member were in jail, and you knew you could clear them, you wouldn't bother to pick up the phone and call the detective to tell them what you knew? It's a very convenient alibi.

"The bottom line is, the evidence is corroborated. As Mr. Gilligan showed you, these crimes corroborate each other. We know that it was one person that committed all these crimes. We know we have DNA evidence that is reliable and consistent, and you know that he has a history of sexual misconduct.

"Ladies and gentlemen, don't be misled. Don't be confused by loaded words that are not backed up by hard evidence.

"We began this by telling you how fortunate we are even to be here. So many things went wrong. But in the end, it was the defendant who left behind evidence that will convict him. It was the evidence taken from the women he strangled, that he raped and controlled, women that couldn't scream because of the ligature he planned and used to kill them. But fortunately, it was those women that contained the evidence to convict him.

"Thank you for your time and your attention. We urge that you find him guilty on all counts and all allegations.

"Thank you."

Seven men and five women retired to a room provided for them at 4:00 P.M., on Tuesday, March 13, 2001, to weigh the evidence and consider a verdict in the case of the *People v. Kenneth Dean Hunt.*

Twenty-four

On Thursday, March 15, sober-faced jurors filed into their rows of chairs and took their seats without looking at Kenneth Hunt. One of them, alternate juror number six, was absent due to illness. A packed gallery watched in silence, as did the assembled attorneys. Hunt, with his right elbow on the table and hand to the side of his face, stroked his jaw.

After discussing the case Tuesday evening, reconvening, and deliberating all day Wednesday and most of Thursday morning, the jury had taken a final vote. Just before noon, they sent a message to Bailiff Bond Maroj to notify the court they had reached a verdict.

Lois Bachrach sat in the second row of bench seats, her fingers crossed, near Barbara Kappedal. Sherry Davis, working on a television series, was unable to attend. There was a touch of irony in the title of the show, *Crime Scene Investigation.*

Dora Green and her daughter Betty Hunt sat in the back row, tense and nervous.

Judge Connor asked if they had reached a unanimous verdict, to which the foreperson stood and said they had, then handed the forms to Maroj. He carried them to Stacey Vickers, who read the verdict aloud.

Kenneth Dean Hunt was guilty of two first-degree murders. All three special circumstances, rape, burglary, and multiple murder were true.

From the back of the courtroom came a shriek. Betty Green was sobbing, "He didn't do it! They lied!" Then she collapsed on the floor.

Bailiffs rushed to her aid and Judge Connor ordered the courtroom cleared.

Reporters hurried outside to file stories.

When the pandemonium had run its course, and the court was reassembled, Judge Connor ordered the lawyers and jurors to return on Monday, March 19, to begin the penalty phase.

Bailiff Maroj escorted Kenneth Hunt through a side door to await the trial in which his fate, life in prison without parole, or death by execution, would be decided.

John Gilligan and Laura Jane Kessner took an elevator upstairs to their seventeenth-floor offices, where they began making arrangements for witnesses to appear the following week. Plans had already been made for the process, on the assumption Hunt would be found guilty. Kessner, while fully dedicated to continuing with the prosecution, also had something else to think about. She had just discovered she was pregnant with her first child.

Mark Windham returned to his office across the street. He would later say, "The toughest challenge in this case was believing I could save Kenneth Hunt's life. I sensed and acknowledged the enormity of the victims' families' losses, and understood in my heart how difficult it was for them. And I also understood the need and reason for mercy. I had to keep reminding myself that it could be done."

Jurors had obviously believed the DNA evidence and had rejected any alibi offered on behalf of Hunt. Four weeks earlier, while they had been questioned during jury selection, most of them had stated they would be able to arrive at a verdict of death in the penalty phase if the aggravating circumstances outweighed mitigating circumstances. Now that resolve would be put to the test.

Sherry Davis later recalled, "When the guilty verdict first came in, no one contacted me. I was on the set of a show, *Crime Scene Investigation,* and somebody paged me before John Gilligan left a message on my home phone. So a friend of mine heard the verdict on the radio and paged me. I felt relieved that Hunt had been convicted, but really dreaded the penalty trial."

Hard facts, forensic evidence, and DNA had been presented in the guilt phase. Now it would be time to hear about the forces that drove Kenneth Hunt to kill two innocent women—two victims who had trusted him to deliver Avon products and to perform handyman services in their homes. Why would a young married man, whose wife and mother-in-law appeared to love him deeply, who had already served prison time for manslaughter, sink into the abyss of rape and murder? Sherry Davis hoped for answers. So did Lois Bachrach and Jean Orloff's family, along with her friends. It would be their duty to testify in a phase called "victim impact" to tell jurors how the tragic loss of the two victims had devastated them.

On Monday morning, March 19, twelve jurors and four of the original six alternates waited eagerly in the conference room to learn what had driven Kenneth Hunt to kill two women.

Alternate juror number five had been excused from
further service. She had previously informed the court
she could serve only a limited time. Alternate number
six would not be there, either. Judge Connor, knowing
the woman was ill, attempted to reach her by telephone. She heard the stunning news that the woman
had passed away over the weekend. Connor made the
decision not to burden the other jurors with such de-
pressing information.

With the seven men, five women, and four remaining alternates seated in the box, and before allowing
the prosecutor to make opening statements, Connor
addressed the jurors. "Good morning. We lost alternate number five because she could stay only a certain
length of time. As to alternate number six, I will let
you know more about her condition, but we are going
to be proceeding without her.

"We will start with opening statements. This part
of the trial is different. We are not dealing with
whether guilt or innocence is proven, but with the
weighing of factors, aggravation versus mitigation. . . .
If you feel the aggravation is so substantial, compared
to the mitigation, then death might be appropriate. . . . You have the choice. The law is not going
to tell you what to do. It's not going to be that easy."
Conversely, if the mitigating circumstances weighed
more, in the jury's opinion, they could deliver a verdict of life in prison without the possibility of parole.

What the judge didn't say is that the jury's verdict
is really nothing more than a strong recommendation.
It's not a widely known fact. In California, the judge
in a capital murder trial has the option to overturn
the jury's penalty phase verdict of death if the evidence, in the judge's opinion, is not strong enough

to merit the death penalty, and deliver a sentence of life in prison without parole. It is seldom exercised, but it remains an option.

"We will start off with prosecution witnesses," said Connor. "They are here to persuade you . . . that the appropriate penalty is death. The defense witnesses will be here on behalf of Mr. Hunt, even though the defendant has been convicted of two counts, and special circumstances are true, that the appropriate penalty is not death but life without the possibility of parole. . . . Those are the only two choices you have.

"Mr. Gilligan."

John Gilligan rose, and spoke no more than ten minutes. He told the jurors he would present testimony as provided in a penal code to show three factors: A) circumstances of the murders, B) criminal activity by the defendant involving the use of force, violence, or threat of force or violence, and C) previous felony convictions. He also would call Sherry Davis, Lois Bachrach, and Barbara Kappedal to the stand to describe the impact on their lives caused by the two murders. There would be several other witnesses as well.

"I will ask you to remember and consider some of the things you have already heard." He named each of the six women who had identified Hunt as the man who attacked and groped them in broad daylight on city streets, and summarized the incidents.

"And there is evidence you have not yet heard that we will ask you to consider. You will hear from Kenneth Hunt's own sister, Gina. She will tell you when she was a little girl, and Mr. Hunt was a teenager, he would force her to orally copulate him by bending her arm behind her back until she complied with his wishes.

"You heard reference earlier to the defendant's prior conviction for voluntary manslaughter in 1992. You will hear the facts of that crime and you will hear from the widow of Mr. Bernard Davis . . . how Mr. Davis died." Gilligan briefly recapped what happened on the day Hunt struck the frail little man, and how he died a few days later.

"Also, you will hear in 1996, Mr. Hunt had a relationship with a woman named Tina Moore and that he assaulted her. You will see evidence of that assault in the form of photographs that were taken when Mr. Hunt was in custody."

Gilligan said he would also present facts about a 1985 burglary conviction against Hunt.

Advising them that they would be presented with evidence in mitigation by the defense, Gilligan said, "I will ask you to look at the evidence critically . . . and see if it really is mitigation that is any way substantial when compared to the aggravation. Because it's your decision, ladies and gentlemen. You decide what weight to give the factors. The law lists them, but it doesn't tell you which are the most important. You've got to decide for yourselves as a group, what is important, what is real aggravation and what is real mitigation.

". . . I am confident that at the end you will be convinced that . . . the only appropriate penalty will be the maximum penalty. Thank you."

Gilligan had followed the strategy of most prosecutors in death penalty cases. That is, open with brief, to-the-point comments, saving the powerful, emotion-packed words until the closing argument.

Mark Windham, on the other hand, spoke extensively to lay the groundwork for his plan. He would show the jury that his client's behavior stemmed from traumatic events during childhood, including abuse, being deprived of parental love, and by a system that not only failed to provide mental-health treatment he desperately needed, but victimized him with unwarranted incarceration.

Opening with a power punch to the midsection, Windham said, "Ladies and gentlemen of the jury, I *disagree* with your verdict!

"The DNA evidence that you heard in this case is not infallible. It's not corroborated in any substantial way, and I do not believe that it was sufficient for proof beyond a reasonable doubt. And I hope that you don't believe that it's sufficient to impose a death penalty."

Repeating his disagreement with the verdict, he said, with some apparent reluctance, "But I accept it."

His words rang loud and clear in the courtroom. Jurors seemed especially attentive. "We turn now to what I believe is the most important part of this trial, the determination of whether Kenneth Hunt should be put to death or given life in prison without the possibility of parole. In order to make this decision, I want to give you a bigger picture of his whole life, not just his crimes, but the entire life of this human being, including the inhuman episodes he endured during his childhood. Only then will you see how he came to be in the position he is in today, accused of two terrible murders, convicted of those murders and begging for his life.

"Gordon Hunt is Kenneth Dean Hunt's father. And

when he was just out of the navy, he liked to drink and take drugs. When he married Kenneth's young mother, Elyse, and when Kenneth was born up north, Gordon Hunt was still married to another young woman.

"When Kenneth was born, his father was in jail for failure to pay child support from yet another relationship." Soon after, said Windham, Hunt Sr. went to work, while Elyse worked in her mother's dry cleaning shop near San Jose. The couple divorced, but Elyse delivered another child on Christmas Eve, 1972, a daughter they named Gina. Little Kenneth had even waited to open his presents until his new sister came home.

"As an infant," the defender said, "he was all right. As soon as he could walk, he became a very difficult child, and the response from his dad was exactly wrong. Gordon Hunt was a drinker and he lost his temper frequently and turned to violence, striking Kenneth with his open hand. And this did nothing to change Kenneth's temperament, but it did help to form his character.

"Gordon Hunt reports that he almost killed Kenneth twice, and now he wishes his son had died. That is his father's feeling about him. The hatred he focused on his son for some reason was palpable. He divorced Elyse . . . because of Kenneth. That is what he said in a probation interview. And the divorce was very bitter, with Elyse moving back to San Jose, to Santa Clara County with the kids. And for some reason, Gordon Hunt [went] to northern California, kidnapped his boy, and brought him to southern California.

"The boy is shuttled back and forth between the

parents, depending on their particular circumstances
at the time. The probation department described
Elyse as an incompetent parent who left him in an
unstructured life situation where he was largely on his
own, unsupervised. But after the divorce was settled,
Gordon Hunt got custody and he remarried. He married a woman named Barbara, Kenneth's new stepmother.

"Kenneth had become a very, very difficult child.
He was in school now. And Los Angeles city schools,
when he was nine years old, diagnosed him as having
a mental illness.

"Meanwhile, Barbara's daughter, Karen, reported
that Gordon Hunt, Daddy, would try to spy on her
when she got undressed and offered to pay her for
naked photographs. He kept sexually oriented maga-
zines lying around and would give sexually suggestive
gifts.

"The boy was so out of control at age nine, that
he was brought to Cedars-Sinai Hospital for psychological treatment. He got it from Dr. Fleming for
about four months. After that, Gordon Hunt and his
wife decided to stop the treatment. But young Kenneth was not well. He would have bowel movements
in his bed at age nine. Did his father take him back
to Cedars-Sinai? No. Did he get another doctor? No.
He decided, and he reported, that Kenneth was just
too lazy to get up and use the bathroom, that is why
he defecated in his bed.

"So he did not get any more treatment. His dad
got so angry with him he almost killed him a couple
of times. And Kenneth kept getting sick and would
vomit at the dinner table. . . . Gordon Hunt made
his boy stop vomiting. He *fed* him his own vomit. He

fed him his own vomit. He bragged about it to the probation department. He had a sense of satisfaction for stopping the boy's behavior without psychological help.

"So Kenneth would run away, repeatedly, from his home. And the police would pick him up and ask why he ran away. And he said, 'My father beats me up every day.' The police checked his body and didn't see any bruises, so they brought him back home to Dad, to Gordon Hunt.

"Well, the behavior continued. Vomiting, defecating in his bed, lighting matches, burning things, cutting things, running away. Finally, his father had him committed. Los Angeles County-USC Hospital took in Kenneth Hunt at twelve years old. He lived there at L.A. County-USC Hospital, downtown, in the mental ward.

"But at age twelve, Kenneth Dean Hunt didn't have just a psychological problem. He had a sexual problem, a sexually assaultive disorder, and L.A. County-USC reported that this twelve-year-old boy was leading the other children in sex play, that he was having the other children copulate him, getting oral sex from the children in the ward.

"Where did he learn that behavior? Did he pick it up himself? The hospital could not handle this boy with a special disorder, so he went to a special treatment program at Sylmar. It was a juvenile hall, a jail facility. Because of his incorrigibility and truancy, he was in the juvenile court system. And the special treatment program at Sylmar really offered some hope. It was a novel program; it was staffed by psychologists, using the latest methods, a ninety-day program. That's right. The state-of-the-art psychological methods for ninety days.

"So they took in twelve-year-old Kenneth and noted this boy has suffered powerful trauma. Because of abandonment by his parents, it will be difficult for him to be treated, since he will be reluctant to form an attachment with his therapist. He needs daily psychiatric care. Twelve years old, he needs daily psychiatric care. And he got it for three months. And then a fourth month. And he started to improve.

"But this boy who is so mistrustful because of his abandonment issues is again abandoned at age thirteen. His program ended after one hundred twenty days. Never again during his childhood was he to receive psychiatric care. He was sent instead to whatever agency would take him. So they sent him out to Redlands, the Guadalupe Home for Boys. No daily psychiatric care.

"After a few weeks, he ran away and he got some help then from Mom. Mom reappeared. This is Elyse. She lived up in Fremont, in the southern part of Alameda County near San Francisco Bay.

"So he joined his mother and her new husband, and little Gina, six years old. He is thirteen and she is six, and with their mom. He is under Los Angeles court's jurisdiction. When he ran away, did the court bring him back to L.A.? No. The probation officer in charge recommended against it. Why? The officer wrote, 'When Kenneth Hunt reoffends, and he will reoffend, he is going to be Alameda County's problem, not Los Angeles County's.' Did the officer or the court inform Elyse that Kenneth had a sexually assaultive disorder, that he would be incorrigible without daily psychiatric care? No, they didn't tell her. And actually, he got along all right for a while. For about four months, he was going to school.

"But after that, Elyse's husband came home one afternoon to find Kenneth forcing his little sister to give oral sex and he found out this had been going on, that [Kenneth] had been having sexual relations of this nature with his sister. So did he tell his wife, Elyse, Kenneth's mother, the girl's mother? You would think so. Elyse says no; she didn't know that her husband had found them and uncovered this sexual relationship. Did he tell a doctor? No. Did he get him treatment? No. Did he tell the police? No. Did he tell the probation officer from L.A.? No.

"But having been discovered, shamed, and humiliated, Kenneth Dean Hunt tried again to run away. He broke into the garage; he took some money; he took a bicycle. He rode away. And when he was picked up by the police, his mother had him placed under arrest for residential burglary, for taking the bicycle. There is no need to discuss the problem of sex with his sister because she had him arrested for the burglary.

"Kenneth got shipped back to L.A., back to juvenile hall. And did Elyse ever see her son? Did she ever visit him? No. Did she ever see him again? No. Tomorrow, when she testifies, she will see him for the first time in twenty years!

"So Kenneth Hunt is in juvenile hall. Nobody knows about the sex disorder. He is not getting treatment. And Dad at first promises him that he can come back home when he is done with juvenile hall. But his dad stops visiting. He stopped writing. And when mail call came, the other boys got mail. Kenneth didn't get any mail. On visiting day, when the other kids got visits from their parents, Kenneth didn't get any visits. Even though the other boys were bad, they got visits. He didn't get any visits, so he must have been worse. No visits from Mom, no visits from Dad.

"Until one day his dad came, supervised by the probation officer. Dad came in and said to Kenneth, 'I hate you. I no longer want you to be my son.' And Gordon Hunt kept his word. He never saw his son again. And when he testifies tomorrow, it will be the first time that he is seeing Kenneth Hunt in twenty years.

"The father sent a letter to the probation department refusing to take him in. Because Kenneth's time was up in juvenile hall, he had to go somewhere. He was still a child at fourteen. So he was sent to whoever would take him. He was taken in by the Pacific Lodge home for boys, over in Woodland Hills in the valley where Kenneth stayed until September 25, 1981. That's when two young boys ran away from Pacific Lodge. One of them was Kenneth Dean Hunt, age fifteen, about five foot eight inches tall. The other boy was Joe Cardenas.

"After four days of living on the streets of the valley, they made it all the way across to Canyon Country. On September twenty-ninth, as these two boys sat on a grassy hilltop overlooking Canyon High School, they talked to each other. And fifteen-year-old Kenneth was very angry. Why? Because although he had a mother and a father, he could no longer live with them. They refused to take him back from juvenile hall. He had to live in this foster home, this group home for boys known as Pacific Lodge."

To stress the emotional damage, Windham took jurors through repetition of the "no visits" part of his speech again. The jury had heard it in his opening statements during the penalty phase, but listened with rapt attention. "He was angry at his dad, his step-mother, and his mom. That is what he told Joe Cardenas.

"As they talked, and Kenneth's anger grew, a girl walked by, fifteen-year-old Arlene Logan. Boiling over like a forgotten pot on the stove, boiling with anger, he saw the girl and said, 'Let's get her.'

"The two boys ran down the hill. Kenneth grabbed Arlene; he pulled her down, pulled off her top, started grabbing her breasts, and covered her mouth as she yelled. And then he stopped. He stopped and ran away.

"Kenneth was arrested, adjudicated, and sent to California Youth Authority at age fifteen, and that's where Kenneth Hunt spent the rest of his childhood.

"The adulthood that you have heard about, and that you will hear about today, followed the childhood, which I have described to you. A childhood during which Kenneth Dean Hunt never healed and never escaped."

As suddenly as he had started, Windham wheeled around, strode to his chair, and sat down.

Judge Connor uttered a quick thank-you. "Call your first witness."

Twenty-five

The first two witnesses were women with whom Kenneth Hunt had engaged in sex, and neither of them was his wife.

As Tina Moore settled into the chair, Judge Connor thought she looked a little pale and unsteady. "Are you OK?" the judge asked.

"I just recently got out of the hospital," said Moore. "So I am a little weak."

"If you need to stop," said Connor, "let us know."

Laura Jane Kessner greeted Moore and asked if she knew [Kenneth] Sonny Hunt. Moore said she did. "How do you know him?" asked Kessner.

"We dated six to eight months."

"I want to take you back to 1986. Is that when you had a dating relationship with him?"

"Yes—I believe it was '96," Moore answered, speaking barely above a whisper.

"I'm sorry, 1996. How did you meet the defendant?"

"He had given me a ride. It was sprinkling rain about eleven o'clock at night. He gave me a ride to my home."

"And you said you had a relationship about six months?"

"Yes, we did."

"Can you tell us what happened?"

"Well, we had an argument because I found out he was married."

"Tell us, what happened during that argument?"

"Ulm, well, I had a couple of drinks. But then I knew he was living with a lady, but like a friend in the same home. And I don't remember how I found out he was married, but it turned out he was. And I was ranting and raving. That is when he backhanded me across the bridge of my nose." At Kessner's request to demonstrate, Moore swept her left hand outward from the center of her chest.

"Just like that. And he hit the bridge of my nose. Of course, he's a big guy and a tall man."

"How tall were you and how much did you weigh then?"

"I was about a hundred to a hundred and five, five feet four. And I believe he's about six feet."

Kessner introduced a photograph into evidence, picturing Moore from the waist up, wearing a sleeveless white T-shirt with an American flag on the front. The flesh around both of her eyes was bruised purple and black. Her nose appeared to be bright red. She held a placard in front of her, giving her name, Hunt's name, a brief description of her injuries, and the name of Parole Officer John Widener. Moore acknowledged the picture was of her.

"Does this photo reflect the injuries you received as a result of this argument?"

"Yes, it does."

"Can you describe for the jury what your injuries were?"

"Like I said, he backhanded me, hit me right across the bridge of my nose. That's obviously why I have raccoon eyes. Everything happened so fast. If I had other bruises, I don't remember that part of it."

Kessner thanked the witness and gave her to Mark Windham, who greeted her courteously before asking, "On the date of that incident, you had been drinking, right?"

"Correct."

"And you were drunk, weren't you?"

"I don't believe I was drunk. I was upset."

"Do you recall speaking with my investigator in January of this year?"

"Vaguely."

"Do you recall telling him you were drunk that night?"

Stammering in a weak voice that faded even more as she spoke, Moore tried to answer. "Again, like I said, I remember having—it wasn't—don't believe it was—"

"You were drunk, weren't you?"

"The night of this January when I spoke with the investigator—or—or, no, the night of this . . . ?"

"The night of the incident. In June 1996, you were drunk?"

"I'd had a few drinks, yes."

"And you were drunk?"

"And I was upset. I don't believe I was drunk. I was upset and that's why I was ranting and raving."

"Mr. Hunt told you that he had to end the affair, didn't he?"

"That . . . I don't remember him telling me. I remember confronting him about the fact—about the lady, when I had found out the lady he was living with turned out to be his wife."

Growing impatient, Windham said to the judge, "Motion to strike. Nonresponsive."

Judge Connor agreed. "It is stricken. Just listen to the question."

Windham asked, "You recall speaking with Parole Officer Widener about this on June 17, don't you?"

"Yes."

"And after you told him what happened, you placed your signature on a statement, didn't you?"

"Yes, I did."

Windham produced the document and read aloud from it. "Because I was drinking and Kenneth told me he wants to cut off our relationship and that he's going back to his wife. . . . You wrote that part, didn't you?"

"Obviously, yes."

"So after he told you he had to end the affair and he was going back to his wife, you slapped him, didn't you?"

"Probably did. I don't remember slapping him. But I—again, like I said, I was upset."

From the document, Windham read aloud another admission that Moore had slapped Hunt. "We started arguing, and I'd had some drinks. So, therefore, I slapped him and he slapped me back." He asked, "When he told you he was ending the affair, and going back to his wife, you hit him in the groin, didn't you?"

"I don't remember that."

"You wrote: 'Because I was drinking and Kenneth had told me that he wants to cut off our relationship and that he's going back to his wife, I kneed him in the groin, and he responded with a back hand to my left eye, causing a bruise.' That's your signed statement from June 17, 1996, isn't it?"

"That—that is my signature, yes."

"And that's what you told the police officer, isn't it?"

"I—like I—I don't remember. It's been so long."

"You were convicted in 1993 of a misdemeanor, weren't you?"

"I believe."

Laura Jane Kessner rose to object to the question as not relevant to the issue. Windham offered a quick explanation that he was trying to introduce "moral turpitude." At a sidebar with the judge, Kessner wanted to know what Windham meant. He explained, "It's prostitution. She has other [offenses] that I won't go into. Possession crimes, but those are not moral turpitude. Although if the court will allow me, I'll go into those as well." His purpose was to undermine the credibility of the witness by demonstrating her moral turpitude, or shameful behavior.

Kessner commented, "The only thing that could possibly be moral turpitude would be prostitution . . . and he doesn't have any sort of facts about it. The conviction, in and of itself, is not admissible. It was a misdemeanor. . . ."

Windham volunteered that "she'll admit that she committed the act."

Judge Connor thought for a moment, then said, "If she admits it, it's not a problem."

Addressing the witness again, Windham asked, "Ms. Moore, you committed prostitution in 1993?"

Regaining some indignant volume to her voice, Moore shot back, "No. It was . . . No!"

Perhaps out of compassion for a woman who had been a victim of life's vicissitudes, Windham decided to drop it. "All right. Thank you. Nothing further."

Kessner announced, "The people call Gina Blake." Hunt's sister, now a twenty-seven-year-old strawberry blonde, dressed in a black suit, took the oath.

After establishing the relationship, and a few facts about their parents' divorce, Kessner asked, "At the time you lived in the same household with the defendant in this case, about how old was he?"

"I think Kenny is seven years older than me. I was in the first grade, about six, I guess. So that puts him, I think, thirteen. I'm not real positive." Her estimates were correct.

"And around that time . . . I assume that there's a big difference in size. Do you remember him being bigger than you?"

"Yeah, because, you know, I'm all of three feet tall at that point, I guess. Kenny always seemed a lot bigger to me. I thinks there's pictures where he's probably twice as tall as I am."

"Tell us, when you were living in that household with the defendant, did something happen?"

"Kenny was in charge of picking me up from school and watching me until my mother came home, and during that time, he took advantage of me by forcing me to have oral sex with him."

"Tell us how this would happen."

"Details are sketchy, but as I recall, it was after school. No one else would be home. I don't remember what he used to get me to do it, like what threat, I guess we could say. But he would turn the microwave on. There was a timer on the microwave. And I had to do these [acts] for so long. Then I could stop."

"What did you have to do?"

"I had to perform oral sex on him."

"And did you perform oral sex on him?"

"Yes."

"And why did you do it?"

"He forced me to. I don't remember why—what he used to force me, but at that time, I was under whatever impression that I had to do it." Gilligan's opening statement had mentioned Kenneth twisting the little girl's arm behind her. If that was the case, she apparently had forgotten it.

"Did he say things to you?"

"He did, but I don't recall at this point what they were."

"And you felt you had to do this?"

"Yes."

"And when he set the microwave, what did that mean?"

"It meant I had to perform oral sex for [a] certain amount of time until I could stop, because I wasn't willing to do this. I was being forced to do it and I would complain. And, OK, you know, at least the timer, there was an end coming, and that's what he used to—"

"When you said you complained, what would you say?"

"I don't recall. I just—I know that I didn't want to do it. I can remember that vividly, but I don't remember what I said."

"How long did this go on?"

"My perception of time is a little skewed, but it could have been a week; it could have been several

months. I don't recall how long he lived with us. . . .
It was at least three or four occasions when this happened. I was . . . on afternoons when I came home
from school, but I don't know specific dates."

"How did it end?"

"As I recall, my stepfather came home and walked
in and caught us in the act . . . and kind of made a
stink and sent Kenny away . . . and tried to sort it all
out. And after that, Kenny moved out. Nothing else
was really said about it."

Kessner thanked the witness. "No further questions."

On cross-exam, Mark Windham showed Blake some
photographs of her and Hunt taken when they were
children, but she couldn't remember where they were
taken. She verified photos of her mother and stepfather, and said they were now divorced.

After a few questions about her real father and her
parents' divorce, Windham asked if Blake had reason
to believe her mother had been told about the oral
sex incidents. Blake said that was true. "And shortly
after this all took place, your brother Kenneth was
arrested, right?"

"I believe so."

"But he was not arrested for what he did to you?"

"No." She had never spoken to the police about
it, nor had she received any treatment or therapy related to the sexual encounters.

"Did your mother ever talk to you about it?"

"No, she would not. But she didn't know about it,
according to her."

Blake left the witness chair with her head held
high. She had been an innocent child when she was

sexually abused by her brother, and had nothing to be ashamed of.

Kenneth Hunt had served time in prison for voluntary manslaughter after having slugged a frail, diminutive man named Bernard Davis, who later died from traumatic injuries he suffered. Now it was time for the jury to hear details from his still grieving widow, Shirley Davis.

In her early seventies, the tiny, gray-haired woman, wearing a light blue suit, seemed nervous and disoriented. Laura Jane Kessner gently led her through the questioning. The witness said her late husband was born on July 28, 1924, and they had been married forty-two years.

"Can you tell us what happened on the day of March 6, 1992?"

Her voice trembling, Davis said, "We were walking toward the market, and the defendant was walking the opposite way. And he had a cocker spaniel with him. He was kicking it."

"Had you seen the defendant before this day?"

"Yes, the day before."

"And what did you see him do?"

"The same thing. He was kicking his dog."

"On the second occasion, what did you do?"

"Well, I told him, 'Don't do that. You shouldn't kick your dog.' "

"And you were with your husband?"

"Yes."

"What happened next?"

"The defendant got very angry and he started using offensive language. He said, 'It's my f-ing dog, I'll do what I like to him.' My husband told him to be quiet, because he knew I didn't like the *F* word. And the defendant came back at us, and first kicked at my shopping cart, which put a dent in it. I was grateful that I had a cart in front of me, or he might have injured me. And then he walked over to my husband and he socked him with his fist, and my husband fell down on the cement."

"Where did he hit your husband?"

"He hit him in the eye, but in so doing, he broke his cheekbone. He fell down and he hit his head. His right eye was closed and his cheekbone was bleeding."

Davis described the ensuing trip to the hospital and her husband's vain struggle for life during the following few days. She had been interviewed by the police and was able to identify Kenneth Dean Hunt as the assailant. When Kessner had completed her direct examination, the defense attorney said he had no questions.

Myra Davis's granddaughter, Sherry Davis, had testified during the guilt phase, but was now recalled to tell jurors how the loss of her grandmother had impacted her life. John Gilligan asked Davis to tell a little bit about the kind of woman Myra had been.

"She was an actress, and continued working in her later years," said Davis. "And she was always trying to make right of the wrongs. She was kind and generous. She would send money to a little boy in Vietnam, a little girl in Africa, a little girl of an Indian tribe." Davis would later describe Myra as very frugal in terms of spending money on herself, but compassionately generous to people in need. "As small as it was, every month she made sure that she sent money to those children. She was kind to her neighbors. If I recall, she even knitted baby clothes for Mr. Hunt's sister-in-law's children. She was very kind to Mr. Hunt's mother-in-law. And if there was a sick neighbor, she would take them soup or bake cookies for them."

"And what was your relationship like with your grandmother?"

"We were very close. I was the only grandchild living in the area. She also took care of her mother, my great-grandmother, until she passed away."

Gilligan posted on an easel several enlarged photos of Myra Davis, and took Sherry Davis through the events when she discovered the body. "Was there a difference, in terms of the impact on you, if she had died of natural causes as opposed to the way she was murdered?"

"Definitely. . . . On the day I found out she was dead and murdered, I was hysterical and shocked. I think the impact of her murder came later and has continued to impact my life to this day. . . . I'm the one who had to deal with the detectives. Also, I would like to say that at the time my grandmother was murdered, I was four months pregnant, and ten days later, I lost the baby. So I had to deal with that on top of all the other problems. And then, having to walk through her home with the detectives . . . and later I had to clean up her house, have it painted, and sell it."

The tragedy had also torn her family apart. "We actually don't see each other anymore. I think that memory is just too painful and some of them just don't want to talk about it. . . . My brothers couldn't come here. They just don't want to sit in the same courtroom with Mr. Hunt. So we just try to forget about it."

Davis spoke of the last time she had seen her grandmother alive, and how the loss deprived her children of having a loving great-grandmother. Myra, she said, had been vivacious and lively. "She was in great health and never complained about being sick. If she was sick, nobody knew about it. So there is definitely a loss. I think when you lose somebody to natural causes, you accept it as part of the cycle of life. But when someone you love is murdered, it just gets to your gut. You never forget about it. I can't even explain it to my children. Should they be afraid of their neighbors? It's something I'm going to have to deal with the rest of my life and the rest of my children's lives."

When Mark Windham took the witness, he didn't try to soften the impressions Davis had given the jury. On the contrary, he reinforced them by asking about her grandmother being an inspiration, a protective and generous woman and a valued member of the family.

Barbara Kappedal came next to tell of her friendship with Jean Orloff. They had known each other more than twenty years. The witness remembered Orloff's love for animals, especially the "very spoiled cat named Frankie." Kappedal said she had suffered because no one would believe her suspicions, after she had discovered the body, that Jean had been murdered. "It was like what I said didn't mean anything. It took away my empowerment, and I started having anxiety attacks. I would wake up during the night with pains in my chest that would go down to my arms. I'd be paralyzed with fear, and I would relive this whole thing and just see her lying there." The mental images tormented her. "There she was, nude, lying on her back. Seeing her face . . ."

The witness had undergone counseling to help her

cope with the psychological trauma. But nothing erased the horror. "It's something that is very isolating, and people want to hear the gory details . . . but they don't want to hear about how you feel." The counseling had helped, making it easier to "look more back at the good things about her instead of just seeing that horrible scene. And then I realized how much I missed her, because she was so much a part of my life. She would yell over the balcony, 'Barbara,'and we would talk. Or she would just stop by. There were so many things about her I just took for granted."

The defense had no questions for Barbara Kappedal.

The last prosecution witness on that Monday was Lois Bachrach, Jean Orloff's sister. In her cultured voice, Bachrach spoke with elegance. "Jeannie was a very youthful sixty-year-old with high energy. Very loving. We are a very, very close family, and Jeannie was kind of the glue. She always held everything together, always optimistic, always cheerful, and incredibly loving. She loved her job; she loved being with people and helping them. If you met her in a store, as a stranger in line at a checkout, she would always start a conversation. She was almost childlike in that she was a trusting soul and always thought there was good in everyone."

The poignant words echoed through the courtroom, raising goose bumps on the skin of spectators.

Bachrach spoke of the good times she and Jeannie enjoyed when spending time together with their mother. "We were kind of like the three musketeers."

One of the most important people in Jean's life, said Bachrach, was her grandson, Andrew McAllister. "Jeannie's daughter and Andy lived down in San Clemente, a good hour and a half by car. Jeannie used to go down there on weekends because she loved to be with Andy."

Replying to John Gilligan, Bachrach told of hearing, by telephone, that her sister was dead, and the horrifying events following.

"The first thing that went through my mind was how I was going to tell my mother. At first, I thought, 'I won't tell her; she is just not going to be able to handle this.' I had been so philosophical about my sister dying from natural causes. I said, 'Body parts give out, and it was her time, and she has gone to a better place.' I thought it was working pretty well. And then, to find out she had been murdered, I didn't know what I was going to tell my mother."

"Why didn't you bring your mother here today?"

"My mother, very slowly over a couple of months after my sister was murdered, slid into a very serious depression. That led to the development of physical ailments, and she was hospitalized for six weeks. And when she came out of the hospital, she wasn't my mother anymore. She is a shell of her former self. She requires round the clock, twenty-four-hour-a-day assistance at home. Usually, she calls me Jeannie, and that's really hard, because what can I say? Can I say, 'No, Mom, I'm Lois. Jeannie is dead'? So it's pretty hard. I've lost my sister and I've lost my mother. I guess I'm the last musketeer."

"What was the impact of Jeannie's murder on your family as a group?"

"Well, all of us have tried to keep her memory alive. We don't want to forget how wonderful she was. We don't want to sweep this under the rug. Holidays are solemn now and tarnished with our grief. They will never be the same." Orloff had always made rice pudding for Lois's birthday. "Now we never have rice pudding on my birthday. We will never have my mother's favorite cake that Jeannie made on her birthdays." Tears welled in Bachrach's eyes and her voice cracked. "This is hard. This isn't something you can handle. It's not like a problem and you have a solution and you are going to handle it. It's hard. . . . I will always miss the unconditional love my sister gave all of us."

Windham showed personal compassion in his brief cross-examination, allowing Bachrach to express how her family loved and missed the woman they all adored.

John Gilligan announced the prosecution would have no more witnesses. It would now be up to Mark Windham to convince the jury they should not recommend the death penalty for his client.

Twenty-six

Dora Green had been supportive of her son-in-law Kenneth Hunt through all of his problems, and continued to express deep affection for him despite everything. Observers wondered if his conviction for raping and murdering two women would change her outlook. She took the witness stand late Monday afternoon as the first defense witness in the penalty phase.

Mark Windham, after establishing the relationship of Green to Hunt, asked if she had known Myra Davis and Jean Orloff. Green said she did—Davis as a neighbor and Orloff as a client in her manicure business.

"Do you miss them?" asked Windham.

"Yes, I do."

"Now I'm going to ask you some questions about Kenneth Hunt. Has he been helpful to you personally?"

She said he had. "Years ago, when I had cataract surgery, I had to have eyedrops put in my eyes. Nobody would help me. They were squeamish. Sonny— we always called him Sonny, always put my eyedrops in. He'd help me. I had carpal tunnel syndrome. He'd cut my food for me."

"Did he help you after you had hand surgery?"

"My shower was leaking in my front bathroom and he decided to fix it. He went and bought a book, tore the whole thing apart, never did this before in his life, and figured out how to fix it, and got it almost finished."

"Was he working on that at the time he was arrested?"

"Yes, he was."

Hunt had also helped her elderly aunt with numerous chores, said Green. And he'd been especially attentive when Green's dog, Ursus, fell ill. On the subject of dogs, Windham asked, "Did Kenneth do anything for your dog Ginger?" Observers knew that Ginger was the cocker spaniel with Hunt during the confrontation with Bernard Davis and his wife.

"It was actually his and his wife's dog, but they lived with me. Ginger had very bad teeth, has lost most of them now. And Sonny used to brush her teeth." Windham produced a pencil drawing Hunt had made of the dog for Green to identify.

He asked if Ginger was a "yapper."

"She was when you walk with her. I got another little dog after Ursus, and if that dog would get in front of her, she would howl because she had to be in the lead. She is a spoiled little baby and she cries and yaps all the time."

"Would she be disobedient when she was being walked?"

"I wouldn't call her disobedient. It's just she wanted to be king of the hill, wanted to be in front."

To illustrate Hunt's skill with pencil drawing, part of the defense plan to show his worth as a person, Windham handed two more sketches to Green. One,

she said, was a portrait of her, and the other was his
rendering of himself and his wife at their wedding.

"You and your family are Jewish?"

"Yes."

"Did Kenneth convert to Judaism in order to marry
your daughter?"

"I don't believe he converted to marry my daughter. I believe he converted to make me happy."

"When you lived with him, did you ever feel fear of
him?"

"Never."

"Do you love him?"

"I love and adore him."

"Thank you. No further questions."

Laura Jane Kessner elicited from Green how long
she had known Hunt, when he married her daughter,
and that he had lived in her home much of the time
since then until he was arrested.

"So Kenneth Hunt was part of the family?"

"Yes, he was."

"And you still love him and supported him and
have felt this way about him as long as you've known
him, right?"

"Yes, I have."

"And even if he got in trouble, went to jail for
something, you still took him back into the home and
gave him a roof over his head, isn't that true?"

"Yes."

"Isn't it fair to say that you have treated him as
well as your own son?"

People with close knowledge of the case had heard
that hard feelings existed between Green and her son,
George, since Hunt had been arrested. It wasn't clear
how much she knew about George's call to Parole

Officer Widener. Dora Green's answer seemed to confirm the rumor. "I'd say that he's closer to me than
my own son."

"Have you helped him out financially?"

"Not really, no. Other than he ate the food in the
house, I feel Kenneth paid his way by fixing and doing
things in the house."

"And throughout this entire relationship, throughout the entire time that you have known him, you
have given him your support, haven't you?"

"Yes, I have."

"Thank you. No further questions."

Observers pondered Dora Green's answers. Apparently, she firmly believed that Kenneth Hunt was innocent of murder, despite the evidence and the jury's
verdict. And she seemed willing to forgive him in view
of evidence about an affair, with Tina Moore, that
ended with physical violence. No one knew whether
to admire her adamant faith in someone she believed
in, or question her judgment.

Jurors and spectators alike could take those questions and opinions home with them, as Judge Connor
called it a day.

Only four witnesses remained to be called by Tuesday morning, March 20, in Judge Connor's courtroom: Kenneth Hunt's mother, a probation officer,
Hunt's father, and a clinical psychologist.

Elyse Smith, Hunt's mother, led off the final inning.

She began by identifying for Mark Windham photographs of her son, daughter, and their father.

"How old were you when you met Gordon Hunt?"

"Sixteen." They were married in August 1965, she
said, and her son, Kenneth, was born on May 29,
1966.

Answering a series of questions posed by Windham about Hunt's father, Smith said he had served time in jail for failing to support a child born to another woman; he was a heavy drinker, though she wasn't certain about drug allegations, and he was emotionally abusive to her. After having another child on Christmas Eve, 1972, she eventually left him, she said, "because I pictured something better in my life than to stick with a man who was continually out with other women, was possibly doing drugs, drinking, and had a violent temper."

"This is kind of personal and private, but I think you understand why I have to ask you this. Did Gordon Hunt have any unusual sexual proclivities?"

"Well . . . he definitely liked sex. I mean, he liked pictures, women dressing that way."

"As far as liking pictures, did he keep pornography in the home?"

"Yeah, *Playboys* and . . ." Some observers would have argued that *Playboy* is not pornography.

"Did he leave that sort of material around the house?"

"All the time."

"Did he draw pictures of naked women?" In the gallery, someone mumbled, "So did every classic artist from Peter Paul Rubens to Henri Toulouse-Lautrec."

"I know that he drew a lot, and he was a . . . very good artist. You kind of shut down things you don't want to remember. I vaguely remember him drawing, you know, those kinds of pictures, but I really can't swear to it."

"Did he want you to dress in see-through clothing?"

"Yes, he did."

"Did he want other people to join in your sex?"

"He would have preferred it."

"Did you stay in Los Angeles for a while?"

"It seems to me I was there probably about six months."

"During that time, did you have custody of your two children?"

"Yes, I had both of them." Asked about child care for Kenneth, she had cloudy recollections of "an older lady" who "kept an eye on him."

After the move to northern California to live and work with her mother, Smith said, Gordon came for what she thought was a visit. Telling her he wanted to take his son out to fly a kite, he drove the boy back to Los Angeles with him. Soon after, the father gained legal custody through a court order.

"Did you feel that your son, Kenny, blamed you for this separation?"

"Oh, absolutely. He told me several times. He didn't want to have anything to do with me."

"So did you write to him when he was living with his father?"

"No, I'm not a great letter writer. I attempted to call, but I was told he didn't want to talk to me."

"When did you next see your son?"

"When he was about thirteen. He had gotten into some trouble in L.A. and somehow I agreed to bring him back into the family to try to help him straighten out."

She was remarried by then, she said. She received no official notification about the trouble Kenneth was in or about his stay in a hospital mental ward.

"Did anyone from the court or the probation department tell that when he was at L.A. County-USC

Hospital, he was making other children give him oral sex?"

Smith's eyebrows shot up. "He was making other children. . . ?"

"Yes."

"Absolutely not!"

"Did they tell you anything about his sexual disorder?"

"No, sir."

"So when you took him in, did you have any reason to take special precautions with your six-year-old daughter?"

"No. He loved his sister."

"Did your new husband ever tell you that he had interrupted Kenneth and his sister in a sexual act?"

"No, not to the best of my knowledge. He never mentioned that."

"Did Gina ever tell you?"

"Not until just a few years ago."

Kenneth, she said, ran away from home about four months after his arrival, after breaking into the garage and taking a bicycle.

"And he took three dollars, right?"

"OK. I mean, I know he had some change. I don't know how much it was."

Smith knew the boy had been arrested and sent back to Los Angeles. "Did you visit him in the L.A. juvenile hall?"

"No."

"And within a year, did you learn that he was ready to leave juvenile hall and needed a place to stay?"

"I never heard that."

"You did not receive an offer to take him back into your home?"

"No, sir." But she had received bills for the destruction he had caused in a radio station and his care in juvenile hall, approximately $10,000. She was unable to pay them.

"Did you come to learn that at age fifteen, he was sentenced to the California Youth Authority for sexual assault on a teenage girl?"

"I did hear that, but I don't remember how old he was." She hadn't visited him at CYA, she said, because she thought he was being held in southern California, not Stockton. There had been no exchange of mail between them, either.

"Did he send a gift to Gina?"

"I don't remember. But I've been told that he sent her a puppet."

Stepping softly into the cross-examination, John Gilligan said, "I know this is hard for you, so I am going to be brief." He inquired about Hunt's age at the time before she left the father, then asked, "Did his father ever sexually or physically abuse Kenneth, to your knowledge?"

"To the best of my knowledge, no."

"Did you ever see him physically discipline Ken?"

"Not to the point where it was abusive, but he did have a temper, and if [the child] was in the wrong, he would correct him."

"Did you love your son?"

"If I was given a chance to thoroughly love him, of course. I'm his mom."

"Do you think his father loved him?"

"Yes."

"You raised your daughter. . . . did she turn out to be a well-adjusted adult?"

"She is wonderful, yes."

"Did the court ever make any finding that you were an incompetent parent?"

"Absolutely not."

"Did you reject your son, Kenneth?"

"No."

"Did you try to contact him after he went to live with his father?"

"I initially tried. Kenny did not want anything to do with me."

"Is that because he blamed you for the divorce?"

"He blamed me for everything because of that."

Gilligan had let some of the air out of a balloon called abuse and desertion. Windham sought to apply some patches during his examination of the witness.

"When you were working at the phone company, and your son was about four years old, his father would be caring for the child and in charge of discipline, right?"

"Yeah."

"So you weren't always there when Gordon Hunt was taking care of the boy?"

"No."

"So you weren't always around to see what kind of discipline was imposed on the child?"

"No."

"You did see him use discipline, didn't you?"

"Well, yeah. I mean, we both would, you know, make sure that he behaved properly and didn't do things he wasn't supposed to do."

"So when he got in trouble, Dad would spank his butt, right?"

"If it was needed, yes."

"And sometimes he would slap him with his open palm, wouldn't he?"

"Yeah."

"At the time, that didn't seem inappropriate?"

"I mean it wasn't . . . He wasn't abusing the boy."

"But he did use physical force to discipline the child in front of you. And you would spank him, too?"

"Yeah. I probably did, too."

"And after his father kidnapped him and took him to L.A., you didn't see what kind of discipline the boy got?"

"No."

"Thank you."

John Gilligan took the last shot. "So until age nine when he went to his father, as far as you were concerned, Kenneth had a pretty normal upbringing and was a pretty normal kid, is that fair to say?"

"Uh-huh."

Elyse Smith stepped down. The jury would decide whether or not Kenneth Dean Hunt had been physically and emotionally abused as a child while still around his mother.

Mark Windham called forward the deputy probation officer (DPO) who had been assigned in August 1979 to handle Kenneth Hunt's case after his release from a mental ward. Alex Ford, now a little grayer than he'd been twenty-two years earlier, testified for two hours about his investigation of the conditions in which the boy had lived and the attempts to place him in a suitable facility. Ford had faced difficulty because of Hunt's sexual quirks, bowel control problems, and tendency to set fires. Finally, he found a group who would accept the boy in Sylmar, the northern sector of the San Fernando Valley. A ninety-day "Special Treatment Program" had been established there. Hunt spent 120 days under therapy and seemed to be improving, but was inexplicably transferred to a different home for boys. From there, his path plunged downhill.

The key question came when Windham asked, "Do you have an opinion about what sorts of things happen to a child, between ages zero to seven, that might help avoid criminality or mental disorder?"

Ford answered, "Let me break it down for you. In the early years in particular, it's consistency of conduct by parents. Parents that respond appropriately to a child's needs are very, very important. Conversely, in those children that I have worked with, the histories overwhelmingly show . . . the child is abused, the parenting skills were inconsistent. Needs of the child were not met. Physical or emotional abuse was given."

"In your experience with Kenneth Dean Hunt, were those factors of inconsistency and abuse present?"

"Yes."

"And you believe that contributed to his behavior as a child?"

"Yes."

Laura Jane Kessner took on the task of dismantling Ford's opinions. "Sir, in the two reports you prepared, can you direct me to where you indicate that there was abuse by Kenneth Hunt's mother?"

Windham's objection was overruled.

"I'm not sure there is anything specific in the reports." He added, though, that he wasn't sure Mrs. Hunt had much control over the boy since he was "shuttled back and forth" between the parents.

Kessner wasn't buying it. "Sir, my question is, did you document in any report that Kenneth Hunt was abused—physically, sexually, emotionally—by his natural mother?"

"I don't recall any specific instance."

"In fact, you never even talked with his natural mother, [correct]?"

"Oh, no, I never did."

"Is there any mention in your reports of abuse by his stepmother?"

"No."

"Is there anywhere in your reports where you say that his father abused him?"

"No."

"When you were reassigned from handling Kenneth Hunt's case, another probation officer would only know what you put into the reports, correct?"

"Yes."

"Isn't it important, then, if you really believe that his father was abusive to him, that you would say explicitly, 'Kenneth Hunt's father is abusive and he should never be back in that home'?"

"Ideally, I would say that to be true."

"In fact, you never made a report against Kenneth Hunt's father, did you?"

"No."

More questions in the same vein produced similar results, so Kessner moved on. "You also indicate that [Hunt] admitted he bases his behavior on whether or not he thinks he will be caught."

"Yes."

"Doesn't that indicate to you that he has insight into the consequences of his actions?"

"Yes."

Probing the assessment made from various tests indicating that Hunt possessed high intelligence, verbal skills, and social skills, Kessner asked if those were Ford's conclusions. He said, "You know, I remember when I wrote the report, I questioned that wording, but that was the words that were given to me, so I wrote it down. That is what I was told, so I wrote it down." He added that he had never seen demonstration of Hunt's social skills.

The placement of Kenneth Hunt in a "suitable facility" fell under Kessner's scrutiny. She asked if Ford had actually recommended a juvenile camp rather than the special treatment program.

Ford spoke for several minutes about how he had tried to put forth his opinions in a report. "I think my supervisor had indicated 'we really don't want your opinion in here.' You know, there were certain political considerations that developed. . . . I was somewhat pressured into accepting suitable placement and the special treatment program as the appropriate recommendation for Kenneth Hunt. . . . I personally would have preferred that it be community camp placement. . . ."

The equivocating answer left Ford vulnerable to another gambit by Kessner. In Windham's opening comments, he had criticized the institutionalization of Hunt when the youth had needed therapy and treatment instead of imprisonment. Kessner asked Ford, "You indicated at one time that you felt Kenneth Hunt should go to California Youth Authority. Why would that be?"

Ford said the CYA had "the greatest variety of mental programs and vocational rehabilitation programs of any agency in the state." Another expert witness for the defense would directly contradict that opinion in a highly critical assessment of the CYA.

Ford answered Kessner's last question about placing Hunt by saying, "I did my very best."

Windham promptly bounced back. "While you did your best, you were never able to find suitable placement for Kenneth Hunt, were you?"

"No."

"And there is no guarantee a young person going into the CYA would get any mental health treatment, is there?"

"No."

That ended the expert testimony of DPO Alex Ford.

Immediately after lunch, Hunt's sister, Gina Blake, took the stand again for a short session. She told jurors that she had felt abandoned by her father when he had taken Kenneth instead of her. Then Windham asked, "How do you feel about what you have heard about your brother's crimes?"

"I'm saddened by them in many ways. I feel very sorry, of course, for the victims' families and sorry that he has had to go through a life that took him to this point."

"How do you feel in retrospect about what he did to you when you were a child?"

"It's not right. I don't condone it, but I understand it. I think—I'm coming from a healthier place now in my life where I can see what led up to that, and I've moved past it. I'm thankful for what I have had in my life and the fact that things weren't worse, and I don't hate him for that. It happened, and we've moved on, and it is sad that he didn't get the help he needed. And it is sad to think your whole life that everybody knows there is a problem, but no one knows. No one ever stepped up to the plate and said, 'Fix this, there's a problem,' yet the problem was screaming at everybody."

"Given what you know now and what you have experienced, what you have lived, do you want the jury to spare your brother's life?"

"I would like that, yes. I've already lost my father. For my entire life I have not known my brother. I don't want to lose any more." Gina Blake's words ironically echoed those of Lois Bachrach, who said she had lost not only her sister but her mother as well.

"Nothing further," said Windham. The prosecution declined cross-examination.

At last, the man who had been criticized as an alcoholic with an unwholesome interest in sex, and a failed parent, stepped up to answer questions. Gordon Hunt didn't appear to be happy about testifying, answering in somewhat defiant, monosyllabic grunts and chewing gum the whole time. He answered yes to a series of questions establishing his marriage to Elyse, while still married to another woman, and being in jail during Elyse's pregnancy. But when Windham asked if he was the father of the child he had failed to support, he answered, "I don't believe I was, no." He also said he had stopped drinking, had been sober since 1981, and had never used drugs.

Windham took him through the early years of the union with Elyse, their employment, residential locations, and his family background. Working his way to the subject of Hunt's son, the lawyer asked, "At some point, did Kenneth's behavior become bad?"

"Well, the indication I got was when he was in first or second grade, maybe third grade. He took a swing at a teacher with a bat."

Windham wanted to go back even further in the boy's childhood. "Do you remember having an interview with a doctor and me earlier this year and telling us that the problems started with Kenneth as soon as he could walk?"

"I don't remember saying that," Hunt snapped back. "Maybe there was problems, maybe crying and stuff like that. But as far as anything else, no. He just seemed bright and alert, so I don't see what you're saying problemwise."

With the question rephrased, Hunt said, "I really can't put my finger on anything. But you know, I don't remember . . . maybe crying at night. A fussy baby, that's about all."

"When he was bad, did you discipline him?"

Shrugging, Hunt said, "We sent him to his room most of the time, yeah."

"Would you spank him?"

"At that age? No."

"But as he got a little older, you started spanking him when he was bad?"

"Yes."

"And he was bad pretty often, wasn't he?"

"Yes, but then again the discipline did not always include spanking. We sent him to his room."

"And sometimes you would slap him with your open palm?"

"No."

"When he got a little bigger, you slapped him with your open hand?"

"No. I never hit him with an open hand or closed fist. If we hit him, it was on his butt."

"But sometimes you'd hit on his butt, and it wouldn't do any good?"

"Nothing ever did any good as far as correcting-wise. So that's basically why he got sent to his room most of the time."

"So it sounds to me like you're describing a difficult temperament in a child? Is that what your experience was?"

"He would always try to push his limits, yeah."

When he and Elyse separated, Hunt said, she took both of the kids. "I went up and took the son back and brought him back down." Observers thought it curious that Hunt didn't say "my" son.

"Did you have a court order to do that?"

"No, I did not."

"Why did you take him?"

"She had no court order, either, and I wanted at least one of my kids. The reason I picked Kenneth is because Elyse, at the time, brought Gina and asked her if she knew who I was, and she said no. So I didn't want to take her away from her mother." Windham wanted to know how that made him feel. "It hurt. But her mother was already living with somebody else and Gina was already calling him Dad. He became her dad. For quite a few years, it was that way."

Hunt admitted that he was living with another woman, whom he eventually married, when he brought young Kenneth to Los Angeles.

"Did Kenneth's behavior problems escalate?"

"Yes, they did."

"Did the school district tell you he had an emotional disorder?"

"No, never."

"But you took him to Cedars-Sinai Hospital when he was nine years old, didn't you?"

"Yes, I did."

"And he got treatment for a mental disorder?"

"It was not a mental disorder. They were trying to find out why he was acting and doing the things he was doing."

"Did you ever lose your temper with Kenneth?"

"Once or twice, yes."

"You almost killed him, right?"

"No, I did not. Never."

"But you . . . He used to vomit a lot, didn't he?"

"I think that was self-induced now that you look back on it, trying to get attention."

"You put a stop to it, right?"

"There's no way to stop that. I may have tried to, but I don't know how."

"You don't recall telling a probation officer that you made him eat it to try to make him stop?"

"No. I have never done that." It was a strong denial of an issue that Windham had emphasized in his opening speech.

When Kenneth had been picked up by police after running away, he had allegedly told them he'd been repeatedly beaten by his father, but no bruises had been seen on his body. Windham brought it up to Hunt, but didn't ask if he had, indeed, beaten the boy.

After admitting that he had committed young Kenneth to L.A. County-USC Hospital, Hunt issued a series of denials to related questions. He couldn't recall exactly how long the boy had been confined there, Hunt himself hadn't received therapy, and he hadn't been notified that his son had forced other children to orally copulate him. "No, they never said that. They said he was just a plain juvenile delinquent, and mental was not his problem."

"When he was [later] at juvenile hall, did you visit him there?"

"We went there once to pick him up, and he didn't want to come home. So we left him there." No, Hunt said, he had never written letters to the boy. And he denied ever telling his son that he hated him.

"Did you ever tell him that you didn't want to be his father anymore?"

"No, I've never told him that, either. I felt it many times."

At a detention facility near Malibu Beach, Camp Kilpatrick, Hunt said, "We went there to visit him and we talked to a camp counselor. They told me he was . . . He should be incarcerated for the rest of his life, basically is what they told me." A probation officer, said Hunt, had advised him not to take Kenneth home.

Windham asked if Hunt had ever wished that Kenneth had been stillborn. "I've never said that." Nor had he ever expressed a wish the child had never lived. "I said it might have been better if he never did, but I never wished that on anybody."

Windham sat down and John Gilligan took over the questioning. He focused first on the homes provided by the father in which Kenneth had his own rooms, privacy, and no overcrowding. There had been no conditions of poverty. Addressing the jail term Hunt had served for failure to pay child support, Gilligan established that it was not for violence, nor had Hunt ever been arrested or convicted for any violent acts. He had no felonies on his record. His only brush with the law, he said, had been for an unpaid traffic citation and a misdemeanor charge of driving under the influence, with no jail involved.

Hunt's marriage to Barbara, Kenneth's stepmother, had eventually ended by her death due to cancer.

"When you took your son to Cedars-Sinai, was that because you wanted to get rid of him, or you wanted to get him some help?"

"I wanted to get him some help, find out what was going on."

"All right. And when you took him to L.A. County-USC, was that because you wanted to abandon him or get him some help?"

"To get him some help."

Regarding the allegation that Hunt had once said, "I almost killed Kenneth a couple of times," Gilligan said, "Now I want to ask you something. Do you understand the difference—and I'm not saying you said it—between a parent in frustration saying, 'I almost killed him a couple of times,' or 'I could have killed him,' as opposed to 'I almost killed him,' meaning 'I put him in the hospital or did physical damage'?"

"Yes, I do," he said, and agreed that if the utterance had been made, it had been in a rhetorical sense, not a serious statement about harming his son.

"No further questions."

Gordon Hunt stepped down and marched briskly out of the courtroom. If he even exchanged glances with the defendant, it went unnoticed by anyone in the gallery.

Twenty-seven

One last witness remained for Mark Windham, a final chance to convince at least one juror that his client did not deserve to die for his crimes. Of course, the defender hoped for a unanimous decision by all twelve jurors to show compassion by voting for life in prison without parole. That would be ideal. But failing that, it would take only one holdout to cause a mistrial, in which case the prosecution would have to make a decision, accept a sentence of life without the possibility of parole, or start all over. The second option would entail impaneling a whole new jury, bringing back all of the witnesses, and presenting a huge volume of evidence again. Plus, it would be an expensive process.

In the gallery, family and friends of the victims prayed for an ending, most of them preferring the death penalty for Hunt.

Windham's final punch would be in the testimony of a clinical psychologist, Dr. David Foy, a professor who had earned his Ph.D. at the University of Mississippi. He had authored more than a hundred articles for professional journals and had testified in twenty trials.

In a cultured voice with a slight southern drawl, Foy said he had been involved in a series of studies regarding problem children, including adolescents incarcerated in CYA and those attending "at-risk" inner-city Los Angeles schools. Conclusions had been reached indicating that young people in trouble with the law had experienced factors such as physical and sexual abuse, domestic violence, family disruption, and family disorganization to a much greater extent than kids who had not fallen into a pattern of lawbreaking.

"Dr. Foy," said Windham, "have psychologists studied the factors representing the greatest obstacle for children to reach normal development?"

"Psychologists and other social scientists certainly have . . . As you might guess, the family environment, the home situation, is the crucible for early development." Foy set up a projector and showed slides to illustrate his comments. "Studies have looked at five areas of family functioning. They're labeled punitiveness, lack of love, laxness, family disruption, and parental deviance."

At Windham's prompts, Foy explained: Punitiveness means using physical punishment in an extreme way. Lack of love—the child is not getting the nurturing, support, warmth, and caring you would hope for. Laxness—the absence of extra attention that must be paid by one or both parents to provide a high level of supervision and monitoring. Family disruption—divorce or protracted separation of the parents, and violence or chronic marital discord in the home. Parental deviance—one or both parents having a criminal record or modeling antisocial behavior.

The defense had attempted to show the presence of all five problems in the life of Kenneth Hunt.

Foy brought up another study examining the relationship between a father's physical discipline practices and his criminality to predict lawless behavior in the child. Windham quickly asked if "criminality" included drunk driving, kidnapping, and abusing a child. Foy said they did. The implied links to Hunt couldn't have been more obvious. "Harsh punishment," said Foy, "is a very profound predictor of criminality in adolescence or adulthood." Eighty-seven percent of children exposed to these elements develop problem behavior.

"In examining the background materials pertaining to Kenneth Hunt, did you find any of these factors?"

"I found *all* of these factors," Foy proclaimed.

The parental criminality, said Foy, stemmed from Hunt's father serving time for failing to pay child support and a DUI conviction, plus a family history of offenses by relatives of the father.

"What parental substance abuse did you see documented?"

"I saw a record of his father's alcohol abuse, as well as use of other drugs, particularly LSD."

"Did you see any evidence of impaired parenting?"

"A lot. Neither his mother nor his father wanted him back after his placement in probation camp. And his stay with one or the other parent was never more than a few months. It was like he was being bounced back and forth between whichever parent would take custody."

"What about family instability?"

"I think this means transience, moving around, not being in the same community over an extended period of time. No roots. No support services that might make up for parental deficiencies—such as a neighbor or church member."

"What about marital conflict?"

"Well, the extreme of that would be divorce, and that happened when he was a youngster. Before that, there was marital discord, particularly his mother's complaints of the father drinking and womanizing, I believe."

Windham asked about severe "punitiveness." Foy said, "There is evidence in the record, for example, when his father was angry at something at the dinner table and Kenneth threw up, his father told several people that he made Kenneth eat his own vomit." The doctor also referred to incidents in which the father allegedly said that he didn't want Kenneth and that he nearly killed him twice. "That would suggest severe unwantedness and severe discipline being meted out."

"Would these things put Kenneth in [a high] category as far as his risk of criminality?"

"As far as the risk, as identified in this study, it would. Yes."

Windham asked if "laxness" showed up in Hunt's childhood. Yes, said Foy. "Laxness can be exemplified in Kenneth's background when neither parent wanted him back and in essence told the probation department that 'he is yours now.' "

"Did you find parental deviance?"

"There was evidence in the records I reviewed that Kenneth's father left pornographic materials around the home, that he was a polydrug abuser, that he had been convicted of several crimes. Those would qualify as deviance."

"What is so bad about leaving pornographic materials around the home?"

"That is a form of sexual abuse. It exposes children to sexuality that is beyond their developmental ability to manage."

The litany of accusations about parental failures against Hunt's father continued, citing use of alcohol, his placing the boy in a mental ward, twenty years of separation between them, and the comment attributed to him about wishing the child had been stillborn. Windham also asked if Foy had seen the report from the father's stepdaughter, Karen, in which Hunt Sr. allegedly had given her "sexually inappropriate gifts, spied on her when she was getting undressed, and tried to pay her for naked photographs."

"Yes, I have seen that report."

"And that he exposed himself to her cousin?"

"Yes."

"And are you aware of the testimony by Elyse Hunt [Smith] of the kinky sexual desires of Mr. Hunt's wanting other people to join their sex?"

"Yes, I saw that."

"Is this report of sexuality significant to you?"

"It suggests, number one, that there has been actual abuse of at least a noncontact form by these images and developmentally inappropriate contact with sexual materials."

Windham next introduced a school document on young Kenneth evaluating him with a behavior disorder, followed by a report from Probation Officer Alex Ford revealing the problem of defecating in the bed. Foy said, "That is very extreme behavior. It suggests that Kenneth may have been afraid to leave his bedroom to go to the bathroom. That would be one possibility. It might also point to extreme self-degradation."

The failure of any follow-up treatment for a youth who had been repeatedly diagnosed as needing therapy filled the next few minutes of testimony, along with criticism of placing him in detention facilities.

"The records confirm, in April 1980, that Kenneth Hunt's stepfather discovered him in sexual contact with his sister, Gina. Was that significant to you?"

"Yes. For somebody who is still quite young to know about oral copulation and to be able to instruct a young sister in doing that, and to think that it is OK behavior, that is very significant." Foy repeated the conclusion regarding Hunt's similar behavior in the mental hospital. "To be experienced enough to coerce others into doing it suggests that he learned it somewhere."

To explore that theme, Windham asked, "How does a child at age twelve or thirteen learn about oral sex?"

"He could learn it in the home with a perpetrator within the family, or he could learn about it from other children who are incarcerated in the same place he was, who may be older or more experienced."

Alex Ford had praised the California Youth Authority, where Hunt spent five years, as having available a variety of mental-health treatment and therapy programs. Windham asked Dr. Foy, "At CYA, is there any record of mental-health treatment?"

"None that I saw."

Kenneth Hunt's childhood structure, said Dr. Foy in summary, represented an unusually high-risk factor for his future behavior.

Before John Gilligan could begin cross-examination, Judge Connor summoned lawyers to a sidebar conference. She realized the prosecutor needed some time to cross-examine Dr. Foy and had one rebuttal witness to call. But one of the jurors needed to leave at 4:20 P.M., so less than one hour remained to conclude all testimony. Gilligan's witness had been waiting all day and needed to leave town that same evening. Connor asked Gilligan if he could squeeze all of his needs into the available time. He said he would.

Gilligan had familiarized himself in considerable detail about the studies to which Dr. Foy had referred. He asked if the risk factors necessarily predicted with accuracy that certain young people would engage in violence.

The doctor admitted that "even though an individual may have a number or all of the risk factors, there will still be some individuals who don't develop offending patterns."

A few weeks earlier, Dr. Foy had written a two-page report summarizing his findings. Gilligan produced it and said, "Now, you list six key family-risk factors, is that correct?"

"Yes. I did."

"And the first is unremitting poverty. Was there any evidence of unremitting poverty in Kenneth Hunt's background?"

"No."

"And the next factor, you list overcrowding in the home. And there is, in fact, no evidence of overcrowding in the home of Kenneth Hunt, is there?"

Foy gave an odd answer. He suggested that it wasn't just the number of people occupying space, but "it's the amount of parenting resources that are available to provide for children that are there."

Gilligan, a little impatient, chided the witness.

"Please answer my specific question. Overcrowding means overcrowding. . . . There is no evidence in these records of too many people living in limited space in Kenneth Hunt's records, is there?"

"In the geographic sense, that's correct."

"Thank you very much," said the prosecutor. "And number three, there is evidence of marital discord, is that correct?"

"Yes, there is."

"How many—what percent of the American population would you say grew up with some marital discord, some problems in their parents' marriage at one point or another?"

"Probably forty percent."

"How many of those people never killed three people?"

"Hopefully, most of them."

"Probably nearly all of them?"

"Correct."

"Now, number four. Is there any diagnosis of specific mental illness in either Kenneth Hunt's mother or father?"

"Um. No."

"OK. Now, parents' criminality, that is number five." Gilligan asked if failure to pay child support thirty-four years ago, and one DUI in the following years, constituted significant criminality. Foy said that such a record would not change his assessment. Possession of marijuana, he said, would also be a mark of criminality. Even when Gilligan asked if there was a difference between these offenses and serious felonies such as murder, Foy clung to his opinion.

"OK. Placement outside the home is number six, right?" Foy agreed. No one could dispute that Kenneth Hunt had been away from both parents' homes many years.

Chipping away from another angle, Gilligan asked, "Now, if the statements about the father's conduct toward his son turned out to be false, would that change your opinion regarding some risk factors?"

"I would have to see which ones were false."

"If the report about the vomiting was false, with no evidence to prove that he had forced his son to eat vomit, would that be significant to you?"

Foy's answer surprised observers. "Probably not."

"If the 'I almost killed him twice' statement turned out to be just a frustrated comment with no real meaning, and in fact no physical violence had taken place, would that be significant to you?"

Again Foy's answer seemed odd. "I think the language speaks for itself."

"Are you telling me that if there was, in fact, no evidence that Mr. Hunt ever physically abused his son in any way, that would not be significant to you?"

"It would. But it would not detract from the seriousness of making an idle comment that said he nearly killed him twice."

Gilligan wouldn't let it drop. "You don't think a parent, a good parent, has ever said, 'I was ready to kill that kid' at one point or another, like when he wrecked the car, when he got drunk, when he whatever? Do you think that is an uncommon occurrence?"

"Before a probation officer, I think it probably is."

In his two-page summary report, Dr. Foy had written its purpose "for use in presenting mitigation in this case." Gilligan asked, "Were you interested in the *aggravating* factors, in his criminal history?"

"As an overall knowledge of the case, yes. As a professional assigned to do a specific thing in this case, no."

Recognizing that Dr. Foy had arrived at his conclusions from reading material prepared by other people, such as probation officers and other officials, Gilligan wondered if the doctor had conducted any independent tests or interviews to verify the data. "In order to check the accuracy of these reports, did you ever interview Mr. Hunt's mother?"

"No, I did not."

"Did you ever interview Mr. Hunt's father?"

"No, I did not." Nor had he interviewed Hunt's sister or stepmother, nor the stepmother's daughter, Karen. For Karen's statement, he had relied on a deposition she had given to the defense team. Gilligan hoped the jury would see a weakness in conclusions made without any hands-on research.

The last hour of the day was slipping by. Judge Connor asked jurors if they could stay a little later. But one insisted she needed to leave no later that 4:20 P.M. Gilligan felt the pressure of time, but agreed to make his best efforts to complete his examination of Dr. Foy and his own brief witness within the limited time left.

"Dr. Foy, how many people have you ever met with no previous risk factors who commit crimes?"

"Not very many."

"Do you believe that if people who have these risk factors commit crimes, they should be treated differently by society? Should they be held to the same laws as people who do not have risk factors?"

With some equivocation, the witness agreed that all

offenders, except mentally disabled ones, should be held to the same standards.

To reinforce the point that presence of risk factors do not necessarily lead to violent crime, Gilligan had an example in mind. "You are familiar with the former president William Jefferson Clinton?"

"I don't know him personally. I may talk like him, but it doesn't mean I know him."

Gilligan wasn't amused by the answer. "In the general sense of the word, you are familiar with him."

"Yes, I am."

"You are aware that he grew up in a broken home, is a child of divorce?"

"I am familiar with that part of his history."

"You are aware that he grew up with an alcoholic, physically abusive stepfather, isn't that correct?"

"That is alleged."

"And further, he grew up in relative poverty, isn't that also true?"

"I think his mother was a nurse. I don't know that I would call that poverty."

"He grew up in a certainly less than wealthy home, isn't that fair?"

"Lower middle class maybe. I will give you that."

"All right. Broken home [and] alcoholic, abusive stepfather, we'll debate the poverty issue. A lot of risk factors, aren't there?"

"Yes, there are. And I will resist commenting on his behavior." A few muffled giggles rippled through the gallery.

"That is fine, Doctor. The fact of the matter is, all levity about personal behavior aside, he went on, despite all the things in his background, to become president of the United States, isn't that true?"

"That is what the record shows."

"A lot of people still wish he was president, isn't that true?"

"I reckon that is so, yes."

"Thank you very much, Doctor."

Both sides had scored strong points through the testimony of Dr. Foy.

Gilligan called the final witness in the trial.

Dr. Ronald Markman, a specialist in forensic psychiatry, looked the part, with a tanned, weathered face and thick, wavy white hair; glasses and a rumpled tan suit completed the image. He had testified hundreds of times for defenders as well as prosecutors.

Gilligan asked if Markman had reviewed Dr. Foy's report. He had.

"And did you receive a court order in this case allowing you to perform a psychological analysis on the defendant?"

"Yes."

Mark Windham knew exactly where Gilligan was going. The prosecutor wanted the jury to know that Kenneth Hunt had refused to speak to Markman. "Objection," said Windham. "May we approach?"

At the sidebar, Windham argued that such information would violate his client's Fifth and Sixth Amendment rights. Gilligan offered to cite case law allowing such testimony. But Judge Connor said, "Don't ask the question right now. I don't want a mistrial."

Disappointed, Gilligan moved on with Dr. Markman, bringing up the studies and reports in Dr. Foy's testimony. Markman said he felt the findings "are rather general in nature." He explained, "These risk factors are too general, and they don't direct them-

selves to being able to analyze a specific individual."
For example, he said, the testimony that possession
of marijuana is indistinguishable from violent crimes
in terms of criminality makes it difficult to make a
valid assessment. "You run into a problem of drawing
strong scientific conclusions with that database."

Gilligan asked if Markman thought it would have
been more sound to verify information by conducting
interviews with the principals. Markman agreed that
would have made the analysis more complete. He also
expressed skepticism about some of the statistical conclusions.

Judge Connor interrupted. "We have to stop."

Gilligan squeezed in one more question, to which
Markman replied that some people who do not have
the risk factors described by Dr. Foy certainly do commit crimes.

Mark Windham made brief, perfunctory inquiries
about Markman's background in statistical analysis and
his history of testifying in trials, and finally said, "Thank
you. That's all."

Gilligan got in the last shot establishing that Markman had testified in many trials "predominately" for
the defense.

Both sides agreed to wind it up. The juror who was
in a hurry to leave rushed out at 4:25 P.M.

On Wednesday morning, the attorneys would present their final arguments to the jury.

Twenty-eight

"Good morning once again," said John Gilligan to the jurors.

"I promise I will be brief this morning. I know this has been a difficult process for all of you. It's been a situation involving brutal crimes, brutal testimony, anguish of victims, their families and friends. This is not *Law and Order* or whatever TV-crime flavor of the month, this is the real thing, and I know it's hard. It's hard for all of us and I know this is probably the hardest part.

"What we've seen in this part of the trial is the reality of horrible violence, not on TV, but in real life; horrible violence being inflicted on innocent people whose only misfortune was they come in contact with Mr. Hunt. That is the reality. Kenneth Dean Hunt has left a trail of death and shattered families. . . . He has left us with a long list, three dead human beings and a long, long list of victims."

The evidence would be summarized on both sides, said Gilligan, and it would show that Hunt had a long pattern of criminal behavior. "He enters this courtroom with a past that qualifies him as a human wrecking ball. . . . He has committed the worst possible crimes that a person can commit." Not only murder, but "raping elderly women, striking and killing a sixty-seven-year-old man whose only crime was to ask Mr. Hunt not to abuse his dog, not to scream profanities at his wife."

Commending Mark Windham as a "very competent defense counsel," Gilligan criticized the theme of what was offered about the defendant. "What do we get? It's not a new tactic in the criminal justice system. It's got a name. It's called the 'abuse excuse.' It's the blame game. . . . You have to blame somebody. You blame Mom. You blame Dad. You blame the system. You blame everybody except the one person who was responsible, the one person who actually committed this parade of horribles."

At a recent movie he and his wife had attended, said Gilligan, they saw a trailer for a film titled *15 Minutes*. "There was a bad guy of some Eastern European background, and he yells out in the middle of doing some dastardly deed, 'I love America. No one is responsible for anything they do in America.' Gilligan said that while he listened to the defense case, and Dr. Foy's testimony, the trailer kept running through his mind. "Is this really the place where no one is responsible for anything they do?

"Ladies and gentlemen, I hope it's not really that easy." Gilligan urged them to take a close look at the evidence of mitigation and aggravation to see what parts were really substantial. Look at the crimes, he said. "This was a brutal, painful death for Myra Davis. He raped her and put that ligature around her neck and tightened it until it began to choke the life from her." Ten years later, he said, the "identical" thing happened with Jean Orloff. "Again someone who

knew and trusted Mr. Hunt. . . . He repays Jean Orloff's kindness with brutal death. He chose to kill her
in the same agonizing fashion in which he killed Myra
Davis."

In both cases, said Gilligan, the victims went
through fifteen seconds of horror before beginning
to lose consciousness. "They knew what was happen-
ing. How long do you think fifteen seconds can be?
Let's count, starting now."

Spectators mentally counted with the prosecutor,
and were amazed at how long it takes to count off
one-quarter of a minute when concentrating on every
tick of the clock.

To drive the stake in even deeper, Gilligan said,
"That's fifteen seconds. Let's go on for a full minute."
Silence hung heavy in the courtroom. One minute—
the time it took each victim to reach the point of no
return seemed interminable.

Turning to Hunt's long string of sexual-battery attacks, Gilligan tolled them off, one by one, naming
the six women and reconstructing what happened to
each one. Then he described events leading to the
death of Bernard Davis. From there, the prosecutor
recapitulated the beating of Hunt's girlfriend Tina
Moore and the molestation of his little sister.

"These are the factors in aggravation," said Gilligan. "The proof of every single one is overwhelming." Had the defense proved their assertions of
mitigating circumstances? Gilligan didn't think so.

The testimonies of Alex Ford and Dr. Foy, said Gilligan, offered no proof of any mental illness or im-
pairment that would mitigate the crimes. "Where is
the proof of anything real, anything tangible, that was

wrong with Mr. Hunt? This is the abuse excuse. That's all it is."

Studies about "risk factors" used by Dr. Foy, said Gilligan, gave no validation to the theories that Hunt's childhood led him to a rampage of murder. "That is because these reports are not for that purpose. They are generalized things. . . ." Naming each of the factors, Gilligan said none of them carried substantial weight. There was no "unremitting poverty" or "overcrowding in the home." As for "marital discord," it is so common that half of all kids grow up with it, so it is "not useful." There was no firm proof of the fourth factor, "mental illness." Foy's definition of "criminality" was too broad, since he could see no distinction between marijuana possession and murder. Regarding the sixth factor, "placement outside the home," Gilligan said, "Dr. Foy finally gets one. There is evidence of instability and that Kenneth lived outside the home."

To put the factors into perspective, Gilligan made some remarkable personal revelations. "Last night, as I was thinking about this case, and about Dr. Foy, and what I was going to say to you, I went to the gym to work off a little of this adrenaline. At the gym, lo and behold, my adult son—I use 'adult' loosely, he is nineteen—was there. And it was kind of a surprise to me because Brendon goes to college and lives there, but he is always coming back home for food or clothes, or whatever, and I don't always know when he is coming home.

"So he comes up to me at the gym. It was an amazing conversation because he didn't ask me for money. And I was thinking about Brendon, and thinking about what Dr. Foy said. Brendon's mother and I were

divorced when he was two and a half. He was shuttled
back and forth between us over the years, custody
changed. Sometimes it was with me, sometimes with
her. On his mother's side, his grandfather is an alcoholic. My sister is a heroin addict who has spent time
in jail. Brendon lived with me when I was in law
school, when I was going to work at night to a
crummy job, going to school at night, and lived in a
one-room studio apartment. Believe me, that place
was overcrowded. And I thought about Dr. Foy's factors. And I thought about Brendon.

"I said, 'criminality,' 'marital discord,' 'substance
abuse,' 'overcrowding in the home.' Four of Dr. Foy's
top six reasons why you should grow up to be an incredibly screwed-up person.

"But there is more. There is more. I also thought
about two years ago when my wife and I went on vacation. Brendon was a little younger then, and a little
more irresponsible. It was the first vacation we had
been on in a very long time. I had just tried a long
case and I was really tired and irritable. We were up
in northern California and I got a call from my wife's
brother, and he was going to look in on Brendon. He
said, 'I hate to tell you this, but Brendon had an un-
authorized party at your house. It's kind of a mess.
On top of that, he took the car, went down to Orange
County, and didn't put oil in it. The engine seized up
and the car is ruined.' So was my vacation.

"I put the phone down, turned to my wife, and
said, 'I'm going to kill him when we get home.'

"You know what? According to Dr. Foy—well, I
guess Brendon is a miracle child. He hasn't raped anybody. He hasn't murdered anybody. Not one. All those

risk factors, plus a terrible father who said he was going to kill him.

"Ladies and gentlemen of the jury, demand proof. Require proof. If they tell you about mitigation, make them prove to you the way we proved aggravation. Does anyone doubt that Myra Davis and Jean Orloff were murdered? Does anyone expect Bernard Davis to come walking through that door? Of course you don't."

There had been no testimony about Hunt being abused as a child, said Gilligan, nor any medical reports of injuries suffered at the hands of his parents. But there was ample word from his mother-in-law that Hunt was given shelter, food, safety, and work opportunities in her home. "He has a wife. Been married for thirteen years. And despite this cocoon of support, Mr. Hunt commits assaults, burglaries, rapes of elderly victims. He killed three people, ladies and gentlemen of the jury—three living, breathing human beings, people who had hopes and lives, [who had] families, children, and grandchildren.

"You have heard about the ripple effects of Mr. Hunt's crimes, the damage to the lives of Sherry Davis, to Barbara Kappedal, to Lois Bachrach. I'm not going to go through it, not going to repeat it. There is no doubt of any of it. None.

"I know this isn't easy, ladies and gentlemen. But at the end of the day, there is always going to be a worse crime and there is always going to be a worse penalty for the worst crime. Mr. Hunt has committed the worst crimes, not once, but again and again. At some point, it's enough. . . . This has been enough. The simple fact is that this case does not cry out for the minimum. The people of the state of California ask you to return nothing less than the penalty of death in this case. Thank you."

Holding the very life of Kenneth Hunt in his hands, Mark Windham stood before the jury, gripping both sides of the lectern. He let a few moments pass in silence as if summoning up the words and power he would need to save a man's life.

With his deep interest in spirituality and world religions, Windham couldn't resist utilizing the knowledge and belief in his appeal to the jury. No greeting was necessary in this final inning.

"Words are so limited," he said. "My words are the least of what I am saying to you in this trial. I want to lift up our level of discourse here. I'm going to lift our hearts beyond factual quibbles. We know what happened. We know what's real and what is not real here. We are talking about a moral decision and moral issues. . . . We need to use our hearts.

"I want to lift up our level of communication here because what we are doing is justice. Justice is sacred, absolutely sacred. . . . We've talked about the value of life and death, and what it is about life that makes it important. See, what I am doing here is much more the job of a priest or minister or a rabbi. I mean, it's not really something that a lawyer, a lawyer's training prepares him or her to do. But we have to do it anyway. We have to make moral decisions here about life and death, and we must do it as we are guided by the law."

Giving a nod to the wisdom of law, Windham stressed that it provides the opportunity for juries to exercise their "God-given right of mercy. So, understand that I am not talking about excuses. . . . I am not talking about forgiveness, nor am I talking about

blame. I am talking about using our law to make jus-
tice in this case, which is our sacred duty. I am talking
about justice for Kenneth Hunt . . . for Myra Davis
and for Sherry Davis. I am talking about justice for
Jean Orloff and Lois Bachrach . . . Bernard Davis and
Shirley Davis." In his appeal for justice, he also listed
Hunt's father and sister, along with Betty Hunt and
Dora Green.

"So don't misunderstand me. Don't hurt me by saying I'm playing a blame game. . . . Blame is false. It
sounds wrong. To say that I am blaming someone
makes me sound wrong, but I'm speaking from the
heart and I'm not blaming anyone." He called blame
a childish emotion and failure to take responsibility.
Calling for understanding, Windham said without it,
it is difficult to show compassion.

"There is no abuse excuse. There is no excuse in
this case for killing. That's not what I am talking
about. I'm talking about justice. And I am not talking
about forgiveness. Who can forgive Kenneth Dean
Hunt? Only Myra Davis or Jean Orloff can forgive
their murders, only they. And they are gone. . . . All
we can do is show mercy.

"Some say the killer did not show mercy. But we
are in a court of law. We have a better concept of
mercy and justice than the killer." Windham still referred to "the killer" in the abstract, not naming him.

"Mr. Gilligan gives you a lot of reason to kill Mr.
Hunt, but you need only one reason to save him.
Mercy."

"The death penalty is reserved for the very worst
of the worst. . . . We know about the Oklahoma City
bombing, where hundreds of people were killed—
men, women, and children, innocent people. We

know about the Night Stalker breaking into homes, raping and killing innumerable people, torturing them, maiming them. We know about Charles Manson plotting out the same kind of terrible, bloody, sadistic murders." Windham left unsaid that Manson's penalty had been reduced to life in prison and he could possibly be paroled one day.

"This is not a case of torture. There is no prolonged intentional infliction of additional suffering beyond the killing. This is not a mayhem murder, nor a dismemberment; no cutting . . . no painful torture of that nature. This is not a murder of children. These crimes are different. The evidence makes them appear spontaneous." The killer had devised ligatures from things he found at hand.

"I thought about the victims when Mr. Gilligan counted off fifteen seconds, and it's terrible. But it was a tremendous force that killed them during that period of time, and in no sense was it prolonged or more torturous than that." Following a brief, thoughtful pause, Windham's voice sounded apologetic as he said he didn't mean to minimize the tragedy of two murders. "Spontaneous or not, they are terrible."

Attacking the DNA evidence again, he reiterated its vulnerability to fraud and contamination. "It's really dangerous to impose a death penalty with this sort of evidence that is not absolute and certain . . . nothing to guarantee in your minds that the DNA test is right. . . . All I'm saying is what if fraud is discovered ten years from now? Kenneth Hunt is dead. Don't let that happen. Don't let that happen."

Six sexual-battery cases and one attempted rape had been presented to the jury as aggravating circumstances. Presenting a brief summary of each one,

Windham said they were not "cold, lying-in-wait assaults," and offered another protest that Hunt had
never received "substantial effective treatment for his
sexually assaultive disorder."

Regarding the injuries Hunt inflicted on his extra-
marital girlfriend, Tina Moore, Windham pointed out
that he had been provoked into retaliation when she
slapped him and kicked him in the groin.

The manslaughter of Bernard Davis, said Windham,
"is disturbing." It started over the dog. "He is disci-
plining his dog, kicking it. He loves that dog. He drew
a picture of it. He brushed the dog's teeth. He loved
it, yet he kicked the dog. Is that how he learned discipline as a child? Is that what you do when a dog
yaps? Is that what you do to a child that yaps? Well,
this dog was in his charge, and maybe it was hard for
him to hear criticism about kicking it. Nobody ever
told his daddy to stop."

Criticism is a catalyst to anger for many people.
Understanding the behavior is important, said Windham. "You understand why someone like that might
kick the dog, and when he is criticized, he gets mad
and he hits Bernard Davis. . . . The point is, it is not
intentional killing. It was wrong and reckless. He
shouldn't have done it, and he went to prison for it.

"It is something you can consider along with the
evidence of rape and murder . . . the fact that he
groped women, that he hit the girlfriend who provoked him. . . . But he is not the worst, particularly
when you look at the mitigation, which is a reason
for mercy. I think it's obvious that childhood matters
in who he turns out to be." Kenneth Hunt's ability
to make choices, said Windham, was encumbered by
a will that was forged early on. "The reason he makes

bad choices is he doesn't have the capacity to make good choices. He is limited by the world he came from."

Going through Dr. Foy's testimony, Windham characterized the studies as useful tools to analyze unlawful behavior and its causes. "I think Mr. Gilligan's criticism is unwittingly misleading." The studies, he explained, were not designed to predict exactly which individual will become an offender or lawbreaker.

Through the entire trial, Windham had aimed sharp criticism at his client's father as a major contributor to the problems. Once again, he railed at Gordon Hunt, taking the jury through allegations of criminal behavior, "a sleazy sexuality," and mistreatment of the child. "And I think Mr. Gilligan, on this one, is as bad as the police who saw Kenneth Hunt when he repeatedly ran away, telling the police that 'Dad is beating me up.'" No bruises had been seen, so the officers had taken the boy back to his father. "What John Lennon sang thirty years ago," said Windham, "is true. 'One thing you can't hide is when you are crippled inside.' The bruises show. Oh, do they ever show."

When Hunt, as a child, had coerced oral copulation from other children in a mental ward, and from his own little sister, it demonstrated sickness, insisted the defender. "This kid is vulnerable. He doesn't process thoughts like other kids. It's a mess. What a recipe for disaster. My God, a kid is damaged psychologically, the dad is deviant, criminalistic, punitive. The mom is gone, and then he gets put into these institutions. Can you imagine what that would be like? A little kid in an institution, twelve years old?"

All of the mistreatment by Hunt's father, said Windham, and abandonment by the mother, combined with locking him up in institutions without effective treatment, had culminated in disaster. "Do you think childhood doesn't matter? Do you think there is no evidence that anything bad happened to this boy? It's obvious. It's clear. It is not made up. It's not a blame game here. This is for the benefit of understanding how all this happened. Some people say, 'Oh, a bad seed,' that he's a bad seed. That's not a theory, it's a cliché. And it is dead wrong. It's a lie. We are not born violent. Someone can change that."

A troubled child, said Windham, can be transformed by someone with an outstretched hand, a big brother, an auntie, or an uncle, maybe a coach. "There was no one to extend a hand to Kenneth Hunt." Gilligan had cited his own son as an example of a child who can withstand the factors spoken of by Dr. Foy. Windham had a response.

"Anyone who has John Gilligan as a father can overcome anything, any obstacle. Anyone who has John Gilligan in his life has someone who cares to the depth of his soul, who will go the extra mile, who will never give up, who will never abandon you. Why don't more children have a father like John Gilligan? Kenneth Hunt didn't."

Admitting that Hunt had unconditional love later in life from his mother-in-law and his wife, Windham said, "Too late. It is too late. When things happen to you between the ages of zero and seven, you're on a bad course. When you are ill and not treated, you're not healed."

Retracing the long road of various institutions in which the child had spent time, and the growing misdeeds in between, Windham posed a series of "What if this hadn't happened?'' questions. Perhaps lives would have been saved, including the life of Kenneth Hunt.

The state of California, Windham charged, had not taken reasonable steps to heal a sick boy in their custody. "They wait until he does something wrong, and then they kill him. That is unethical. That is wrong. That is a reason not to give him the death penalty."

The punishment for Hunt should be imprisonment, not another death, the defender said. "Life without the possibility of parole is not leniency. It is a man-made hell. He is socially dead. He has no choices. He doesn't turn on the lights in the morning or turn them off at night. He's told when to eat. He's told when to exercise. No choices. He loses all life's pleasures. He does not walk on the beach. He will never know the touch of a woman. No holiday or birthday dinners with his family. No lying on the grass and seeing billowing clouds above. He will be socially dead in a dark, grim, bleak world, ten years from now, twenty years from now, thirty years from now. No hope. No possibility of parole. This is punishment. It's the severest form of punishment, and society is protected.

"I want to talk to you about the victims in conclusion. I'm going to put their pictures up, and I'm not afraid. The value of their lives is not measured by whether or not you give a death sentence. The value is . . . how they lived, the kindness and love they showed. . . . A death penalty would be a poor memorial to the unconditional love of Myra Davis and Jean Orloff. The death penalty is no way to measure their lives.

"Let us have justice here. That's what I ask of you.

That's what we have to do." Citing the forgiveness shown by Hunt's sister, Gina, Windham expressed hope it would be contagious.

Turning toward the gallery, he addressed two women. "Sherry Davis and Lois Bachrach, my aspiration is that you will know from this trial how it happened, how it came to be that you lost your loved ones. My hope is that you will get understanding from this, and you will know justice in this way."

To the jury, he said, "You will never regret choosing life as long as you live. You will never look back and say, 'I wish I had given Hunt the death penalty.' You will never feel bad about that. You will never regret choosing life. I hope that you will have an understanding of how this tragedy happened, and I hope that we can learn from this so that little children are not abused, so that older people are not victimized. There is too much suffering in this world already.

"And by doing justice in this case, true justice, which means compassion and mercy, by doing justice in this case, we are fulfilling our sacred duty."

At 11:45 A.M., Wednesday, March 21, Mark Windham turned, walked to his chair, and virtually collapsed into it. It would now be up to seven men and five women to make the most difficult decision of their lives. The four alternates would stand by, ready to be called if any juror needed to be replaced.

Jurors sometimes return verdicts within a few hours, or take weeks to make a decision.

Twenty-nine

Sherry Davis, after sitting though Mark Windham's passionate, emotion-laden speech, thought it had been a bit dramatic. Once, in the hallway during a break, she had chatted with him briefly and told him he had missed his calling. With his looks, voice, and flair for theatrics, he should have been an actor. Windham smiled.

A few weeks earlier, she had been working out in a gym, and had run into him there. They had conversed briefly. Later a trainer at the facility, who had seen them together, asked if she knew Windham. Davis told of her grandmother's murder, and said Windham was defending the accused killer.

"Oh, you're the girl in that case!" he said. Windham had told him about the pending trial, and mentioned the victim's granddaughter, but not by name. The trainer volunteered a few comments to Davis about the attorney. Windham, he said, had been suffering migraine headaches from stress related to the case, and that he had been "agonizing" over the issues involved.

With honest respect for Windham, in recognition of his intelligence, dedication, and dramatic skills,

Davis said, "I certainly think he is the right man for the job."

As if the long trial of Kenneth Hunt wasn't enough for Davis to endure, she would soon be called to the Criminal Courts Building to serve jury duty. The first panel in which she sat for questioning was for a murder trial. She later recalled, "One of the prospective jurors was a real loon." He had given bizarre answers to questions by the lawyers. Two days later, on a different panel, she saw him again, and to her astonishment, the man gave completely different answers to the lawyers' questions, and was selected. Incredulous, she said, "He told a completely different story about himself on that second panel. So, obviously, he was lying on one or the other."

Relieved not to be serving on a jury with the individual, Davis ran into another familiar face during an elevator ride. The woman had also been on both panels, and had been picked to serve. She asked Davis, "Do you think I should tell the lawyer or the judge about how that guy changed his story? He's weird." Davis never learned what happened on the case, but the incident shook her faith in the system.

"If I had been selected," she later said, "I darn well would have told them this guy was lying. It made me wonder how many people lie to get on juries with some kind of a mission in mind, maybe to impose a personal agenda against the death penalty. I think the law should be changed to allow a majority of jurors to decide on life without parole or death, so that some wacko doesn't get on just to disrupt things. There are too many hung juries due to one person who just won't listen to reason against eleven others."

In the ninth-floor deliberating room of Department 109, Judge Jacqueline Connor's court, twelve people discussed, argued, read papers, examined exhibits, and took the first of six votes. On the first ballot, they were split evenly, six for death, six for life without parole. Debating, reasoning, and more discussion followed. Another vote resulted in eight for the death penalty, four against it. When they adjourned on Wednesday afternoon, little progress had been made toward breaking the deadlock.

On Thursday morning, they pored over the evidence again and scrutinized the judge's instructions. After heated discussion and reviews, they took another vote. Now the gap had closed—ten for death, two against. Frequent breaks became necessary to relieve the tension. Frustration wore on a few of them, while others spoke with quiet resolve. The day ended with the same ten-to-two split.

Assembling again on Friday morning, March 23, they reexamined the reasoning they had used, looked again at the evidence, considered what attorneys from both sides had said, and took another vote.

Two members of the panel were frustrated at the behavior of juror number eight. They both sent notes to Judge Connor, who summoned the waiting attorneys into the court. She told them, "I have two notes from jurors, just given to me by the bailiff. One says, 'We feel it is conduct on the part of juror number eight, whom would not state what their reason was for coming to a certain conclusion.' The second one says, 'Juror number eight was resistant to making an open-minded decision. All the other jurors were open-minded on basis for their reasons and basis for their decisions.' "

John Gilligan asked to have a hearing for the purpose of understanding the problems.

"I don't know who wrote these," said Connor.

Windham commented, "I think we should bring them out and ask them."

Connor replied, "Let's do a general inquiry and then decide whether anything further might be appropriate."

Five minutes before noon, the weary jurors filed back into the box and took their seats. Connor spoke to them about the deliberations, and then called the foreperson to the sidebar. Connor spoke. "I have a couple of notes. I don't know if one is from you, but some concern about juror number eight being resistant in discussing their feelings, and I want an overview from you. You look surprised, so it doesn't look like it came from you?"

"It did not come from me."

"Did you feel there was any refusal to deliberate? Not just a difference of opinion, but refusal to deliberate?"

"I think everybody really put forth their best effort. At the penalty stage, it is more of a moral issue than anything."

Connor agreed. The foreperson had more to say. "You have some individuals who are of a sympathetic capacity. Others just don't see it that way, and you have to give them that right. We went over the instructions, over and over and over again. And to be perfectly honest with you, I felt as a foreperson everybody honestly put forth their best effort to make a decision. I always asked the other jurors if there is anything we can discuss that may help a person come to a better decision, not necessarily through persuasion, but basically with everything we had. We went over and over it, and when a person stands firm on their decision, there is nothing more we can do."

The judge asked if the jury had felt rushed.

"No, no. In this particular phase, we need to take as much time as necessary so that everybody can come to their own conclusion, and we did tons of discussion, votes, back and forth. Everybody was very open."

Satisfied no misconduct had occurred, Judge Connor sent the foreperson back to her seat.

The jury's final vote had been eleven to one. Eleven people wanted Hunt to die for his crimes, but one adamantly held out for life without parole.

In open court, Connor asked each juror if additional deliberations could possibly result in a unanimous verdict. Each one of them answered with an unequivocal "No."

Judge Connor declared a mistrial, dismissed the jurors, and set a hearing for April 24 to decide if the penalty phase would be retried.

Families and friends of the victims, the lawyers, and the general public had mixed reactions. Many felt that Kenneth Hunt should be sentenced to death. Others felt that all the effort, inconvenience for witnesses, horror for new jurors, plus the astronomical expense of another trial, just wasn't worth it.

For some, the reasoning stemmed from California's administration of capital punishment. Voters had twice overwhelmingly approved reestablishment of the death penalty following a Supreme Court decision in the early 1970s that nullified existing laws

providing for execution. Every condemned inmate in
California, at that time, had been resentenced to life
in prison and were all eligible for parole, including
notorious convicts such as Charles Manson and Sirhan Sirhan.

With new laws in place, death row began filling up
once more in 1978. By the time of Kenneth Hunt's
trial, 705 killers had been sentenced to death in California. Nine had been executed at San Quentin, the
site of the state's death row, and one sent to Missouri
to face execution for a murder he'd committed there.
More than 600, including twelve women remained on
death row. Nineteen had died while waiting for the
long, drawn-out process—some due to violence in
prison, others from natural causes. Thirteen more had
committed suicide. Appeals courts had overturned the
death penalty for fifty-seven condemned men, and a
few of them were set free.

Skeptics about California's capital punishment complained that it virtually didn't exist, so why bother to
spend all that money, the resources, and time to hold
penalty trials? If so few killers were going to be executed, why not save millions of dollars by eliminating
the penalty phase, and send them to prison without
possibility of parole? Forty men had been living on
death row twenty years or longer! So sentencing killers
to death certainly did not mean they would ever be
executed.

Still, a number of people vehemently wished that
heinous murderers would suffer the supreme penalty.

John Gilligan explained the process he faced. The
decision whether to forge ahead with another penalty
trial, he said, is made by a special committee of senior
people in the district attorney's office. "When Laura

Jane Kessner and I finished the trial, we wrote a memo giving all the details and the jury results. We included our evaluation regarding the likelihood of another jury reaching a unanimous verdict. The fact that Mr. Hunt had been hospitalized as a child, more than once, was something to seriously consider. We realized that some jurors might just sit there and say this guy was damaged goods from the beginning and question applying the death penalty to him. If someone is institutionalized three times as a child and a teenager, people are going to take that quite seriously. I can show pretty effectively this guy was bright and didn't have any real mental retardation or organic brain damage. He has a high IQ. And obviously, the majority of the jury didn't think he deserved any special consideration."

The committee, giving considerable weight to the jury split, a very close eleven-to-one vote, decided to proceed with a second penalty phase.

Evidence presented to the new jury would have to include all the testimony and exhibits used in not only the penalty phase of the first trial, but everything in the guilt phase as well. It would be necessary to lay it all before the new jurors so they could understand how Hunt had been convicted. Only then would they have adequate facts to consider a penalty of death. The second penalty trial, then, would last as long as both phases of the first trial.

Jury selection began in early July. On the eleventh, the first of twenty-seven prosecution witnesses, all of whom had previously appeared, began testimony to educate the new jury. Gilligan rested his case on July twenty-eighth. Mark Windham called ten witnesses, replacing Dr. Foy with two other experts. He concluded the defense on July twenty-third. A rebuttal witness for the prosecution completed the process the next day. Arguments by Gilligan, Kessner, and Windham were finished by midday of July 25, and the second jury began deliberations.

On Monday, July 30, tension filled the court once more when the foreperson announced the results.

The jury had argued for several days and could not reach a unanimous decision. They were deadlocked again—ten for the death penalty, two for life without parole.

Enough was enough. Lois Bachrach and Debby McAllister, along with Sherry Davis, told John Gilligan they did not want another trial. In his report to the death penalty committee, he included their wishes.

In a hearing on September 6, the prosecution announced they would accept a sentence of life in prison without parole for Kenneth Dean Hunt.

Two months later, a scowling Hunt entered the courtroom for the last time. In place of his slacks, white shirt, and suit coat, he wore a bright orange jumpsuit. Chromed manacles encircled his wrists. The mane of neatly styled hair seen during the trial had been shaved off, leaving him with a shining bald head. He had gained weight over the months. Bailiff Bond Maroj and another deputy kept close watch on Hunt during the hearing.

In the gallery sat Lois Bachrach and her husband Chuck, Barbara Kappedal, Virginia Hauhuth, Detective Ron Phillips, a writer, and several reporters. Television newsman Stan Chambers, a fixture on Los Angeles channels since the 1960s, stood near a TV cameraman.

Mark Windham, in a stylish dark pinstriped suit, sat

next to his paralegal assistant, Eric Johnson. John Gilligan, Detective Francene Mounger, and a very pregnant Laura Jane Kessner occupied the remaining chairs at counsel table.

Conspicuously absent were Hunt's wife and mother-in-law, who had attended every previous session. Had the unconditional love and support been bled dry? Only they knew why they had chosen to skip the final act.

Before Judge Connor delivered the sentence, she allowed Lois Bachrach to voice some thoughts. Standing near the prosecutors, she said, "On behalf of my sister's friends and family, I would like to take this opportunity to offer a few words. First I would like to commend the LAPD, especially Francene Mounger and Ron Phillips, for the incredible work they did in apprehending Kenneth Hunt. I'd like to also express our dismay at the Los Angeles County Coroner's Office for the errors early in the case."

Turning toward the convicted killer of her sister, Bachrach intended to publicly tell him about her hopes for his future, but he cut her off.

"Fuck you, bitch!" he shouted.

Judge Connor interceded, saying to Bachrach, "Please address your comments to me." To the defendant, she ordered, "Mr. Hunt, be quiet."

If Hunt's outburst bothered her, Bachrach showed no signs of distress. She expressed gratitude that he would finally "be put away forever. His life, we hope, will be difficult. We think they won't like him where he is going. We hope that every day of his pitiful life, he will wake up knowing pain because of his actions. We hope he suffers degradation in a maximum-security prison, never having food he likes,

never having a woman's touch or any of life's pleasures. We hope his family no longer supports him.
We offer our sentiments to his wife and mother-in-
law, both of whom lost their good friend, my sister."

Turning again toward the fuming convict, Bachrach's voice spewed poison as she ended her brief
diatribe with a simple but vitriolic "Good luck, Mr.
Hunt." She wheeled and walked back to a seat beside
her proud husband.

Chuck Bachrach bristled with anger, still furious
about the errors committed and the failure of the
system to give Jean Orloff's murderer a death sentence.

Judge Connor perfunctorily read the sentences.
Count I: life without the possibility of parole. Count
II: life without the possibility of parole.

When court was adjourned and Hunt had been escorted back to a holding cell, Mark Windham, embarrassed at Hunt's behavior, hurried over to Lois and
Chuck Bachrach. "I'm so sorry about that," he said.
"I apologize. It was completely unexpected." The couple nodded their appreciation. It was a sincere and
classy gesture by a decent man.

John Gilligan also spent a few moments with the
Bachrachs, Kappedal, and Hauhuth. He courteously
explained what was immediately in store for Hunt.
County jail would keep him approximately thirty days
until a formal probation report was filed, as required
by law. Then he would be taken to a Department of
Corrections reception-and-classification center, and
ultimately to one of the high-security prisons.

The assembly broke up with handshakes, hugs, and
good-byes.

At last it was finally over.

Sherry Davis had waited thirteen years from the time she discovered her grandmother's body to the final act.

Lois Bachrach had spent more than three years attending hearings and trials. She, too, said it was time to put it all behind them.

Some felt bitter that Kenneth Hunt would not die for his savage crimes. Others wondered if life without a chance of parole was perhaps even a harsher punishment. Rapists and killers of women, especially when the victims are mothers and grandmothers, are not well treated by other inmates. If he had been sentenced to die, he would have been housed on death row, where convicts do not circulate in the general population. But Hunt will be among some of the most brutal, violent, and callous men in the country, and subject to whatever treatment they choose. Endless days in such an environment could be hell on earth.

It has often been said that the concept of "closure" is false, a meaningless cliché. But if the victims' families didn't have closure, at least they could get on with their lives, facing no more hectic trials and taking comfort in the knowledge that the souls of Myra Davis, Jean Orloff, and Bernard Davis could at last rest in peace.

Debby McAllister held fond memories of her mother. Jean Orloff's beloved piano occupied an honored place in McAllister's home. And her son, Andy, now a teenager, kept perfect care of the car he had inherited, his grandmother's red-and-white Chevy Malibu.

McAllister found a special way to honor her mom. When Jean Orloff had died, her "snobby" cat,

Frankie, was "traumatized." McAllister recalled that "Frankie didn't like anyone except Mom and Barbara Kappedal. Most cats adjust, but Frankie never adjusted." She took him home to San Clemente. But the beige-colored chocolate-point Balinese, Frankie, didn't get along well with McAllister's other three cats. So when a girlfriend, Erin, said she would be happy to adopt the independent little fellow, McAllister gave Frankie to her. "Surprisingly, he bonded with Erin and her mom."

A few months later, Erin's husband ended his tour in the Marine Corps at Camp Pendleton, near San Clemente, and decided to move to Texas. They took Frankie with them.

McAllister laughed when she recalled the incredible change in Frankie. "I couldn't believe it. He became an indoor-outdoor cat! Mom would have scoffed at the idea. He was always a spoiled house cat. But in Texas, Frankie lived happily the last days of his life hanging out under a tree."

When Frankie succumbed to old age in the spring of 2001, McAllister had an idea. Her mother had been cremated and the urn rested in a nook at a Los Angeles mortuary. In the nook, McAllister had placed the pit passes used by Jean to attend a Rolling Stones concert, a letter from Debby's son, Andy, a pen Jean had used, the ashes of Frankie's predecessor, Tiffany, and a few family photos. Now Debby McAllister wanted one other item to rest beside her mom in the sealed nook. It would be a posthumous Mother's Day gift.

She contacted Erin in Texas and arranged for Frankie's remains to be cremated. Erin shipped the ashes to McAllister, who took them to the mortuary.

"They put him in a little baby urn," said McAllister. "They reopened the nook and put Frankie in there with her. And now she has her little family, forever."

AUTHOR'S NOTES AND ACKNOWLEDGMENTS

One of the reasons I chose to write this book is my long-standing interest in classic movies. When I heard that one of the murder victims, Myra Davis, had worked in the motion picture and television industry most of her life, and had been involved in making *Psycho,* I couldn't resist the opportunity to investigate the case.

As I systematically learned the facts, I became absorbed in a key question that preoccupies most true-crime writers. What forces or circumstances drove the killer into the abyss of rape and murder? At the trial, I made extensive observations, took reams of notes, and conversed with a number of the principals. Gradually, the remarkable and shocking explanations for the defendant's behavior spilled onto the pages of my notebooks.

Courtroom dramas have always intrigued me. As a movie buff, I relished the conflict and tension portrayed in *Anatomy of a Murder, Witness for the Prosecution, Inherit the Wind, To Kill a Mockingbird, A Few Good Men,* and many others. The trial in this case, in addition to revealing insights into the killer, contained all the dramatic elements of a good movie. So I elected to present much of the story through events and voices at the trial. In the text, I have quoted courtroom testimony liberally to retain the integrity of what was said, while trying to be selective about what I chose from nearly 10,000 pages of transcripts. It should also be noted that lawyers' questions to witnesses were far more numerous than those I've used to exemplify key points.

Perhaps the most difficult challenge in developing the full story was how to present information about DNA evidence. The so-called "genetic fingerprinting" was a central issue in the case, but I realize that it's not a gripping, suspenseful topic for most true-crime readers. I tried to walk a narrow line, balancing the need to make clear the use of DNA, while not going into tedious detail. I know that for some, a single paragraph on the subject might be tedious, while other inquiring minds might wish to understand more about the technology. I hope I have satisfied both needs, without shortchanging either one.

This is a true story. To the best of my knowledge, I presented the facts as they happened, without fictionalizing any part of it. To protect privacy and avoid embarrassment to certain individuals, I changed several names of people involved in the events told herein.

Names also presented another problem, especially keeping separate everyone with the surname Davis. Myra Davis was a murder victim, and Bernard Davis, no relation, was the victim of manslaughter. Myra's granddaughter, Sherry Davis, even though married, retains the name for professional reasons. The third victim, Jean Orloff, could have been named Davis, too. When her mother remarried, she wedded Myron Davis, who legally adopted Jean. But he never changed her name. If he had, and if she had taken her maiden name following her divorce, all three victims, all unrelated, would have been named Davis. Strange twists in true crime never cease.

I am deeply grateful to a number of people who courteously gave their time to sit for interviews. Lois Bachrach, charming and graceful, hosted me in her beautiful home and told me about her sister, Jean Orloff, with admirable clarity and sensitivity. Sherry Davis did the same in relating details about the life and death of her grandmother, Myra Davis. Jean Orloff's daughter, Debby McAllister, demonstrated a terrific sense of humor and great personality as she reminisced about her mom. All three women generously provided photographs as well. Both attorneys, John Gilligan and Mark Windham, invited me into their offices, where they spoke with impressive intelligence and candor. Gilligan's coprosecutor, Laura Jane Kessner, tried her best to sit through a personal interview, but the baby she was soon to deliver protested, so we finally completed our conversation by telephone. Investigators Ron Phillips and Francene Mounger nearly put out an arrest order on me after I missed two appointments. When I finally sat in the interview room with them (the same room in which Kenneth Hunt had been interrogated), they both chatted like I'd known them forever.

Thanks also to my brother, Bob Lasseter, for his input regarding personal experiences while employed by the California Youth Authority.

If writing about DNA is the toughest part of the job, meeting and befriending people like those listed above is the best part.

Don Lasseter

HORRIFYING TRUE CRIME
FROM PINNACLE BOOKS

MORE BONE-CHILLING STORIES
FROM PINNACLE TRUE CRIME